Irish Migrants in Modern Wales

Irish Migrants in Modern Wales

Edited by
Paul O'Leary

LIVERPOOL UNIVERSITY PRESS

First published 2004 by
Liverpool University Press
4 Cambridge Street
Liverpool L69 7ZU

British Library Cataloguing-in-Publication data
A British Library CIP record is available

ISBN 0–85323–848–0 hardback
     0–85323–858–8 paperback

Typeset by Servis Filmsetting Ltd, Manchester
Printed and bound in the European Union by Bell and Bain Ltd, Glasgow

Contents

Notes on Contributors

Neil Evans is joint editor of *Llafur: The Journal of Welsh People's History*, and has published extensively on Welsh history, especially on racial and ethnic issues.

John Hickey was Emeritus Professor of Sociology at the Dominican University, Chicago, Illinois, USA. Sadly, he died in 2002 before this book appeared in print.

Peter Jones is a former PhD student at University College Chester.

Louise Miskell is a Lecturer at University of Wales, Swansea and was formerly a research assistant at the Department of History, University of Dundee.

Frank Neal is Professor in the School of English, Sociology, Politics and Contemporary History, University of Salford.

Paul O'Leary is Senior Lecturer in the Department of History and Welsh History, University of Wales Aberystwyth.

Jon Parry is a former Vice-Principal of the Working Men's College in Camden, London.

Chris Williams is Professor at the Centre for Modern and Contemporary Wales at the University of Glamorgan, Pontypridd.

Introduction – Towards Integration: The Irish in Modern Wales

Paul O'Leary

Until relatively recently immigrant and ethnic minority groups were relegated to one of the silences in the history of modern Wales. Where they were mentioned at all it was as outsiders who added a dash of colour and exoticism to the story of the majority but who had little to contribute to our understanding of developments in the 'mainstream' of society. In recent years this picture has begun to change, not only in terms of the increased volume of research on immigrants and minorities but also in the way the study of such groups poses searching questions about the nature of society as a whole. Historians, sociologists, novelists and the media have all begun to pay sustained attention to the immigrant and ethnic minority experience. Although the former silence has hardly become a cacophony, there is now a real sense of a debate taking place in the wider culture about the nature and implications of a plural society.[1] It is a debate in which the Irish experience should occupy a prominent role.

There is inevitably a degree of tension between a perspective that takes as its starting point a close examination of the Irish in a particular society and the recent tendency to explore the similarities and differences between Irish migrants in different parts of the globe, a development that has paralleled an interest in 'globalisation' among social scientists and cultural critics. The conceptualisation of Irish migration in terms of a global diaspora has yielded many valuable insights.[2] Most fundamentally, it holds out the prospect of a reconceptualisation of Irishness in terms of a more inclusive identity, and one that is not restricted to the territory of Ireland itself.

Such perspectives on Irish migration have been shaped decisively by developments outside of academia. Perhaps inevitably, our ways of understanding the Great Famine and its consequences owe an enormous amount to the experiences and preoccupations of the 1990s, when a determined effort was made by Irish people to comprehend the magnitude and ramifications of the crisis that occurred during the second half of the 1840s. It is at this point that the intersection of a perspective rooted in the idea of diaspora and exploration of the specificity of place come into fruitful contact.

This point is reinforced by an examination of the unveiling of a monument at Cardiff in 1999 commemorating those who died during the famine years. As on most such occasions nowadays, the accent was on reconciliation, in an attempt to achieve closure of a difficult and painful past, reflecting the tenor of former Irish president Mary Robinson's attempt to reach out to the Irish around the globe by taking seriously the pain and suffering caused by the demographic upheaval of the nineteenth century.[3]

The events surrounding the unveiling can be stated briefly. On an unseasonably warm and sunny St Patrick's Day in 1999, several hundred people gathered in Cardiff's Cathays cemetery for the event, organised by the Wales Famine Forum. It was a model of symbolic inclusiveness and inter-faith harmony. The monument itself, in the form of a Celtic cross on a plinth, was fashioned from Irish stone and Welsh slate and was jointly unveiled by the newly appointed Irish consul general at Cardiff and a minister of state at the Welsh Office. Participants in the service of dedication included Roman Catholic bishops, a representative of the Anglican Church in Wales and ministers of a number of other Protestant denominations, as well as a gaggle of individuals who defy easy classification. The latter included Tyrone O'Sullivan, an emblematic figure in south Wales who led a successful workers' buy-out of Tower Colliery, Hirwaun, during the 1990s, an episode that has since become the subject of several television documentaries and an opera. Speeches, prayers, poems and hymns were recited and sung by contributors who shifted easily between the English, Irish and Welsh languages.

The unveiling ceremony represented the culmination of a number of years of endeavour on the part of the Wales Famine Forum in its attempt to bring the history of the Irish in Wales, and of the experience of the Great Famine in particular, into sharper contemporary focus. Commemorations of the Great Famine during the 1990s created a context in which modern-day Irish migrants and the descendants of migrants (often many generations removed from the experience of migration itself) could symbolically reunite themselves with connections in their Irish past. Such commemorations responded to stimuli from Ireland, with its concerted attempt to come to terms with the tragic historical legacy of famine, as well as to a cultural dynamic arising out of the accumulated historical memory of the migrant communities themselves.

In some ways, however, the unveiling of the memorial at Cathays cemetery raised as many questions as it answered. Memory is a complex phenomenon. Its silences and elisions often reveal as much about the past as what is actually said and done. This point is underlined by the unveiling of another plaque with Irish connections in Wales in 2002. This time political events were centre stage. On 29 June 2002 about one hundred people assembled in wet and windy conditions to witness the unveiling in the remote village of Frongoch, where 1,800 Irishmen – Michael Collins among them – were interned after the Easter Rising in Dublin of 1916. The plaque was organised by the Liverpool branch of Conradh na Gaelige (the Gaelic League) and a local group called CANTREF. This memorial also used the Irish, Welsh and English languages, but with its emphasis on republican politics the unveiling lacked the cultivated inclusivity of the ceremony in Cardiff three years earlier. The presence of the socialist and republican Starry Plough banner evoked a very different tradition of Irish history, and one that does not fit easily with current political and historiographical concerns.

Commemorations take place in that twilight world between collective memory and the fuzzy imprint on that memory of changes in historical writing. Both elements are subject to revision over time, though the process tends to be a more self-conscious and reflective one among professional historians. Each of the contributors to this book brings to his or her research an acute awareness of the contradictions and complexities of the lived history of Irish migrants that are revealed by a juxtaposition of the two commemorations described above. Their contributions demonstrate that there is no easy narrative of Irish migration to which a stubbornly untidy and contradictory past can be made to conform, no simple story of either total alienation or complete segregation. To this extent, these essays, while focused specifically on the Irish in Wales, constitute a contribution to wider debates about the Irish diaspora. They cohere around four principal themes: migration, settlement, conflict, and integration.

In a valuable opening contribution on the interaction of maritime trade and migration, Frank Neal amplifies his more general work on the famine migration to Britain with a detailed study of the experience of south Wales. He provides a detailed analysis of shipping patterns between Ireland and south Wales, thus underlining the importance of an approach adopted in some of his earlier work which concentrates on distinctive regional experiences.[4] His careful analysis of the nature, scale and spatial distribution of the influx of Irish famine refugees in Wales during the years 1845–49 uncovers the appalling hardships of their journeys. He constructs a detailed picture of the reaction of local authorities to the crisis and pays particular attention to the scale of the typhus epidemic of 1847 and the consequent deaths among the refugees. His contribution reminds us that there was an enormous human and financial cost to the famine migration.

By comparison, the industrial settlements of north Wales experienced little Irish migration during the famine years, in spite of the proximity of the region to Ireland. This point is illustrated by the fact that of all the Welsh counties that of Merioneth in north-west Wales registered the smallest number of Irish-born men and women in the 1851 census. The Irish made their greatest impact in this county in a brief period during 1916. As Jon Parry points out in his intriguing chapter on the internment camp at Frongoch for rebels of the Easter Rising, these were involuntary 'migrants' who had no voice in their destination. Their extraordinary conditions of life in the camp ensured that a temporary community of exile, composed entirely of men, was forged in adversity. In many ways, it bore all the hallmarks of an imagined community and, as Parry demonstrates, it held sway over the imagination of some groups of politicians in both Wales and Ireland long after 1916, thus extending its significance way beyond the actual circumstances of its creation and dispersal.

Although there were Irish migrants in Wales before the Great Famine,[5] that momentous event provided such a stimulus to migration that most research has focused on the years of disruption that followed it. In particular, most studies of Irish settlement and community life in Britain have concentrated on the mid-nineteenth century, a period that is treated fully in this collection of essays. Nearly forty years after he published his pioneering study of the Irish in Cardiff,[6] John Hickey, who sadly died before this book was published, provides a fresh overview of Irish settlement in that town. He describes the growth of the migrant settlement, the establishment of churches and schools, the operation of religion as a binding force and the leadership role undertaken by the clergy. In a complementary, but methodologically different essay, Chris Williams provides a detailed demographic study of Newport, a town which bore the brunt of the famine migration in south Wales, by exploiting the data available in the census enumerators' books. He also explores the avenues by which the Irish participated in the public culture of this Protestant town, paying particular attention to the role of the church and societies as well as the interventions of members of the Irish middle class and the participation of the working-class Irish in the labour movement.

While Cardiff and Newport are familiar to historians of Irish migration, Peter Jones's contribution explores an area not usually associated with this movement of people, the small town of Wrexham in north-east Wales. Here the Irish – most of whom hailed from the counties of Mayo, Sligo and Galway in Connaught – were a small but significant and observable element in the town's life. In spite of their small numbers the Irish did make an impact on public life, as is shown by the fact that Wrexham's first Irish mayor was elected in 1876, whereas Cardiff – with a much larger Irish contingent – did not elect an Irish mayor until 1894. Jones's work is part of a growing interest in the experience of the Irish in the small-town context, which provides an essential counterpoint to the study of the large cities of England and Scotland.[7] What the Irish found and created in the great conurbations of Liverpool, Glasgow and Manchester (or even middling towns such as Cardiff, Swansea and Newport) was in marked contrast to their experiences in places such as Wrexham.

A discussion of settlement patterns raises the question of the extent to which the Irish were integrated into the wider society. This is a difficult process to analyse and assess historically. Recent interpretations of the Irish in Britain have questioned the extent to which 'ethnic fade' occurred from the 1870s and have emphasised those factors, such as the growth of the Orange Order and the persistence of communal violence into the twentieth century, which conspired to prevent the Irish from achieving integration. Donald MacRaild, in particular, has cast doubt on the 'assimilationist' view. He argues that the centrality of the Irish Home Rule issue in British politics in the 1880s led to a resurgence of Orangeism not only in Britain, but in all British colonies also.[8] It is an argument based primarily on conditions in the north of England and in Scotland, and current research indicates that these conclusions do not apply to Wales, especially south Wales, where the Orange Order was weak and marginal. Moreover, the overwhelming dominance of Gladstonian politics in Wales, combined with the weakness of Conservatism, ensured that the espousal of Home Rule politics by the Irish in the region created an issue that united the majority of Welsh Liberals and Irish Home Rulers. In spite of the continuing vitality of popular Protestantism in Wales, appeals to Protestant sectarianism went largely unheeded.[9]

Contributors to this volume adopt different approaches to the question of integration, partly as a consequence of the timescales they have adopted for their individual studies. John Hickey describes a process of assimilation of the Irish into Cardiff society and the virtual disappearance of an identifiable Irish 'community' in the town by the end of the twentieth century. Such an approach is consistent with an interpretation that emphasises ethnic fade, according to which ethnicity is of decreasing importance to the descendants of migrants. According to this interpretation, the community institutions that sustained the Irish before, say, the 1920s either cease to exist or take on a less obviously Irish complexion (as in the case of the Catholic Church). It can be argued that a crucial factor in this development was the decline of Irish migration to Cardiff in the twentieth century, particularly when compared with some other cities in Britain.

For those who concentrate on the period before the First World War, it is not ethnic fade but the integration of the Irish into the wider culture while retaining a distinctive identity that is the most salient development. In the case of Newport, Chris Williams finds little explicit hostility to the

Irish as a group and, in a town where the question of national identity was never simple, the Irish were frequently seen as making a distinctive contribution to what locally constituted 'Britishness'. This is an infrequently studied aspect of Irish integration in Britain and one that requires further attention. Perhaps it can be best studied in a comparative perspective with the experience of the Irish in the USA.[10]

Paul O'Leary examines the extent to which sections of the migrant community came to subscribe to the mid-Victorian cult of respectability, a topic rarely broached by historians of the Irish in Britain. Unlike the case of the Irish in the USA, where the 'lace-curtain' Irish are an established part of the picture of the ethnic community, the cult of respectability in mid-Victorian Britain has usually been seen as irrelevant to the experience of a group characterised by lower-status occupations, irregular employment and high geographical mobility. This chapter makes claims for the plurality of the Irish migrant experience in south Wales and charts the evolution of a 'respectable' Irish identity. It also raises questions about a minority's use of public space in the nineteenth-century town.

When taken together, these studies raise the unresolved question of whether successful integration without subsequent top-up migration inevitably leads to ethnic fade. It would be misleading, however, to see integration as a trouble-free process. In her detailed study of the incidence of anti-Irish rioting between the 1820s and the 1880s, Louise Miskell discerns a distinctive and durable tradition of anti-Irish rioting in Wales which did not necessarily resemble the pattern of anti-Irish behaviour that has emerged from big-city studies in England and Scotland. She argues that an interpretive framework different from that used in the existing literature is needed to understand fully the causes and patterns of anti-Irish disturbances in Wales, a framework that places ethnic disturbances in the context of customary forms of popular protest. She demonstrates that anti-Irish rioting can be interpreted as one strand of the strong traditions of community regulation in south Wales manifested in the activities of, for example, the 'Scotch Cattle' and the Rebecca rioters. By making this link between patterns of anti-Irish violence and regional traditions of popular protest, this chapter offers a new perspective on the study of anti-Irish behaviour in Britain as a whole.

This book does not claim to be comprehensive in its treatment of the Irish in Wales, and there are obvious omissions in terms of subject matter. For example, none of the contributors gives sustained attention to the impact of the Irish on the Catholic Church in Wales (or of the Catholic Church on the Irish), though it is mentioned in passing on several occasions.[11] More work is required on the nature of Irish settlement, especially relating to the towns of Swansea and Merthyr Tydfil and the smaller centres of Irish settlement in the south Wales coalfield.[12]

Other ongoing research, on topics as diverse as Irish doctors, the nature of Irish criminality, and sport and the Irish, will stimulate debate about the role of an Irish middle class and the extent of Irish working-class alienation respectively.[13] Moreover, there is room for further studies of a comparative nature that illuminate the extent to which the experience of the Irish in Wales was distinctive or whether it reflected developments elsewhere. In the meantime, however, this book reflects the current state of research and marks an important stage in the development of the study of the Irish in Wales.

Notes

1. Charlotte Williams, Neil Evans and Paul O'Leary (eds), *A Tolerant Nation? Exploring Ethnic Diversity in Modern Wales*, Cardiff, University of Wales Press, 2003.

2. See Donald Akenson, *The Irish Diaspora: A Primer*, Belfast, Institute of Irish Studies, 1996; Andy Bielenberg (ed.), *The Irish Diaspora*, Harlow, Pearson, 2000. The important series of six volumes of essays edited by Patrick O'Sullivan under the title *The Irish World Wide* has also contributed to this process. On the historiographical background, see Alan O'Day, 'Revising the Diaspora', in *The Making of Modern Irish History: Revisionism and the Revisionist Controversy*, ed. D. George Boyce and Alan O'Day, London, Routledge, 1996; and Roger Swift, 'Historians and the Irish: Recent Writings on the Irish in Britain in the Nineteenth and Twentieth Centuries', in *The Great Famine and Beyond: Irish Migrants in Britain in the Nineteenth and Twentieth Centuries*, ed. Donald M. MacRaild, Dublin, Irish Academic Press, 2000.

3. See her speech to the two houses of the Oireachtas, 2 February 1995, 'Cherishing the Diaspora', http://www.emigrant.ie/emigrant/historic/diaspora.htm.

4. See especially Frank Neal, *Black '47: Britain and the Famine Irish*, London, Macmillan, 1998. For a supporting argument in favour of a regional analysis of Irish settlement, see Paul O'Leary, 'A Regional Perspective: The Famine Irish in South Wales', in *The Irish in Victorian Britain: The Local Dimension*, ed. Roger Swift and Sheridan Gilley, Dublin, Four Courts Press, 1999, pp. 14–30.

5. See Paul O'Leary, *Immigration and Integration: The Irish in Wales, 1798–1922*, Cardiff, University of Wales Press, 2000, pp. 15–72.

6. John Hickey, *Urban Catholics: Urban Catholicism in England and Wales from 1829 to the Present Day*, London, Geoffrey Chapman, 1967.

7. John D. Herson, 'Irish Migration and Settlement in Victorian Britain: A Small-Town Perspective', in *The Irish in Britain, 1815–1939*, ed. Roger Swift and Sheridan Gilley, London, Pinter, pp. 84–103; *idem*, 'Migration, "Community" or Integration', in Swift and Gilley (eds), *The Irish in Victorian Britain*, pp. 156–89;

Louise Miskell, 'Irish Immigrants in Cornwall: The Camborne Experience, 1861–82', in Swift and Gilley (eds), *The Irish in Victorian Britain*, pp. 31–51.

8. Donald M. MacRaild, *Culture, Conflict and Migration: The Irish in Victorian Cumbria*, Liverpool, Liverpool University Press, 1998; *idem*, *Irish Migrants in Modern Britain, 1750–1922*, London, Macmillan, 1999.

9. O'Leary, 'A Regional Perspective', passim. See also *idem*, 'A Tolerant Nation? Anti-Catholicism in Nineteenth-Century Wales', in *From Medieval to Modern Wales: Historical Essays in Honour of Kenneth O. Morgan and Ralph A. Griffiths*, ed. R.R. Davies and Geraint H. Jenkins, Cardiff, University of Wales Press, 2004; *idem*, 'When was Anti-Catholicism? The Case of Nineteenth- and Twentieth-Century Wales', *Journal of Ecclesiastical History*, forthcoming.

10. For important comparative essays on Britain and the USA, see MacRaild (ed.), *The Great Famine*. Mary Hickman's work on England is of relevance here; see her 'Alternative Historiographies of the Irish in Britain: A Critique of the Segregation/Assimilation Model', in Swift and Gilley (eds), *The Irish in Victorian Britain*, pp. 236–53.

11. This theme has been addressed elsewhere: Paul O'Leary, 'Irish Immigrants and the Catholic "Welsh District", 1840–1850', in *Politics and Society in Wales, 1840–1922*, ed. G.H. Jenkins and J.B. Smith, Cardiff, University of Wales Press, 1988, pp. 29–46; *idem*, 'From the Cradle to the Grave: Popular Catholicism among the Irish in Wales', in *Religion and Identity: The Irish World Wide*, ed. Patrick O'Sullivan, London, Leicester University Press, 1996, pp. 183–95; Trystan Owain Hughes, 'Archbishop Michael McGrath, 1882–1961: A 20th Century St David? The Irishman who Came to Wales', in *Contrasts and Comparisons: Studies in Irish and Welsh Church History*, ed. J.R. Guy and W.D. Neely, Llandysul, Gomer Press, 1999, pp. 135–53.

12. However, see the following unpublished theses: Ursula Masson, 'The Development of the Irish and Roman Catholic Communities of Merthyr Tydfil and Dowlais in the Nineteenth Century', MA thesis, University of Keele, 1975; Louise Miskell, 'Custom, Conflict and Community: A Study of the Irish in South Wales and Cornwall, 1861–1891', PhD thesis, University of Wales, 1996; Peter Jones, 'The Irish in North-East Wales, 1851–1881', PhD thesis, University of Liverpool, 2002.

13. In particular, Veronica Summers, 'Criminals or Scapegoats? The Irish and Crime in Nineteenth-Century Cardiff', *Llafur: Journal of Welsh Labour History*, 8.2 (2001), pp. 63–73; and Louise Miskell, 'The Heroic Irish Doctor? Irish Immigrants in the Medical Profession in Nineteenth-Century Wales', in *Ireland Abroad: Politics and Profession in the Nineteenth Century*, ed. O. Walsh, Dublin, Four Courts Press, 2003, pp. 82–94; Neil Evans and Paul O'Leary, 'Playing the Game: Sport and Ethnic Minorities in Modern Wales', in Williams, Evans and O'Leary (eds), *A Tolerant Nation?*, pp. 109–24. See also the autobiography of a Cardiff doctor, recently reprinted: James Mullin, *The Story of a Toiler's Life* (1921), ed. Patrick Maume, Dublin, University College Dublin Press, 1999.

South Wales, the Coal Trade and the Irish Famine Refugee Crisis

Frank Neal

An aspect of the Irish famine that, understandably, has received relatively little attention until very recently is the famine refugee problem in those British towns that bore the brunt of the exodus from Ireland.[1] Large numbers of destitute Irish, men, women and children, fled to Britain to escape the nightmare being enacted in Ireland, hoping to obtain relief and the possibility of work and a new life not characterised by extreme hardship. This massive movement of people was only possible because of the existence of well-established shipping lanes between Ireland and Britain. The most important British ports of entry were Liverpool and Glasgow.[2] This chapter sets out to establish the evidence concerning the role of the coal trade in facilitating the movement of Irish refugees into south Wales during the famine years. In particular, I shall argue that the industrial developments in Britain that were already drawing pre-famine Irish to its industrial areas also made possible the flight of large numbers of Irish to south Wales, seeking to escape the death, disease and suffering of a famine-stricken country. This essay sets out to place the Irish famine refugee crisis in south Wales in the context of the regional economy and its economic nexus with the south-eastern counties of Ireland. It should be noted that the term 'Wales' used here includes Monmouthshire, despite the fact that in the census reports Monmouthshire data are kept separate from those of the other 12 Welsh counties.

I

For thousands of years the mineral ore deposits lying under the surface of the hills and valleys of south Wales were, literally, useless. This lack of utility ended, for all practical purposes, in the latter half of the eighteenth century, when various technological developments and their commercial exploitation coalesced to transform the coal and ore deposits into valuable economic resources.[3] In essence, the development of the steam engine increased the demand for coal for industrial use while the emergence of iron and copper as materials in both construction and consumer products accelerated the mining activities in the region. The successful exploitation of these mineral deposits could only take place if there was a simultaneous provision of transport facilities. Ore and coal needed to be moved to the foundries; finished products had to be transported to their markets and, in the case of exports particularly, this meant the provision of canals, dock facilities and ships. In south Wales, the building of the canals was crowded into a twenty-year period. The Glamorgan, Neath, Monmouthshire and Swansea canals were built between 1794 and 1799, while the Brecknock and Abergavenny canals were operating by 1812. The Marquess of Bute opened the docks at Cardiff over the period 1832–39, while the Newport docks began to receive vessels in 1841. By the 1840s, the anthracite field behind Llanelli, Swansea and Neath was connected to those ports by railway and in 1841 the Taff Vale Railway opened, joining Cardiff and Merthyr.[4] All these developments meant that by 1845, the year in which the potato blight made its appearance in Ireland, south Wales was a booming economic region, offering the hope of jobs to many Irish wishing to start a new life outside Ireland.

Central to the themes of this chapter are the close economic links that existed between south Wales and Ireland, in particular the ports of south-eastern Ireland, most significantly Cork, Wexford and Waterford. The primary cargo out of south Wales to these ports, and others, was coal, cinders and culm (anthracite slack). This trade engaged a fleet of vessels (colliers) used specifically for carrying such cargoes. These vessels were usually small sailing ships owned by partnerships, often consisting of two to six persons, and many of them were registered in the Irish ports. In order to address the issue of which ports in Ireland and south Wales became the points of exit and entry for the famine refugees, it is necessary to establish the scale of the traffic between the two countries. This can only be done using government records. Unfortunately these were not kept on a systematic basis and so we have to use what is available. Turning first to the ports of south-east Ireland, Table 1 shows the imports of coal, cinders and culm twenty years before the famine crisis.

The obvious feature of Table 1 is the primacy of Cork as the port handling the largest volume of imports of these raw materials, followed by Waterford. As the tonnage handled is closely related to the number of ships involved, this is of significance given that the colliers returned, usually in ballast, to south Wales. This point brings us to the question of which ports in south Wales were at the other end of the shipping route. The official statistics do not enable us to identify the volume of coal from a particular Welsh port that went to a specific Irish port. However, we

Table 1 *Tonnage of coal, cinders and culm imported from Britain through the ports of south-east Ireland during 1825*

Port	Coal and cinders	Culm	Total
Cork	88,713	2,243	90,956
Wexford	16,286	1,598	17,884
Waterford	39,010	4,594	43,604
Youghal	10,584	9,979	20,563

Source: PP 1826 XXII, Accounts and Papers.

Table 2 *Tonnage of coal, cinders and culm exported through ports in south Wales to Ireland during 1825*

Port	Coal and cinders	Culm	Total	% of tonnage
Swansea	24,579	19,080	43,659	25.9
Newport	96,668	–	96,668	55.6
Cardiff	11,644	–	11,644	6.7
Llanelli	20,399	–	20,399	11.7
Milford Haven	472	991	1,463	0.9
Total	153,762	20,071	173,833	100.0

Source: PP 1826 XXII, Accounts and Papers.

can establish from which ports in south Wales vessels carried coal to Ireland (see Table 2). In 1825, 56 per cent of all the coal exported from south Wales to Ireland went from Newport, with Swansea being the next in terms of volume. It is therefore highly likely that Newport and Swansea were, at this time, the primary ports of entry for the pre-famine Irish migrants into the region. There is no doubt that the availability of passages in the colliers would influence the movement of people to Wales. The greater the number of voyages, the greater the potential number of passengers.

An obvious question to ask is: what was the tonnage of shipping, *other than colliers*, trading between these Welsh ports and Ireland? The answer is, as Table 3 shows, very little. Between 1824 and 1826, 5,826 voyages took place between the three ports and Ireland and, of this total, 54 per cent went from Newport, 36 per cent from Swansea and only 10 per cent from Cardiff. Equally noteworthy is that of all the voyages made 90 per cent of them were carrying coal, cinders and culm. The relative importance of Newport, Swansea and Cardiff with regard to coastwise trade had not changed by 1841, on the eve of the famine (see Table 4). By this

Table 3 *Numbers of vessels cleared outwards from the ports of Swansea, Newport and Cardiff, bound for Ireland, in 1824, 1825 and 1826*

	Swansea			Newport			Cardiff		
Year	Colliers	Others	Total	Colliers	Others	Total	Colliers	Others	Total
1824	542	5	547	973	64	1,037	105	80	185
1825	626	22	648	889	67	956	150	61	211
1826	881	8	889	957	175	1,132	125	97	222
Total	2,049	35	2,084	2,819	306	3,125	380	238	618

Source: PP 1826–27 III, Accounts and Papers.

Table 4 *Numbers and tonnage of vessels cleared outwards coastwise from the ports of Wales in 1841*

	Sailing vessels		Steamers		Total	
Port	Number	Tonnage	Number	Tonnage	Number	Tonnage
Aberystwyth	221	9,433	–	–	221	9,433
Beaumaris	1,087	31,704	124	11,815	1,211	43,519
Cardiff	2,434	157,668	298	18,268	2,732	175,936
Cardigan	85	2,464	–	–	85	2,464
Llanelli	2,221	129,251	6	384	2,227	129,635
Milford Haven	1,537	54,543	81	11,409	1,618	65,952
Newport	8,707	471,313	–	–	8,707	471,313
Swansea	6,398	370,437	238	26,288	6,636	396,725

Source: PP 1842 XXXIX, Accounts and Papers.

time, steam vessels had established their reliability on short-haul routes. Table 4 also demonstrates that, as late as 1841, sailing vessels still dominated the Welsh shipping routes. This situation contrasted with the situation in Liverpool, where the Irish cross-channel traffic was overwhelmingly carried by steamers. For poor Irish migrants travelling as deck passengers, the journey by sailing ship was a longer, even more miserable trip than was the case using the faster steamers.[5]

II

Given the scale of the coal trade between south Wales and Ireland before the famine, what were the size and spatial distribution of the Irish

Table 5 *Irish-born populations of the Welsh registration counties in 1841*

County	Males	Females	Total	County total as % of Welsh total
Anglesey	70	67	137	1.6
Brecon	163	119	282	3.4
Cardigan	35	35	70	0.8
Carmarthen	100	63	163	2.0
Caernarfon	130	162	292	3.6
Denbigh	184	132	316	3.9
Flint	207	163	370	4.5
Glamorgan	1,936	1,238	3,174	38.7
Merioneth	33	19	52	0.6
Montgomery	55	40	95	1.2
Pembroke	150	142	292	3.6
Radnor	17	16	33	0.4
Monmouth	1,707	1,218	2,925	35.7
Total	4,787	3,414	8,201	

Source: PP 1841 census, Enumeration Abstracts, M.DCCC.MLI. Summary of Wales, p. 458.

migrant population in Wales? The 1841 census was the first to record the place of birth of the enumerated population and so we are able to establish whether the pre-famine Irish settlements, in terms of numbers, mirror the pattern of economic development described above (see Table 5). Not surprisingly, 39 per cent of all pre-famine migrants in Wales were found in Glamorgan, the area of maximum industrial development, closely followed by Monmouthshire with 36 per cent. What is striking is how widely and thinly spread were the Irish settlements *within* Glamorgan (see Table 6), though there were further clusterings within the country which, again, reflected the pattern of economic development achieved by 1841. The Hundred of Caerphilly together with the boroughs of Swansea and Cardiff accounted for over 79 per cent of all the Irish-born in the county. The attractions were the employment opportunities offered by the docks at Swansea and Cardiff and the foundries in Caerphilly. Within the Hundred of Caerphilly was the parish of Merthyr Tydfil, which experienced a significant population increase, rising by 59 per cent from 21,933 in 1831 to 34,977 in 1841. The census report of 1841 stated that the expanding iron trade was responsible for this growth and so Merthyr became a goal for many Irish migrants.[6]

Table 6 *Distribution of the Irish-born population in Glamorgan in 1841*

Hundred or borough	Males	Females	Total	Irish-born as % of hundred population
Caerphilly	725	403	1,128	2.5
Cowbridge	21	12	33	0.6
Dinas-Powis	11	9	20	0.4
Kibbor	13	12	25	0.1
Llangyfelach	20	6	26	0.1
Miskin	88	53	141	0.9
Neath	90	42	132	0.7
Newcastle	124	70	194	1.2
Ogmore	24	16	40	1.0
Swansea	24	18	42	0.3
Cardiff (borough)	554	411	965	10.4
Swansea (borough)	242	186	428	2.6
Total	1,936	1,238	3,174	

Source: PP 1841 Census Abstract of Answers and Returns under the Population Acts 3 & 4 Vic. C.99, Enumerations MD.CCC.XLI.

III

The failure of the Irish potato crop in 1845, though causing hardship, did not result in widespread deaths or emigration, but the following year witnessed the beginnings of a catastrophe. The bad winter of 1846 triggered an increase in the flow of refugees leaving Ireland, reaching a peak during 1847. In that year, the government's decision to close the soup kitchens caused a further increase in the numbers of people leaving Ireland for Britain.[7] By this time, a significant change had taken place in the trade pattern between south Wales and Ireland. The opening of the Taff Vale railway in 1841 resulted in a greatly increased volume of coal being shipped out through Cardiff, with the result that Newport no longer dominated the coal export trade.

It can be seen from Table 7 that 442,065 tons of coal and cinders were shipped coastwise through Cardiff in 1846, almost reaching Newport's tonnage of 493,582. In 1847, the two ports were almost level in terms of coastwise exports of coal. The significance of this is that the number of vessels trading out of Cardiff for Ireland was no longer fewer than the number leaving Newport. By 1851, Cardiff's dominance over Newport was complete. Table 8 illustrates that as late as 1851, when the famine exodus was continuing, the coal trade was still carried on primarily in sailing ships. The port of Beaumaris included Holyhead, hence the rel-

Table 7 *Tonnage of coals, cinders and culm shipped coastwise from Welsh ports to other parts of the United Kingdom during 1846 and 1847*

Port	1846				1847			
	Coal	Cinders	Culm	Total	Coal	Cinders	Culm	Total
Cardiff	438,781	3,284	–	442,065	429,448	3,278	–	432,726
Newport	493,582	–	–	493,582	436,099	–	–	436,099
Swansea	256,960	1,337	196,053	454,350	212,484	486	160,337	373,307
Llanelli	169,006	–	67,155	236,161	165,650	–	38,741	204,391
Milford Haven	20,939	–	47,552	68,491	17,319	–	35,394	52,713

Source: PP 1847–48 LVIII.

Table 8 *Numbers and tonnage of vessels that cleared outwards coastwise from Welsh ports in 1851*

Port	Sailing vessels		Steamers	
	Number	Tonnage	Number	Tonnage
Aberystwyth	245	9,541	–	–
Beaumaris	502	20,250	511	118,401
Caernarfon	312	10,816	48	6,537
Cardiff	5,866	391,298	624	58,458
Cardigan	59	1,711	–	–
Llanelli	2,888	172,964	125	15,182
Milford Haven	1,269	88,713	108	32,526
Newport	7,228	107,904	–	–
Swansea	5,601	353,215	490	58,690

Source: PP 1852 XLIX, Accounts and Papers.

atively large number of steamer departures, reflecting the mail traffic between Holyhead and Dublin.

The inter-censal decade, 1841–51, covered the famine years and witnessed unprecedented numbers leaving Ireland. The results of this flight for Britain were mirrored in the 1851 census returns. Table 9 shows that after the influx of Irish famine migrants, although most Welsh counties still had small Irish settlements, all had experienced increases in number. The pre-eminence of Glamorgan was further emphasised – not surprisingly, given the pace of economic development in south Wales. For example, in 1851, of all the Irish-born persons in Wales, 17,885 (86

Table 9 *Increases in the Irish-born populations of the Welsh counties, 1841–1851*

County	1841	1851	Increase	% increase
Anglesey	137	340	203	148
Brecon	282	674	392	139
Cardigan	70	279	209	299
Carmarthen	163	514	351	218
Caernarfon	292	583	291	100
Denbigh	316	1,036	720	228
Flint	370	612	242	65
Glamorgan	3,174	9,737	6,563	207
Merioneth	52	77	25	48
Montgomery	95	205	110	116
Pembroke	292	703	411	141
Radnor	33	90	57	173
Monmouthshire	2,925	5,888	2,963	101
Total	8,201	20,738	12,537	153

Source: PP 1841. Census Enumeration Abstracts, MDCCCMLI. Summary of Wales, p. 458. 1851 census, Div. XI, Monmouthshire and Wales, birthplaces of the people, pp. 887–91

per cent) lived in south Wales and of those living in north Wales 58 per cent lived in Flintshire and Denbighshire, drawn by the coal mining of Wrexham and the nearby ironworks. All of this supports the proposition that the overwhelming majority of Irish migrants gravitated to industrial areas; escape from Ireland and the possibility of employment in established Irish settlements were their objectives. This feature of Irish inward migration is emphasised when the data concerning registration districts are examined. Table 9 shows the Irish-born populations of counties, but in the census reports each county was further subdivided into registration districts and each of these was almost identical in area and population to the corresponding Poor Law Union. This becomes significant when attempting to measure the financial consequences of Irish inward migration during the famine. For example, Table 10 shows that the population of the Merthyr Tydfil registration district in 1851 was 76,804 and the number of Irish-born persons was 3,646. The town of Merthyr Tydfil, with a population of 63,080, accounted for 82 per cent of the population of the Merthyr district. The Irish-born population of the town was 3,051, or 84 per cent of all the Irish in the district. Similarly, the borough of Newport contained 2,078 Irish-born persons, which accounted for 76 per cent of all the Irish in the Newport registration district. Lastly, 96 per cent of all the Irish-born counted in the Swansea

Table 10 *Irish-born populations in the principal registration districts of south Wales in 1851*

District no.	District	Total population	Irish-born	Irish-born as % of total
578	Abergavenny	59,229	1,733	2.9
579	Pontypool	27,993	1,018	3.6
580	Newport	43,472	2,737	6.3
581	Cardiff	46,491	3,317	7.1
582	Merthyr Tydfil	76,804	3,646	4.7
583	Bridgend	23,422	412	1.8
584	Neath	46,471	993	2.1
585	Swansea	46,907	1,389	3.0
586	Llanelli	23,502	182	0.8

Source: 1851 census reports, birthplaces of the people.

registration district lived in the borough of Swansea. The published census returns do not give the numbers of the Irish-born for towns other than Merthyr, Newport and Swansea. However, they do give data for registration districts and the evidence is clear enough: the Irish settled principally in the burgeoning industrial areas of south Wales.

IV

Having established the scale and direction of the coal trade in this region and identified the correlation between Irish settlement and industrial development, we are left with the question of how many famine refugees came ashore along the south Wales coast during the Irish famine. The simple fact is that we do not know. In December 1846, the Home Office asked the authorities in the ports of arrival to count the persons disembarking from vessels entering inwards from Ireland. Only the port of Liverpool kept records of this phenomenon, covering the years 1847–53 inclusive. Swansea, Neath and Cardiff kept none, while in the case of Newport such data were recorded only for the years 1849–53 inclusive (see Table 11). We do not know how accurately the arrivals from Ireland at Newport were logged nor how the numbers broke down into paupers and others. We do know that the situation in 1847 was far worse than in subsequent years. There is also considerable anecdotal evidence that many Irish were landed clandestinely, unknown to the customs officers (see below). Given all these qualifications, the data in Table 11 clearly understate the number of arrivals and also suggest that the exodus from

Table 11 *Numbers of passengers landed at Newport from Irish ports, 1849–53*

| | | | Year | | |
Month	1849	1850	1851	1852	1853
January	21	43	–	52	85
February	344	195	33	135	65
March	169	705	178	43	150
April	259	438	342	602	1,558
May	534	421	744	1,183	1,344
June	345	157	978	564	1,005
July	–	34	909	342	377
August	–	34	297	40	52
September	–	40	80	12	58
October	–	21	106	47	18
November	–	32	59	32	–
December	30	20	13	–	–
Total	1,702	2,140	3,739	3,052	4,812

Source: PP 1854 LV.

Ireland of refugees continued unabated at least until 1853. This would reflect the situation at Liverpool.[8] The numbers of Irish-born resident in any region revealed by the two censuses of 1841 and 1851 are given numbers at particular moments in time, but what affected the life of ports most was the flow of Irish refugees passing through; the snapshot figures do not give any sense of the scale of the problem. The majority of the Irish coming ashore eventually moved on; for many, the objective was to reach Birmingham or London. The Irish landing at or near Newport reduced the mileage they had to cover when setting out for the metropolis or the industrial hinterlands. While these transients were in the ports, however, they added to the problems of overcrowding and disease. For these people, the Poor Law Unions at Chepstow, Gloucester and Cheltenham provided overnight stops where food and shelter could be obtained. However, the fact remains that we have very little hard evidence of the numbers involved.

By contrast, there is a great deal of anecdotal evidence of the scale of the crisis and its consequences, or the perceptions of such in the minds of those involved in coping with events. There is a remarkable consistency in the constant reiteration of the view that the colliers were the culprits. Important sources of such evidence are the witnesses appearing before the Select Committee on Poor Removal, which took evidence in 1854, when events were still fresh in the minds of the witnesses. Evan David had been the chairman of the Cardiff Board of Guardians in 1847. Asked where in Ireland the Irish came from, he replied:

Chiefly from Cork, they are over in the coal vessels from Cardiff. We have a large export of coal from Cardiff to Cork and vessels generally return in ballast and they are enabled to bring back deck passengers, of course, at a very low rate, and we have them in very large numbers; we have had them as many as 100, 150 and 200 landed at once, all in the most wretched condition . . .

David was further questioned about where the Irish came ashore, and was asked in particular whether they came ashore at Cardiff. He offered the following opinion:

They were formerly landed at Cardiff but our Union ascertained that the Captains of these vessels had no licences for carrying passengers, and they offered a reward for informations against them. After considerable difficulty they fined only one; we then found that they left the paupers on the coast near Cardiff and went on themselves to Newport, consequently we were unable to get at the captains. We find the paupers very reluctant to state by what vessel they came over or the name of the Captain . . .[9]

David's evidence is interesting on a number of counts. First, it implies that the Cardiff Guardians quickly took a tough line regarding the illegal carrying of passengers from Ireland, offering rewards for informers. The fact that only one captain was fined suggests either that the system did not produce many exposures of law-breaking or that evidence was hard to get, in particular given the reluctance of paupers to act as witnesses in court. A probable explanation is that the masters began to drop passengers off up-river, between Cardiff and Newport. Asked whether a labour shortage in Cardiff was causing Welsh employers to advertise for labour in County Cork, David replied:

I am not aware of any. The relieving officer of our Union states that the paupers have told him that the placards have been posted up in Cork, stating that there are parties who will meet them at our docks and will employ them there at very high wages; but we have had nothing of the kind in Cardiff and our officers are of the opinion that those placards were posted by the Captains of the vessels, who were anxious to take them over, for the small payment which they received for their passage, as they came over as ballast . . .[10]

It could have been predicted that the ships' masters would exploit the demands of those seeking to flee Ireland at this time. Given the nature of the trade, the return trip to Wales was usually without cargo, therefore ballast, often limestone and shingles, was needed and was not available at zero cost. The refugees could provide ballast free of charge. In fact, since they were charged, they paid for the pleasure of being ballast, and for the ship's master their fares were pure profit.

John Salter was the relieving officer at the Newport Union and he claimed to have spoken with hundreds of Irish paupers about their reasons for coming to Newport and the conditions under which they were carried. The Committee asked Salter about the practice of ships' masters putting the Irish ashore at isolated spots on the coast. He stated:

> There is a place within three miles of Newport called the Lighthouse: it is invariably the practice (so I am told by the poor people who have been so used) to put them ashore there; many of them have been called upon by the Captain to get out at that part of the river and have been told it would be much better for them, that there was not water enough to take them to Newport and that they would get to Newport much better and obtain relief much sooner by getting out there. Sometimes they send from 20 to 30 out of the vessel at this place before they come to Newport, and when the Customs House officer comes to the vessel in Newport to examine whether the captain has more than his licenced number, of course he finds that his number is invariably under the licence because the number who exceeded the licence have been unshipped within three miles of Newport . . .[11]

The events revealed in these anecdotes are what we would expect. The ships' masters were not wealthy men and were often hard pressed to find profitable cargoes. Salter went on to say that the reason for this unloading of passengers in quiet spots, which itself was not illegal, was to avoid the charge of carrying passengers without the necessary licence and also to avoid the hostility of the townspeople of Newport, who were worried both by the rising expenditure of poor relief and by the risk of typhus. Useful anecdotal evidence is to be found in the document entitled *Reports and Communications on Vagrancy*, published in 1848 in the midst of the famine refugee crisis. John Box Stockdale, the superintendent of police at Cardiff, stated that early in 1847 the Cork vessels were landing 13 or 14 persons per vessel, but as conditions in Ireland deteriorated, the number increased, reaching 200 in one case.[12]

A further source of evidence concerning the events of 1847–53 is the correspondence of the Poor Law Unions with the Poor Law Board in London. In 1847, the Cardiff Poor Law Union consisted of 43 parishes and the town of Cardiff. By 1849, the financial consequences of the influx of Irish paupers were beginning to expose potential conflicts of interest between various categories of persons eligible to pay the poor rate. In essence, the source of strain arose from the fact that a large proportion of the Board of Guardians was elected from the rural parishes, while the greatest number of Irish in the Union lived in Cardiff town. In 1848, an Act was passed (11 and 12 Vic. Cap. 110) which stated that, from 30 September 1848 to 30 September 1849, all cases of sudden illness among vagrants must be charged to the common fund of the Union, to which all parishes had to contribute. There was a fear among the ratepayers in the parishes that this temporary legislation might become permanent. On 29 November 1849, the Cardiff Board of Guardians met and adopted a memorial to be sent to the Poor Law Board in London. The gist of the document was that most Irish vagrants lived in the town of Cardiff but the parishes were having to pay into the common fund to provide Irish relief. As always, the complaints were prefaced by a statement referring to the role of the shipping interests in bringing the Irish paupers to Wales:

> The town of Cardiff is the shipping port for the export of coal and iron from the adjoining mineral districts and some of these districts are within the Cardiff Union; and as the coal trade is to a large extent with Ireland, the coal vessels bring over destitute Irish in very large numbers, who come to seek employment in this most desirable country. They partially find employment in the manufacturing districts, and from the cheapness of their labour, are also numerously employed in the agricultural parishes. At Cardiff, there is scarcely any work for them and they seldom find employment there but because they find houses to dwell in the town, they return to Cardiff to lodge. This is also the case when they are landed on the coast in this Union, which is of very frequent occurrence in the industrial parishes, they always flood the towns . . .[13]

Thus the Board of Guardians, many members of which represented rural parishes, objected to these parishes having to contribute to the common fund to support the Irish in Cardiff town. The coal vessels were bringing Irish migrants to Wales when, in the view of the Guardians, there was no work in Cardiff and hence they finished up claiming poor relief and swelling the bill for medicine. Some among those who paid the poor rate in Cardiff were outraged at the Guardians' action and called a meeting of ratepayers. At this a memorial was drawn up, to be sent to the Poor Law Board:

> Your memorialists beg to state their conviction that in no Union in the Kingdom did there exist a greater necessity than that of Cardiff, for distributing relief over a wide area. The cost of relief to the casual poor, inhabiting but not settled in one locality, insomuch as the large trade carried on between Cardiff and Ireland affords great facilities for the migration of Irish in large numbers, the males making Cardiff the home for their wives and families whilst they find employment in the surrounding country, as agricultural labourers . . .

The memorial went on to complain that the farmers enjoyed the benefit of cheap Irish labour but were objecting to paying medical bills when those labourers fell ill while working on the farms.[14] The Cardiff Guardians retaliated by sending a petition to the House of Commons, claiming that as a result of requiring parishes to contribute to the Common Fund when vagrants fell ill in the parishes, the small farmer would be seriously burdened. The petition also reminded the Poor Law Board:

> In addition, very large importations of Irish paupers are periodically conveyed to the port of Cardiff, in vessels trading there for coal, from Ireland and as rural parishes cannot exercise control in the town, checking these immigrants (many of the parishes being eight or nine miles distant from Cardiff) your petitioners deem it to be a most grievous hardship that they should be compelled by the above [legislation] to maintain either these Irish poor or those who have been employed . . . in work unconnected with them . . .[15]

The Guardians seem to have been labouring under the misapprehension that the movement of Irish migrants to Wales could be stopped by the Cardiff authorities. It could not, because it was entirely legal. The only action open to the Guardians was to stop the carrying of Irish people to Wales in unlicensed vessels and the carrying of numbers of passengers in excess of the licensed number. However, as noted above, they had tried to stop such violations of the law and failed. To sum up, the body of anecdotal evidence is consistent in claiming that large numbers of Irish paupers landed in the region over the period 1847–53. All those offering such views stressed the role of the colliers in facilitating this large inflow and the profiteering of the ships' masters in carrying migrants in excess of their permitted numbers. The fact remains that we cannot give exact numbers, but it is reasonable to conclude that the impact of this influx of Irish famine refugees on south Wales was much greater than can be inferred from the number of Irish-born residents recorded in the 1851 census.

V

What evidence is there, if any, of the actions taken by the customs authorities to stamp out the carrying of unlicensed passengers? Any attempt to understand the official reaction must be based on an appreciation of the legislation available to customs officers in the ports of departure and arrival. On 25 June 1823, a bill was introduced into the House of Commons for regulating vessels carrying passengers between Great Britain and Ireland. This Act, 4 Geo.IV.88, laid down that in vessels under 200 tons register, no more than 20 passengers could be carried unless licensed to do so by the collector of customs at the port of departure. The penalty imposed on the master and owners of a vessel carrying passengers without a licence was £50, a considerable sum. In the case of carrying passengers in excess of the number permitted by licence, the penalty was £5 for each person, again a sizeable amount. Vessels could be detained until the fine was paid. This was a particularly

Table 12 *Numbers and tonnage of coastwise vessels entering the port of Newport, 1842–51*

Year	From Ireland		Others	
	Number	Tonnage	Number	Tonnage
1842	254	21,774	728	29,027
1843	243	18,220	888	35,520
1844	209	18,192	902	38,965
1845	267	20,097	1,017	50,573
1846	289	22,534	1,464	64,941
1847	257	19,409	1,583	73,402
1848	299	22,712	1,335	65,069
1849	291	22,620	1,065	53,302
1850	273	22,601	1,118	50,621
1851	285	25,125	993	48,742

Source: PRO, Cust./71/130, 'An account of Coasting Vessels'.

damaging imposition as a detained vessel was not earning revenue. In the next session, the law was extended to vessels with a register tonnage of 200 tons or over.

As with all legislation, its efficacy depended on the rigorous enforcement of the law. In this case, the responsibility fell on the customs officers at the ports. Their ability to enforce the law would depend on such factors as the availability of manpower, the volume of traffic and the determination of the collector of customs in each port of entry to enforce the law. In the case of Newport, for example, two thirds of all coastal vessels arriving were not from Irish ports (see Table 12). The arrival of large numbers of vessels from non-Irish ports would tie up customs officers in routine duties, thus diverting attention from Irish vessels. At the port of Cork, the majority of the persons took vessels to south Wales and the south coast of England, including London. The alternative route was to Liverpool, but there were far fewer sailings to Liverpool. For example, during 1847, there were only 55 sailing ships and 50 steamers entered inwards at Liverpool from Cork. In the case of vessels from Waterford and Wexford, the corresponding numbers were 24 and 63, and 24 and 22 respectively.[16] In each of these ports, steamers accounted for most of the tonnage entering outwards for Liverpool. In addition, vessels trading from Cork, Waterford and Wexford to Liverpool did not need ballast arising from a lack of cargo. Economic forces determined the choice of routes out of Ireland: the typical fare to Liverpool was ten shillings, far beyond the means of most famine refugees. By contrast, the need of the coal vessels for ballast on their return trip to Wales meant that the shipmasters could afford to offer passages at low prices. In many cases, the price of a passage fell to two shillings and sixpence, or lower. The need to enforce the law was increased when the public became aware of the conditions under which the Irish were brought over. This concern was at its height in the first half of 1847, before 'compassion fatigue' had set in. The medical officer of health for Cardiff, writing in 1854, stated: 'these poor wretches are brought over as ballast, without any payment for their passage. The Captains, it appears, find it cheaper to ship and unship this living ballast than one of lime or shingle.'[17]

From November 1846 onwards an increasing proportion of Irish migrants arriving at British ports were in bad physical condition, exacerbated by the voyage to Britain. Worse, many were already in the grip of typhus, requiring hospital treatment immediately on arrival.[18] The *Cardiff and Merthyr Guardian* of 12 February 1847 carried a report from its correspondent at Newport, dated 8 February:

> a vessel named the *Wanderer* just arrived here with nearly two hundred of the wretched famished creatures, chiefly from Skibbereen, huddled together in a mass of wretchedness unparalleled. On examining the crowded vessel, it was found that between twenty and thirty starving men, women and children were lying on the ballast in the hold in dying condition. Their state was most deplorable and had it not been that surgical and charitable aid was rendered the moment the vessel came alongside the wharf, it is said that many would have been brought ashore dead.

Following the removal of the people from the hold, five died. This was the worst case reported and increased the calls for control of the trade.

The case of the *Industry* of Cork provides a more typical example of the passenger trade at this time. The *Industry* was a small sailing vessel of 86 tons. She left Cork on Monday 29 March, bound for Cardiff to pick up a cargo of railway lines. Her master was John Hart and there were four other crew members. She carried 150 sheep and ballast and it is not clear whether or not she was licensed to carry passengers. The vessel had no food for passengers and no medical equipment. Before sailing the master took on board about 35 Irish men, women and children. The adults paid two shillings and sixpence each for the voyage. They clearly had no idea what the voyage entailed; they had provisions for the journey, but several asked the mate how long the trip would take. The *Industry* left Cork bound first for the New Passage, then Penarth and finally Cardiff. Soon after leaving Ireland, the passengers began to suffer from seasickness. On Wednesday 31 March some of the passengers asked the master for food and water. He gave them some biscuits and a water allowance of four pints a day. The mate complained that the Irish were roasting salt fish and this was making them particularly thirsty. On Thursday 1 April, an Irishman who had boarded alone complained of feeling ill and vomiting. He asked the master for some bread, as he had none. On 1 April the *Industry* reached the New Passage and the sheep were put ashore. Several Irish went with them to help drive them to Bristol. Some of the remaining passengers then left the deck and stayed in the hold. The same night, the unknown Irishman died on the deck of the *Industry*. The inquest was held at Cardiff on 4 April and the verdict was 'died by the visitation of God'.[19] This example – a small vessel, probably unlicensed, refugees unprepared for a journey – is almost certainly typical of the south Wales immigrant traffic during 1847. The inquest verdict made no reference to malnutrition, although this was probably the single most important factor contributing to the man's death.

The ships' masters incurred a great deal of hostility in the south Wales ports.[20] Essentially, during 1847, the resentments were twofold: first, the rising level of concern over the amount of relief spent on the Irish immigrants, and second, the fear that the Irish were bringing typhus with them. The favourite place for putting the Irish ashore was called the Lighthouse, about three miles out from Newport harbour. It was claimed that the immigrants were usually told that by going ashore at this point they would reach Newport more quickly and obtain poor relief much earlier. In practice, being disoriented, many finished up in Cardiff or did not reach Newport until days later.[21] Many put ashore in this manner were in a weak physical condition and, not surprisingly, some died. This was not a short-term phenomenon. In May 1849 a vessel called the *Three Brothers* was observed making its way along the Welsh coast, landing 300 Irish migrants, all in a bad physical condition. A man named Donovan died after being put ashore and his wife, assisted by other migrants, buried his body in the mud. The corpse was washed ashore at Peterstone. At the subsequent coroner's court, an inquest was also held on the body of an Irishman who had been put ashore and who had died of starvation soon afterwards. In July 1849, the secretary of state wrote to the mayor of Cardiff, saying that the coastguard officers of the Swansea district had been instructed to keep a look-out for vessels landing Irish passengers and to check whether they had infringed the law. This confirms that a sense of crisis was not confined to the year 1847.[22]

We do not know how many vessels the customs officers checked to see whether they were carrying unlicensed passengers, nor do we know how many owners were fined because their vessels carried such passengers. What we do know is that some ships' masters petitioned the customs authorities in London after being caught breaking the law.

The customs' service files at the Public Records Office provide the only available official evidence of the activities of ships' masters caught breaking the law. On 13 February 1847, Edward Bell, the collector of customs at Newport, wrote to the Commissioners of Customs in London regarding a vessel called *Maria*, whose master was named Henry James. The ship had arrived from Cork carrying 65 passengers as well as a cargo of 62 hides and 500 skins. When questioned by customs officers, James could not produce a licence to carry this number of passengers. The 65 passengers included 17 children under seven years of age. James claimed that the owners of the vessel also owned several other ships and probably had the licence and stated that he would write to them immediately.[23] Meanwhile, the customs at Newport placed the vessel under detention, a severe sanction. This case provides further evidence that early on in the crisis the customs officials at the ports in south Wales were taking steps to stop the traffic in unlicensed passengers. On 17 February, Henry James wrote to the Board of Customs:

> In reply to your letter of this day's date, calling upon me to show cause why I should not be proceeded against for the penalty incurred by me under sec. 3 of the Act Geo. 4. Cap. 88. for having onboard the *Maria* passengers from Cork beyond the number of 20 without a licence, I humbly beg to state that I left the port of Cork on the 9th Instant, where a number of poor people were assembled and praying for a passage to England and I took them aboard, not being aware that I was acting contrary to law by carrying passengers from Ireland to England. I had on board 60 men women and children. I now humbly pray that the Assistant Collectors of Customs will take my case into their merciful consideration and that they will not proceed against me for the penalties which I have ignorantly incurred, also that the vessel may be released upon my making a report or giving you any security.[24]

James implies that he broke the law by carrying passengers from Ireland to Wales. This was not true; he was in trouble because he could not produce a licence to carry more than 20 persons. He also implies that he did not know that he needed a licence. This is highly improbable: he was trying to wriggle out of any fines that could be imposed. It transpired that he had landed some of the Irish well below the landing stage at Newport, before the tide surveyor (customs officer) had boarded the vessel when it entered the port of Newport. This disembarking of passengers on the coast was not illegal but, clearly, James wanted to prevent the excess passengers from being noticed by the customs officers. When the tide surveyor at Newport boarded the *Maria* he was told that the ship carried six passengers, but on searching the vessel he found 41 men, women and children. James was prosecuted, having been caught out lying, although his letter implies that he was doing the passengers a favour.

At about the same time, similar cases provided further evidence of customs officials enforcing the law. The *Elizabeth and Sara* entered at Newport, James Bowen, Master. The vessel's home port was Cork.

When the officials at Newport boarded, Bowen stated that he carried six passengers but a search of the vessel revealed the number to be 40. The vessel was detained and proceedings were invoked against Bowen.[25] On 21 February 1847, the *Thomas and Mary*, of Cork, John Sullivan, Master, entered at Newport. The customs officials found that Sullivan did not have a licence to carry the number of Irish on board. The vessel was detained. Sullivan immediately wrote to the Board of Customs in London:

> 22 February 1847
> Newport.
> I arrived at this port yesterday on the *Thomas and Mary* of, and from, Cork, myself the master, having on board a cargo of bacon, butter, porter and with between 30 and 40 persons onboard, men women and children for which latter I do not have a licence. I am now called upon by the Customs House to show cause why I should not be proceeded against under the third section of 4 Geo. 4. Cap. 88, for the penalty I have incurred for having onboard my vessel passengers beyond the number of twenty without a licence. I must respectfully beg to assure you that I was not aware that I require a licence to carry the number of passengers I had onboard between Ireland and England and that I acted in ignorance of the law, in consequence of which my vessel is now detained by officers of Her Majesty's Customs, which will raise serious loss to the owners and myself. I therefore humbly pray that your Honors will give direction for the release of the vessel on my paying any expenses that may have been incurred.

Sullivan got away with a caution although, again, it is difficult to believe that a master did not know the law regarding the carrying of passengers. The fact that he could not quote the precise number of people he carried suggests that the crew may have been left to take passengers on board.[26]

The *Lady Ann* of Kinsale arrived at Cardiff in April 1847. The master had been observed landing 40 Irish paupers on the coast and he was arrested, appeared before the magistrates and was fined £10 for carrying unlicensed passengers. The customs officers impounded the vessel until the fine was paid. As in some of the cases cited above, John Page, the master, wrote to the Board of Customs in London, hoping to avoid any penalty. The letter is dated 12 April 1847, Newport.

> That your memorialist was applied to whilst lying at Kinsale, in Ireland, in ballast, bound for Penarth Roads, seeking employment for his said vessel, by several Irish men, women and children, who implored your memorialist to give them a passage as they were given to understand that employment was to be procured at Cardiff and Newport. That your memorialist, from feelings of humanity, consented to convey them to Penarth Roads. That after your memorialist had proceeded to sea, he discovered the Irish were short of

provisions and at considerable expense to himself and the owners of the said vessel, supplied the poor creatures with food otherwise they must have perished. That your memorialist was wholly ignorant that a licence was required for conveying people and did so without any intent whatsoever of defrauding the Revenue. That your memorialist has already paid the sum of nineteen shillings for light duties for having the said Irish onboard, in addition to the £10 inflicted . . . That your memorialist is in very low circumstances with nothing but a small monthly sum and wages to support himself and an aged mother . . .

John Page's plea of ignorance of the Passenger Acts is also hard to believe. He, like some other masters, projected the image of a good Samaritan helping the unfortunate. This may have been true but it is difficult to overlook the fact that any money he may have received would not have needed to be recorded, nor paid to the owners. In this instance, the vessel had already acquired ballast before taking passengers aboard. Also of interest is his statement that the Irish wanted to go to Wales because of the expectation of finding work.[27]

The *Argyle* of Cork arrived at Newport at 5 pm on 18 February 1848, from Clonakilty. Her cargo consisted of three cows, two horses, 20 sheep and four tons of potatoes. This last named item is evidence, if it were needed, of the continuing export of food from Ireland even though people were still suffering from malnutrition. The *Argyle* had been observed putting 79 people ashore, one mile down-river from the passenger station at Newport. On the ship's arrival at Newport, the customs officers found another 15 adults and six children onboard. Michael Driscoll, the master, told the officers that he had carried 12 adults and 30 children free of charge.[28] The *Argyle* was a small sailing ship of 79 register tons, with a crew of four including the master. Driscoll was in trouble on two counts. He did not have a licence to carry over 20 passengers and he had not entered up his cargo in the ship's cargo book. He was heavily fined, £50 for carrying passengers and £50 for not entering his cargo in the cargo book. In addition, he was fined £5 for every passenger carried over his licensed number. In his defence, Driscoll claimed that he landed some of the Irish outside Newport because it was late in the evening and it was better to land them before it got dark, and because the tide was fast-running. The customs officials dismissed these excuses. Driscoll was in even greater trouble when his claim to be ignorant of the law was proved false, when it was established that he had previously been master of a ship with a passenger licence. He broke under questioning and admitted his lies. He called on the Board of Customs to take into account that he was a poor man with a wife and six children.[29] The officers at Newport wrote to the Commissioners of Customs in London, on 19 February 1848:

We respectfully report that the master [Driscoll] now confesses that he was not ignorant of the law requiring him to have a licence for bringing those passengers, having formerly being master of another vessel called the *Isabella*, in which he had brought passengers from Ireland to this country, having then a licence for the same but states that Clonakilty, being 32 miles from Cork, it would have put him to great inconvenience and delay.

Thus he picked up passengers in Clonakilty but could not be bothered to go to Cork for the requisite licence. Edward Bell, the collector of customs, asked the Commissioners of Customs in London to impose a severe fine on Driscoll because the number of Irish paupers brought over in 1847 had caused a 'great increase' in the poor rates.[30] The fines imposed on Driscoll were very heavy and must have had some deterrent effect when the news went round the maritime community. However, the evidence after the *Argyle* case is that, despite the efforts of the customs officers in south Wales, the masters of colliers continued to carry more passengers than they were licensed for.

Early in July 1848, the vessel *Star of the Sea*, from Clonakilty, was observed standing-to three miles below the landing stage at Newport. The customs officer reported this fact and then boarded the vessel to see whether the master, McCarthy, had a problem because a flood tide was running. When he got aboard, the officer found 18 adults, mainly women, and 40 children, nearly all under seven years of age. In addition, it turned out that McCarthy had already landed 53 persons since standing-to. On being questioned as to why he had done this, he replied that he did not like to proceed up-river with all of the passengers because he was frightened of being abused by the people at Newport.[31] This reply is revealing, providing hard evidence of the growing resentment of the indigenous population towards the ships' masters, who, having made a profit, dumped Irish paupers on the Poor Law Unions at the ports of arrival and in the surrounding areas. As it happened, McCarthy had a licence and so the customs officers took no action.

On 7 September 1848, the *Emma*, a schooner of Bideford, arrived at Newport from Glandore, in the port of Skibbereen. Unusually, the ship carried only passengers, and the customs officers detained it because the master, Richard Barment, did not have a passenger licence. Barment pleaded ignorance of the law, stating that he had been a master for only five months and that this was the first occasion on which he had carried passengers. He claimed that the customs officers at Glandore had told him that he could carry passengers and on that basis he had brought them to Newport. The customs officers at Newport believed Barment's story and released the vessel.[32] On 22 May 1849, the vessel *James*, also of Kinsale, arrived at Newport, weighing 78 tons and licensed to carry 98 persons. In fact the ship carried 119 adults and 78 children (three children counting as one adult for the purpose of fares), in addition to 16 horses and 30 sheep. This was a case of gross overcrowding. Captain James Savers was charged with carrying an excess number of passengers and fined £200 or two months in prison. The severity of this sentence suggests that the authorities were becoming even more determined to stamp out overcrowding of vessels. Even if each of the 199 adults had paid 2s 6d, this would have amounted to just under £15, nowhere near the cost of the fine.[33]

VI

The long established folklore of south Wales, in which large numbers of Irish famine refugees were said to have escaped to Wales in coal-carrying ships short of return cargoes, is, in fact, strongly supported by all the available evidence. It is not possible to determine how many made the trip but it must have been a considerable number, given the scale of the suffering in Ireland and the volume of shipping traffic going to Wales from Cork, Wexford and Waterford. This outflow of destitute refugees was at its height during 1847. In the pre-famine years, the colliers carried some passengers to Wales, but the flight from Ireland over the years 1847–53 provided the ships' masters with an unprecedented opportunity to make extra profit.

Unlike the steamship companies, the colliers were owned by small partnerships, which often included the masters. In general, masters and seamen were not well paid and the chance of extra income was too good an opportunity to ignore. Given human nature, it was inevitable that some exploitation took place, in the form of charging the maximum that the refugees could pay and in overcrowding the vessels. The carrying of passengers in excess of licensed numbers was illegal and there is over-whelming evidence that some ships' masters were putting people ashore outside the recognised landing stages to avoid prosecution for carrying excess numbers. This occurred mainly on the coast between Cardiff and Newport. The customs authorities at Newport did bring prosecutions against masters found breaking the law but, again, we do not know how many arrests were made or anything of the deterrent effects of such pros-ecutions. The evidence suggests that the Newport customs officers were mostly involved, the customs files containing no references to Cardiff or Swansea over the period under review. Many of the Irish coming ashore at the ports of the region made their way inland to the ironworks and coalmines of the valleys, but even larger numbers set off to the English Midlands and London.

Space does not permit an analysis of the impact of this passenger trade in Swansea, Cardiff and Newport. In any case this has been done elsewhere.[34] It seems reasonable to assert that although conditions on the colliers were bad, the coal trade did give a chance of escape to desperate people, which otherwise would not have been available at such a low cost. Had the customs authorities stamped out the carrying of excessive numbers of passengers, many Irish paupers would have been unable to leave Ireland at this time of crisis. Whether or not they would have been better off remaining at home is a moot point.

Notes

1. For the first account of the impact of the famine refugees on British ports and towns see Frank Neal, *Black '47: Britain and the Irish Famine*, Basingstoke, Macmillan, 1998. Included is a detailed analysis of the problems posed for the authorities in, among other places, south Wales.

2. Neal, *Black '47*, chapter 3.

3. An excellent survey of the development of the iron industry is J.R. Harris, *The British Iron Industry 1700–1850*, Basingstoke, Macmillan, 1988.

4. H.J. Dyos and D.H. Aldcroft, *British Transport History from the Seventeenth to the Twentieth Century*, Leicester, Leicester University Press, pp. 96, 183. For the mineral ports of south Wales see G. Jackson, 'The Ports', in *Transport in Victorian Britain*, ed. M.J. Freeman and D.M. Aldcroft, Manchester, Manchester University Press, 1988, pp. 230, 238–39.

5. The passage of famine refugees to Liverpool is analysed in detail in Frank Neal, 'Liverpool, the Irish Steamship Companies and the Famine Irish', *Immigrants and Minorities*, 5.1 (March 1986), pp. 28–61. See also *idem*, *Black '47*, chapter 3.

6. PP 1841 census [XI, Welsh Division], South Wales–Glamorganshire –Population, p. 23.

7. The recent principal works on the catastrophe are: Cormac Ó Gráda, *The Great Irish Famine*, Basingstoke, Macmillan, 1989; C. Kinealy, *This Great Calamity: The Irish Famine, 1845–52*, Dublin, Gill and Macmillan, 1994; Cormac Ó Gráda, *Ireland Before and After the Famine: Explorations in Economic History, 1800–1925*, Manchester, Manchester University Press, 1993 (2nd edn); *idem*, *Ireland: A New Economic History, 1780–1939*, Oxford, Clarendon Press, 1994; Cathal Póirtéir (ed.), *The Great Irish Famine*, Cork, Mercier Press, 1995; E.M. Crawford (ed.), *The Hungry Stream: Essays in Emigration and Famine*, Belfast, Institute of Irish Studies/Centre for Emigration Studies, Ulster-American Folk Park, 1997; Patrick O'Sullivan (ed.), *The Meaning of the Famine* (*The Irish World Wide: History, Heritage, Identity*, VI), London, Leicester University Press, 1997; Cormac Ó Gráda, *Black '47: The Great Irish Famine in History, Economy and Memory*, Princeton, NJ, Princeton University Press, 1999; Peter Gray, *Famine, Land and Politics: British Government and Irish Society, 1843–1850*, Dublin, Irish Academic Press, 1999.

8. Neal, *Black '47*, p. 61. The number of paupers recorded as arriving at Liverpool in 1853 was 71,353. In 1854 the figure fell dramatically to 6,679.

9. PP 1854 XVII, Select Committee on Poor Law Removal (referred to hereafter as 'SC 1854'), Minutes of Evidence, E. David, pp. 474–45, qq. 6471–73.

10. SC 1854, Minutes of Evidence, E. David, qq. 6551–53.

11. SC 1854, Minutes of Evidence, J. Salter, p. 492, q. 6740.

12. PP 1848 LIII, *Reports on Communications on Vagrancy*, p. 30.

13. PRO, MH12/16248/1850, pp. 29–30, 'Memorial to the Poor Law Board, London'. The meeting was held on 29 November 1849 but the memorial was only signed on 10 January 1850.

14. PRO, MH12/16248/1850, p.34, 'A memorial of the ratepayers of the town of Cardiff drawn up at a public meeting held to complain about the memorial of the Guardians of the Poor'.

15. PRO, MH12/16248/10771/1849, petition from the Guardians of the Cardiff Union to the House of Commons. This petition was actually approved on 2 March 1850.

16. Neal, *Black '47*, Table 3.3, p. 55.

17. SC 1854, Minutes of Evidence, E. David, q. 6482. David quotes from a report written by Dr Paine in January 1854.

18. SC, 1854, Minutes of Evidence, E. David, pp. 475–76, q. 6482.

19. *Cardiff and Merthyr Guardian*, 10 April 1847. PRO, Cust./71/49. Letter to the Customs House, London from Newport, dated 21 July 1849. The captain of the *Industry* on this occasion had arrived without completing the necessary customs documents.

20. SC 1854, Minutes of Evidence, J. Salter, p. 493, q. 6741.

21. SC 1854, Minutes of Evidence, J. Salter, p. 492, q. 6740.

22. *The Times*, 2 July 1849.

23. PRO, Cust./71/5/Newport/1847.

24. PRO, Cust./71/5/Newport/1847, p. 31.

25. PRO, Cust./71/5/Newport/1847. Letter dated 15 February 1847, Collector of Customs to HM Board of Customs, London. See also PRO, Cust./71/49/1847. Letter from HM Board of Customs, London, dated 16 February, saying vessels should be detained.

26. PRO, Cust./71/5/Newport/1847. The vessel carried 24 adults and 24 children under seven years of age. See also PRO, Cust./71/22/1847. Letter dated 25 February 1847, HM Board of Customs, London to Collector of Customs, Newport, asking him to caution Captain Sullivan about his future behaviour.

27. PRO, Cust./71/1847, pp. 56, 58, 59.

28. PRO, Cust./71/6/Newport/1848, p. 155. Letter dated 19 February 1848, Edward Frost, Tide Surveyor, Newport, to HM Board of Customs, London.

29. PRO, Cust./71/6/Newport/1848, p. 155. Letter dated 19 February 1848, Driscoll to HM Board of Customs, London.

30. PRO, Cust./71/6/Newport/1848, p. 156. Letter dated 19 February 1848,

Edward Bell, Collector of Customs, Newport, to HM Board of Customs, London.

31. PRO, Cust./71/6/Newport/1848. Letter dated 6 July 1848, Edward Bell, Collector of Customs, to Edward Frost, Tide Surveyor, asking him to take action against the master of the *Star of the Sea*. Letter dated 7 July 1848, Tide Surveyor to the Collector re boarding of the *Star of the Sea*.

32. PRO, Cust./71/6/Newport/1848, p. 256. Letter dated 4 September 1848 from the coastguard at Glandore, Port of Skibbereen, certifying that the *Emma* was carrying passengers only. Letter dated 7 September 1848, Captain Barment to the Collector at Newport, stating his case.

33. PRO, Cust./71/Newport/1849.

34. Neal, *Black '47*, chapter 3, also pp. 113–15, 166–73, 259.

Irish Settlement in Nineteenth-Century Cardiff

John Hickey

The background to the Irish immigration into Britain in the nineteenth century – including the operation of the 'push' (economic necessity) and 'pull' (economic opportunity) factors – has been explored elsewhere in this book. This chapter focuses on Irish settlement in Cardiff. It examines, in the context of the founding and development of the settlement, the process of upward social mobility experienced by the group and the consequent movement of its members from a position of relative isolation to that of integration and eventual assimilation into the host society.

There were other urban areas in south Wales where the Irish immigrants settled during the nineteenth century and have made their contribution to the social, economic and civic development of the societies they entered. The most important of these are Merthyr Tydfil–Dowlais, Newport and Swansea. Here the Irish immigrants and their descendants first established their own communities and then spread out, eventually, into the host population to become part of the general social structure of the towns. Paul O'Leary analyses these developments in his recent work on the Irish in Wales and provides an excellent overview of the spread of Irish urban settlement in south Wales in particular.[1] Cardiff, however, merits special attention. The size of its population, its social structure and its history of growth and development during the nineteenth century make it similar to other urban areas in which the Irish settled in Britain. It could be claimed, as a result, that Cardiff is reasonably typical of the Irish urban immigrant settlement in the nineteenth century and that a study of the Irish experience in Cardiff provides insights that may be used to explore the patterns of settlement in urban areas of Britain as a whole.

It is useful, at this point to address the question of the 'ghettoisation' of the urban Irish immigrant population. O'Leary also considers this concept and is highly critical of the references to 'Irish ghettos' in the works of earlier historians of the Irish in Britain.[2] Sociologists rarely use the term 'ghetto'. Strictly, it should apply only to groups of people living together in clearly demarcated geographical areas who have little or no contact with people outside. In a real ghetto there will be few, if any, non-members of the group. The ghetto itself will provide all the physical and social needs of its members including housing, work, religious practice and entertainment. Therefore, they can live in isolation from the rest of the urban population. Although there were clusters of Irish immigrants living close together in parts of neighbourhoods there were no Irish settlements that remotely approached 'ghettos'.

Cardiff as a city is a product of the industrial developments that took place in south Wales during the nineteenth century. Throughout the eighteenth century Cardiff remained a small community, containing approximately 1,000 people and existing as the centre of the agricultural area of the Vale of Glamorgan. In common with many other small ports along the coast of south Wales, Cardiff engaged in the shipment of coal and it was this activity that provided the key to its future development as a thriving industrial settlement. During the nineteenth century there was a progressive development of the coalfield that spread across the valleys of south Wales, and an outlet had to be found for the shipping of this coal not only to other parts of Britain but also to many countries abroad. It was to meet this need that Cardiff was developed. A canal was dug and a railway built to link the town with the coalfield and a network of docks was constructed in the town itself to cope with the vessels needed for transporting coal.

Work of this nature demanded an increasing amount of labour, which could not be supplied by the small population of eighteenth-century Cardiff. The result was that there was a steady immigration of workmen and their families from the surrounding counties of Wales and England and from the south-east counties of Ireland. These people settled in Cardiff and, as commerce in general and the coal industry in particular flourished during the nineteenth century, the town grew in size, until by the middle of the twentieth century its population amounted to almost a quarter of a million (see Table 1).

To fill in the demographic picture a little more it is helpful to look very briefly at the occupations of the inhabitants of Cardiff at different times, particularly in the first half of the nineteenth century when Irish immigration reached its peak. The *Cardiff Records* show that, at least until 1835, there was no class of merchants or manufacturers in the town.[3] Until Cardiff began to be transformed by the industrial developments that occurred after the first quarter of the nineteenth century its occupational divisions remained fairly static. There was a small number of 'gentry' in the town (though the *Report to the General Board of Health* of 1850 takes pains to point out that Cardiff was not a town that 'gentlemen' would find attractive to live in), a number of yeomen farmers and small tradesmen (including mercers, hat makers, tobacconists and journeymen carpenters) and a labouring population made up of farm

Table 1 *Total population of Cardiff, 1801–1951*[4]

Year	Population
1801	1,870
1821	3,521
1841	10,077
1861	32,954
1881	82,761
1901	164,333
1921	200,184
1931	223,589
1951	243,632

Table 2 *Percentage of labour employed in different trades in Cardiff, 1851*[5]

Trade	Percentage
Agriculture	4.7
Iron and steel	7.0
Shipbuilding	3.2
Coalmining	5.0
Railway	2.2
Canals	2.5
Building	17.0
Occupations connected with the sea	58.4

workers and men connected with the slight activity of the port. By 1851, however, the working population was beginning to reflect the increased activity in the town and was becoming more diversified (see Table 2). The Irish were engaged mainly in the unskilled sectors of all these trades except agriculture and coalmining. In this they followed the general pattern in south Wales.

The following examination of Irish settlement in Cardiff has been divided into two sections, the establishment and the development. In the period of establishment, immigration was continuously rising and there was apparently no ordered community among the newcomers; in the period of development, immigration steadily declined and the group began to take shape. The dividing date, 1861, has been chosen because in that year immigration had already reached its peak and because St Peter's church was opened – an event that symbolises the beginning of an era in which Irish settlement entered a phase of rapid institutionalisation.

The Establishment of the Irish Settlement in Cardiff, 1800–61

It is difficult to make accurate estimates of the numbers of Irish immigrants who came to settle in Cardiff in the first decades of the nineteenth century. The census reports of the period are not sufficiently precise in this regard, partly because the census boundaries within which Cardiff was contained changed during the period, but also because of the difficulty of keeping track of the large number of immigrants who made temporary stays in the lodging-houses in the town, many of them owned by their compatriots. Census-takers at the time found difficulty in tracing the movements of these people and it would be unreasonable to expect totally reliable population figures from them.

There are, however, other reliable sources to be used. Almost all of the Irish settlers were Roman Catholics and, to a greater or lesser degree, church attenders, so parochial records give a good indication of their numbers. In Cardiff the first church to be established during this period was St David's, followed by St Peter's in 1861. The parochial records of both churches are used, in combination with the census reports and the Cardiff Diary of the Fathers of the Institute of Charity, to estimate the size of the Irish settlement in Cardiff. During the first three decades of the nineteenth century, births, marriages and deaths had to be registered in the Church of England, regardless of religious affiliation. The appropriate church in Cardiff was St John's, so parochial records there have been consulted for the appropriate periods. From this combination of sources the following picture emerges.

For the first three decades of the nineteenth century there was a steady but very slow increase in the number of Irish immigrants settling in Cardiff. From the one identifiable Irishman, James McLoughlin, residing in Cardiff prior to 1822, the number of settlers increased to around 50 by 1830. After that date the rate of settlement increased very rapidly throughout the decade, so that by 1841 there were 1,200 persons on the register at St David's. This sudden and dramatic increase was due mainly to the considerable work that was being done to develop Cardiff as a port for the export of coal from south Wales and to serve the ironworks in the south Wales valleys. The building of the Bute dock occupied the middle years of the 1830s and the work was completed in 1839. At the same time, the Taff Vale Railway, designed to link Cardiff with the coalfield, was being constructed, a project that was completed in 1841. The demand for labour that these schemes produced accounts for the increase in the Irish population up to 1841. Employers looked to Ireland to supply labourers, and the proximity of south Wales to the Cork and Waterford areas of Ireland made immigration to Cardiff a fairly simple matter.

After 1841 there was a decline in the numbers of the Irish in Cardiff. This was probably caused by the completion of the docks and railway so that by 1845 the figure had dropped to 900. From 1845, however, there was a steady increase. This is shown by the evidence from the registers of St David's and St Peter's. In 1848 there were 2,300 on the register of St David's; by 1850 this number had increased to 3,700, and by 1861 the combined total of St David's and St Peter's had reached 10,800. This influx of immigrants may be attributed to two major 'push' and 'pull' phenomena. The 'push' resulted from the need of the immigrants to escape from the effects of famine; the 'pull' was the prospect of steady work and a reasonably reliable income. There is little doubt that the Irish who streamed into Cardiff from 1846 to 1851, in particular, were the victims of the disaster that had befallen their homeland and came in search of refuge and the hope of achieving some sort of security for the future. The pull in Cardiff was real at the time. Cardiff's docks were being extended during that period and in 1855 the East Bute dock and basin were both completed.

Social Status of the Immigrants

The general picture of the social status of the Irish immigrants during this period is depressing. Their status was directly related to their occupations and it was reported that their work was 'usually of the roughest, coarsest and most repulsive description, and requiring the least skill and practise'.[6] As a result, the Irish were relegated to the bottom of the social scale, on a level with the poorest of the indigenous population. In Cardiff, in the early 1840s and before the post-famine flood, there were reports in the local press of mendicant Irish. One newspaper, for example, in 1840 and 1841 reported cases of Irish people seeking money from the courts to pay their fare home. By 1842, however, the number of such cases was so high that the editor no longer thought it worthwhile to publish an account of them. The affairs of these 'gentry', he felt, were not, in any case, of sufficient value to merit the attention of his readers.[7]

Further evidence comes from the Commissioners on Education in Wales, who noted in 1847 that there was little permanent poverty in the town except among the Irish.[8] Their view is supported by the evidence of Fr Patrick Millea at Cardiff, who stated that the members of his congregation were, with few exceptions, 'of the labouring class and many of them the poorest of the poor'.[9] This view of the Irish is repeated frequently by officials reporting on conditions in the town.

For example, the author of the government report on the sanitary condition of the town in 1849 comments on the influx of Irish immigrants as follows: 'the worst of these straggling accessions to the local population is, that they too generally consist of the most wretched members of the society from which they have, as it were, been cast forth – generally in a starving condition, often already afflicted with disease, or carrying the seeds of it about with them'.[10] During the years 1846–49 there were outbreaks of typhus and cholera in Cardiff. The main weight of the blame for these was laid at the door of the Irish. In 1849 the medical officer of the Cardiff Union stated that the main cause of the increase in disease was 'the immense invasion of Irish destitute labourers, navigators and others, who had been brought over to this town by public works'. His assistant went so far as to say that the majority of cases of fever 'may be said to have been imported direct from Skibbereen and Clonakilty'.[11]

Social Divisions among the Immigrants

It would be an oversimplification, however, to create the impression that the Irish constituted a completely destitute group of refugees from famine. There were divisions among the Irish themselves. Those who had arrived prior to the Great Famine contained among them persons of a different type from those who arrived in such great numbers after 1847. Evidence of this is available from a number of sources. The first settlers, that is those who came between 1822 and 1847, were not all illiterate. The registers of St John's show that some of them, at least, were capable of reproducing signatures in very fair handwriting. They had, furthermore, a concern for education. Fr Millea mentions the existence of a school that must have been there since the early 1840s at the latest. Classes were held 'in a room or two in some back place only fit for cattle', yet the subjects taught included 'arithmetic, geography, English grammar, reading, writing etc.', a not unambitious programme for the children of the poorer classes at the time. Before the opening of St David's chapel in 1842, centres of worship – admittedly small and unsatisfactory – were set up, indicating that attempts had been made from the start to bring the Irish in Cardiff into close contact with their religion, even though they were few in number and resources and could ill afford to rent premises and support a pastor.

It was in the early 1840s, also, that the Ancient Order of Hibernians was formed. The appearance of a branch of this national organisation in Cardiff at such an early date is of some significance. Among the aims of the Ancient Order of Hibernians was the encouragement, through savings and insurance schemes, of the virtues of thrift and a concern for the future. There must, therefore, have been Irishmen in Cardiff at that time who possessed these virtues, so highly esteemed by their fellow-townsmen, and who, as a result, must have felt that a gulf existed between them and the new arrivals after 1847.

The evidence quoted shows that there was some attempt, prior to the famine-related influx, to organise the Irish along sound lines and to begin building for the future. It also indicates the existence of a group among the immigrants themselves who were prepared to accept the responsibilities of leadership. It was from among these people that the clergy, who were mainly responsible for leading the later organisation of the Irish community, drew their support. In the early 1840s their numbers were not large and later in that decade they were confronted by a sudden and massive increase in the numbers of their compatriots. Nevertheless they were able to play an active and valuable part in the stabilisation of the settlement and its continuing development.

The Nature of the Settlement in Cardiff

In the first years of the settlement, between 1822 and 1841, the Irish established themselves close to the centre of what was then still a small town, with houses and businesses clustered on the southern side of Cardiff castle, a building that dominated the whole area. The registers of St David's and St John's show them located in Tunnel Buildings, Union Buildings, the Hayes and Bute Street, all within easy walking distance of the castle. After 1841 there was also a concentration of Irish around St David's chapel, which was located in Bute Terrace, slightly further away from the castle but still within easy walking distance. After 1847, it was in this area that the famine immigrants lived and which became the centre of the settlement. Throughout the remainder of the nineteenth century the Irish spread outwards from here.[12]

In 1850 one street, Stanley Street, running north–south alongside St David's, was occupied almost exclusively by Irish immigrants. Large concentrations of them were also to be found in adjacent streets. The result was that by 1850 the area of settlement lay roughly between the Taff Vale Railway, running north–south and forming the Eastern boundary, and St Mary Street, then the main street of the town, on the west. To the north, the cut-off point was Ebenezer Street, and the South Wales Railway formed the boundary to the south. At this time Newtown, located within a quarter of a mile south-east of St David's – and which was to become the centre of the Irish population in Cardiff in the twenty years following 1850 – consisted only of about 100 houses but it was developing steadily.

The reports of the medical officer of health for Cardiff, the earliest of which is for the year 1853, trace the spread of the Irish into Newtown, an area that lay immediately to the east of the Taff Vale Railway. It was thus within one hundred yards of Stanley Street and the streets adjacent to it and was the natural area to which the Irish moved. In 1853 Newtown's streets were 'improved' and by 1854 a large number of the immigrants were living there. The report for this year indicates that there were at least 1,500 Irish living in Newtown.[13] In 1855 the majority of houses in this area were Irish lodging-houses.[14]

It is difficult to give a precise estimate of the number of Irish living in the areas outlined above. Most of the houses there, at the time, were used as lodging-houses and consequently had a varying number of occupants who stayed in them for varying lengths of time. Prior to 1850 no check was kept on the numbers of people who lived at any given time in these houses and so no accurate figures are available. After 1850 an inspector was appointed to visit these lodging-houses and a maximum number of occupants was laid down for each house. This regulation, however, applied only to places *registered* as lodging-houses and, therefore, did not cover all the residences where lodgers were taken in.

Probably the most reliable guides to the actual numbers living in the areas are the estimates in the reports based on the figures given by the landlords of the houses or by neighbours. Using these as a basis, it appears that in 1850 there were approximately 3,000 Irish immigrants concentrated into the area around Stanley Street and the site of St David's. Between 1850 and 1859 the total Irish population of Cardiff had increased to 8,900, and the process of spreading out from the original area of settlement into Newtown had begun. This was the result of both fresh immigration and some movement on the part of the Irish. By 1859 there were about 2,000 immigrants living in the streets recently built in Newtown.

The number of Irish living in these two areas, then, in 1859 was approximately 5,000. This figure is almost certainly an underestimate, however. Although the medical officer made regular checks on the houses registered as lodging-houses, the landlords, as he ruefully admits in the reports of 1858 and 1860, took every opportunity to increase the number of occupants between inspections. The actual number of Irish who occupied the lodging-houses was likely to be substantially higher than the estimate made. To them must be added the immigrants who lived in lodging-houses that were not registered and therefore not inspected.

To add to this brief sketch of the settlement before 1861, some description of the type of housing the immigrants occupied may be helpful. One official report shows that in 1850 the type and quality of the houses built in Cardiff varied considerably.[15] Those occupied by the small number of 'gentry' and the professional and merchant class lay immediately south of the castle – the old part of the town – and were of as high quality as conditions permitted. Most of the town was built at sea level and on swampland. The highest part of Cardiff was named (appropriately enough) High Street, where the Town Hall was located, and was a mere sixteen feet above sea level. Consequently, and not surprisingly, the houses were subject to flooding and the inhabitants vulnerable to what was described at the time as 'ague and miasma'.[16] These were among the reasons why Cardiff had been described as not a fit place for gentry to live.

The newcomers did not occupy this area but were located further south and east where the environmental and health problems were even worse. As a general rule most of the houses built in the Stanley Street and Newtown areas in this period, including the lodging-houses, were two- or four-roomed cottages and of greatly inferior quality to the houses in the old part of the town. Because of the rapid influx of workers and their families, not only from Ireland but also from the surrounding rural areas of Wales and England, there was an acute housing shortage between 1840 and 1861. Such a situation attracts speculative building with an eye mainly on quick and short-term profit rather than on the comfort and convenience of the occupants, and this was certainly the case in Cardiff. By 1849 the demand for housing had become so great that the town surveyor reported that 'houses of the lower class . . . are now commonly let before even the first stone is laid'.[17] He goes on to say that as these houses were built without any regard to level or uniformity it was almost impossible to construct decent roads and pavements between them and that in those streets that had been paved the floors of the houses were often below the level of the paving. The drainage problems that resulted contributed substantially to the conditions that produced the outbreaks of typhus and cholera during the period.

Although the quality of the housing was low the rents were not. The town surveyor reported that '[the] rents of the cottage property throughout the town are very high. The very lowest class of cottages – those in Stanley Street, for instance – which have only two rooms each, and the building of which would not have cost more than £40, let for £6 10s. a year; very inferior cottages let as high as £10 a year'.[18] In 1857 the medical officer of health reported that houses in Newtown that had been built at a cost of between £105 and £110 were being let without difficulty at rents between £15 and £16 per annum.

It was these factors that brought about the increase of lodging-houses in the town, occupied largely by Irish immigrants. The rents of the cottages were so high that they were beyond the pockets of the majority of wage earners and certainly beyond the reach of the impoverished immigrants who arrived after 1845. It became a common practice, then, for

Irish immigrants who had been in Cardiff before 1845 to take over the tenancy of houses where the Irish settled and to take in their compatriots as lodgers. This enabled them both to meet the high rents and to provide the new immigrants with at least a minimum level of shelter. The use of such small cottages as lodging-houses, however, inevitably resulted in very severe overcrowding; this, along with inadequate or non-existent drainage, resulted in dire living conditions which encouraged outbreaks of typhus and cholera. These conditions persisted throughout the 1840s and 1850s. After 1860, however, when the immigrants were becoming adjusted to urban living, beginning to achieve some level of prosperity and moving out of the original areas of settlement, the quality of their lives began to show steady improvement.

These conditions were not endured by all the Irish, however. As was indicated earlier, there was a small section of the community composed mainly of immigrants from the pre-famine years whose standard of living was at least on a par with that of their working peers and who aimed at achieving high status in the town. The influence of this section upon their less able or less fortunate compatriots was already being felt before 1861. The membership of this group looked for their leadership to the Roman Catholic clergy appointed to attend to their spiritual welfare. Such leadership extended into other areas of life beyond the spiritual, two of which, education and social activities, are briefly considered below.

Prior to 1850 a start had already been made on the task of providing educational facilities for the immigrants. Mention has already been made of the school opened in David Street by Fr Millea in 1847 and reported on by the Commissioners on Education. The schoolroom is described in the report as measuring 40 feet by 19 feet and possessing an 'open roof, three good-sized windows, four skylights, two fireplaces, and a bricked floor'. There was a dwelling-house attached to the school and 'sufficient outbuildings, the whole structure being held on a lease for 999 years'.[19] The school opened at a time when the flood of destitute Irish had been reaching Cardiff for about two years and it is reasonable to suppose that the financial support necessary to establish the school came from the more firmly established members of the community. (There is no mention in Fr Millea's report of any one substantial benefactor.)

It appears that Fr Millea had a considerable struggle to persuade the majority of the Irish that education was beneficial for their children, particularly when the parents discovered that they would have to pay for it. Of the estimated 220 school-age boys and girls in the settlement in 1847, fewer than 80 or 90 attended the school regularly. Millea writes that the parents of these children complained that they were not well able to pay for their children's schooling. The highest sum charged was four pence per week; this was done in order to leave the parents no cause for complaining, yet they considered it too much for their means; hence we may conclude that the greater part of the children of my congregation would want a gratuitous education.[20]

Economic factors forced many parents to send the young members of the family out to work at the earliest possible age and they looked upon time spent at school beyond that age as time wasted. As might be expected, this attitude caused Fr Millea some feelings of frustration, and he commented that the parents felt that 'if their children can read, that is enough – they should thank providence and be satisfied – that should be the *ne plus ultra*'.[21] By patient effort, however, the rate of attendance was steadily improved. By 1856 there had been an eightfold increase in the Irish population in the town and in that year the school premises were extensively enlarged. As the settlement grew after 1860, many more schools, again through the agency of the clergy, were opened in other parts of Cardiff, but it took years to eradicate the impression from the minds of many of the Irish that education beyond the elementary stage was a luxury to be afforded only by those who had no need to engage in more productive tasks. This was one attitude, at least, that they shared with their non-Irish contemporaries.

Some organisation of social activities was also attempted, and here again the lead was taken by the clergy, assisted by members of the pre-famine settlement. The mode of life of the majority of the Irish severely limited the scope for recreation. For many of them, the only release from the unpleasant realities of their existence was to be found in the taverns. Consequently, drunkenness reached serious proportions and became a matter of concern for the clergy, particularly at times such as Christmas when it became more prevalent. Eventually, on 17–18 December 1859 Fr Richardson visited Cardiff from Newport in order to establish the Roman Catholic Association for the Suppression of Drunkenness.[22] This Association had only a limited effect, however, for it was necessary for further measures to be taken at different times during the next twenty years.

Apart from discouraging drunkenness, efforts were made to provide opportunities for the Irish to spend their leisure hours in a more constructive and rewarding fashion than by merely frequenting the taverns. It was felt that the best way of doing this was to provide a means by which the members of the settlement could undertake activities in common. Thus, in February 1859 Brother Colton, a member of the Institute of Charity, which had by now taken over the care of the Cardiff mission, came to Cardiff and founded a night school at which he taught.[23] No record exists of the number of students who attended these classes and so no reliable judgement can be made of the appeal that they may have had to the immigrants. In order to influence as wide a section of the Irish as possible, Brother Colton also formed a fife and drum band, an organisation that would have been very familiar to the immigrants and that may have provided them with a link to their homeland. Again, no records of this band are extant but the tradition established in Cardiff lasted for eighty years: an Irish fife and drum band existed in the city until 1939.

Attempts like these to provide some organised social activity within the settlement are indicators of future developments. Though small and probably short-lived, they set the pattern for similar developments that were to take place during the latter half of the nineteenth century and the first quarter of the twentieth. In this regard they are important as forerunners of communal activities – parish social and religious groups, the Ancient Order of Hibernians, city-wide celebrations of St Patrick's Day, among others – that provided the Irish settlement with a sense of communal identity and, at the same time, marked it off from other sections of the population of Cardiff.

The Development of the Irish Settlement in Cardiff after 1861

The years following 1861 saw fairly rapid developments in both the size and the organisation of the Irish settlement in Cardiff. The movements of the Irish outside the original area of settlement may be tracked through the locations in which Catholic churches and schools were built and Catholic parishes established. The vast majority of the Catholics in Cardiff were Irish in origin or descent throughout the nineteenth century and this provides the justification for using the sites of Catholic churches as the main means of tracing the movements of the Irish throughout the town. Making reliable estimates of the actual size of the Irish settlement, including Irish-born immigrants and their descendants, has, however, proved to be much more difficult. Although the figures quoted above from the parish registers of St David's and St Peter's, relating to the original settlement, may be regarded as reasonably accurate the same cannot be said of the records of parishes founded later in the century.

It has not been the practice of parish priests generally to keep yearly records of the total number of parishioners; the work involved in taking regular censuses is beyond their resources of time, cash and available labour. Numbers would fluctuate in any case because of the increasing incidence of 'short-stay' parishioners – Irish workers who came to take advantage of the relatively high wages paid for short-term construction work and then returned to Ireland, an alternative not available to their predecessors during the famine years. After 1861, also, there is not the

Table 3 *Irish-born residents of Cardiff, 1861–1951*[24]

Year	Total Cardiff population	Irish-born
1861	32,954	5,000
1881	82,761	4,259
1901	164,333	3,655
1921	200,184	3,100
1931	223,589	2,332
1951	243,632	2,033

abundance of official reports, with their detailed descriptions of both the numbers and the living conditions of the immigrants as extra sources of information. Consequently, only rough estimates can be given from the available evidence. Firm figures can be extracted from the official censuses and these are shown in Table 3. They relate, however, only to Irish-born residents of Cardiff and give a profile of the pattern of immigration but not the full picture of the size of the settlement.

After the peak year of 1861 the number of Irish-born people in Cardiff declined slowly. The flow of immigrants subsided and the influx of Irish into Cardiff in the second half of the nineteenth century and the first half of the twentieth century was not as great as it was in many of the large English cities. The main reason for this is that Cardiff is not a centre of manufacturing industry in the same way as, for example, Birmingham. Consequently, the demand for labour was not consistently high during the period but fluctuated. Most of the demand came from the increased volume of trade through the docks and the building of the Guest Keen Steel Works in the second half of the nineteenth century, both of which demanded a large supply of unskilled labour.

The majority of the immigrants, both men and women, who arrived in the second half of the nineteenth century were aged between 20 and 25.[25] Consequently, the Cardiff settlement received a constant, if declining, supply of fresh blood during the 90 years following 1861. The bulk of these immigrants seem to have settled easily into the life of the community, many of them going to live and work with relatives and friends who had sent for them. Many of the men married Irish women who had emigrated at the same time and founded families in Cardiff, so that the settlement grew steadily in size and strength.

During the second half of the nineteenth century the living conditions of those of the Irish who remained in the original area of settlement steadily improved. A number of factors were responsible for this. The increase in the number of houses in Cardiff meant that there was a movement out of the settlement and a consequent reduction in overcrowding. Also, the area, along with all other parts of the town, came under the strict supervision of a succession of able and active medical officers of health, who ensured that standards of cleanliness and public hygiene were maintained. Finally, the local authority, using the powers granted to it by parliament, was able to enforce higher standards of drainage and paving and to improve the quality of the streets and housing generally.

Two other factors should also be taken into account. The fact that Irish immigration into Cardiff reached its peak in 1861 and declined slowly thereafter meant that there was no repetition of the sudden influx that followed the famine into an area that was not sufficiently developed to offer the migrants adequate living space. Also, the immigrants who came in the second half of the century did not arrive in the state of destitution so characteristic of their predecessors and were better able to improve their living standards. In the Newtown and Stanley Street areas the combined effect of these factors was to produce a steady change from conditions of squalor to those nearer to the general level existing in the working-class areas of the town built in the last decades of the nineteenth century.

The Irish who lived in this area made an effort themselves to improve their own living conditions. For example, under the leadership of the clergy they formed an association aimed at raising standards of hygiene and impressing upon the immigrants the importance of maintaining adequate sanitary facilities.[26] Also, the misery of those among them who were unable to find employment was relieved to some extent through the work of an organisation that had been formed to give help in times of distress.[27]

The effects of the increased supply of housing were being felt by the middle of the 1870s when some of the congestion in the area of settlement was being relieved. The most rapid improvement, however, came in the 1880s. For example, by 1882 overcrowding had been considerably reduced from the 1869 figure and by 1885 the number of overcrowded houses was insignificant, in spite of the fact that rents remained high.[28] Improvements in the standards of cleanliness and the resultant decline in the incidence of disease among the Irish were maintained and there was no repetition of the large-scale outbreaks of typhus and cholera of 1847 and 1849.

During these years of improving living conditions the community itself took shape. As the population grew, the church that had been built in 1841 became inadequate, so a chapel was opened in Newtown in 1873 in order to meet the needs of the Irish who had moved there. In turn, this proved very quickly to be too small, and in 1893 St Paul's church was opened and the area was made into a separate parish. By this time the original St David's church had been replaced by a larger building in Charles Street, which was consecrated in 1887 and which was to become St David's Cathedral. The interval between the building of these churches – symbols of the increasing economic prosperity of the immigrants – also saw a considerable increase in the educational facilities available to the Irish. By 1865, for example, there were two schools in David Street, where the first schoolroom had been established, and the number of children attending them had increased to approximately 1,000.[29]

By the end of the nineteenth century conditions in the original area of settlement were comparable to those in any other working-class area of the town. Improvements in living conditions had been accompanied by a rise in the provision of formal education and a general movement out of the conditions of apathy and squalor that had prevailed in the mid-century years. During the second half of the nineteenth century the increased commercial importance of Cardiff brought about a rapid expansion of the town. New areas, particularly around the docks and other centres of industry, were developed as suburbs to house the working class while, at the same time, more substantial buildings began to be erected close to the town centre for the prosperous merchants and traders.

As the town grew, so did movement by Irish immigrants. Sections of the Irish community moved into the new working-class neighbourhoods that were being built. The numbers of those who moved from Newtown and Stanley Street into Roath, Canton, Grangetown and, later, Splott, were increased by new immigrants from Ireland during the second half of the century. These newcomers sought accommodation in the areas close to their places of work and many settled with relatives or friends who had come to Cardiff earlier. As a result, the later years of the nineteenth century and the first quarter of the twentieth century saw the development of a number of Irish sub-communities in the town, linked together by organisations common to them all. In the second and third quarters of the twentieth century the increasing affluence of many of the immigrants' descendants enabled them to move into the middle-class residential areas of the city.

The initial founding of the settlement and the first movements out have already been described. By 1861 further developments had taken place, for in that year a substantial number of Irish were living in Roath, outside the original area of settlement. By the middle of the 1860s Irish families were also located in Canton and Grangetown, two new districts that were developing practically simultaneously. Twenty years later, there had been a tremendous increase in the size of the Roath district and a thriving Irish community was established there. Grangetown and Canton had already grown in size and at this time the Irish groups in both districts were over 1,000 strong. The concentration of a number of industries near the Roath dock had led to the building of workers' houses nearby and, as a result, the district of Splott had come into existence.

At the end of the nineteenth century, Roath, Canton, Grangetown and Splott had been completed, except for minor additions made during the first half of the twentieth century. In each of these districts there was a group of Irish families concentrating their activities around church and school, two organisations that were symbols of their existence as communities.[30]

The twentieth century saw the development of areas on the outskirts of the city – residential areas and council estates. At the end of the first decade of the century Penylan had come into existence and the residential area around Victoria Park on the other side of town was in the process of development. During the course of the following twenty years extensive building was carried out on the northern, eastern and western outskirts of Cardiff, so that by 1930 Birchgrove, Cyncoed, Rumney, Fairwater and Heath had found their places on the map, Llandaff and Whitchurch had increased in size and a start had been made on the council estate at Ely. In each of these areas members of the Cardiff Irish community were to be found, although, as might be expected, prior to 1951 there were heavier concentrations of them in the working-class districts of Roath, Canton, Grangetown and Splott than there were in the leafy suburbs of Whitchurch and Cyncoed. Movement into these areas came later in the century when the Irish had become assimilated into the general population of the city, had proved to be successful in the professional, business and political life of Cardiff, and had ceased to be an identifiable group within the population as a whole.

The development of the Irish community was not restricted to the building of churches and the establishment of schools. Some account has already been given of attempts to organise leisure activities among the people before 1861 and these efforts were continued on a larger scale during the second half of the nineteenth century. 'Social activities' should be taken to cover not only recreational activities but also activities that were undertaken in common and aimed at improving the general level and quality of life of the immigrants. During this period the initiative in organising these aspects of life was still being taken by the clergy. The Irish accepted them as spiritual leaders, but given that the average Catholic clergyman had a level of education and administrative experience substantially higher than most of his flock, the clergy's leadership role extended far beyond the spiritual.

In order to strengthen the sense of community among their flocks and to ensure that the latter played as full and active a part as possible in the life of the church, the Roman Catholic clergy placed great emphasis on the importance of parochial organisations. Once the essential building programme of church and school was completed, attention was focused on providing a suitable meeting-place for the people of the parish. In many cases where funds were not sufficient to meet the cost of building a parish hall, the school or even the church itself was used for this purpose. Thus, in each district where groups of Irish settled, organisations were set up with their headquarters on church premises, and in this way the church became the focal point of an important aspect of the lives of the people. During the second half of the nineteenth century and the first half of the twentieth, many such organisations were established, most with branches in each parish, and others catering for the special needs and interests of their members.[31]

One city-wide organisation deserves special notice. The Ancient Order of Hibernians, formed and directed solely by lay people, was in existence, as noted earlier, in the early years of the life of the settlement. The original members of the Order continued their activities during the second half of the nineteenth century, and as membership grew due to the community's increasing prosperity, so the organisation itself expanded. By 1874 sufficient progress had been made for the establishment of the Hibernian Benefit Building Society.

The work of this society had two main aspects. The 'Benefit' section provided a scheme whereby, in return for small weekly payments from its members, payment was made during sickness or unemployment. The 'Building' section existed to encourage home ownership among members through the advance of loans for house purchase. Unfortunately, no records are available of the scope of these activities before 1896, the date of the oldest extant balance sheet of the Building Society. At this date the building and benefit sections, though still occupying the same offices and remaining under the control of the Order, had been divided into two self-contained organisations. The Hibernian Benefit Society remained in existence until National Insurance legislation made its work unnecessary. The Building Society, however, increased its activities until its balance sheet for 1957 showed the amount of £408,000 on loan for house purchase, at a time when a three-bedroomed, semi-detached house in a prosperous, middle-class suburb in Cardiff could be bought for £2,000. For a small society, strictly local in its activities, this is not unimpressive.

Since it was not the practice of the society throughout the nineteenth century and into the twentieth to advertise for business or to attempt to make its name known outside the Irish community, it is fairly safe to assume that the bulk of its lending was restricted to members of that community. Consequently, the steady growth of loans throws an interesting sidelight on the increase in home ownership among the Irish and is some indication of their growing prosperity.

Until the middle of the twentieth century, the two branches of the Hibernians were controlled by a group of men drawn from within the

Irish community. Their occupations varied but most of them were skilled workers or small tradesmen who devoted their spare time to the affairs of the two societies. Both societies are remarkable examples of self-help and initiative on the part of men who were, for the most part, unversed in the skills of finance, yet who were prepared to take the risk of lending money to their compatriots to provide them with homes. The technical difficulties involved in house purchase presented some problems at first but fortunately the Hibernian directors were able to obtain the services of a solicitor who was also a prominent member of the community. Other aspects of the work – such as surveying and valuing the properties – they performed themselves. The suitability of the candidates for loans, apart from their financial resources, was tested by the standing of their families in the community or by a character reference from one of the clergy.

The importance of the Hibernians was not restricted to the activities described above. The Order also acted as a social body that united, in its functions, all the more prosperous members of the Irish community. The Hibernians' celebrations on St Patrick's Day were the social events of the year and were much commented upon by the local press. The Hibernians played a prominent part in the St Patrick's Day procession during the nineteenth century and their custom of holding a dinner on that day was followed until well into the twentieth century.

Conclusion

In conclusion, this brief survey of the establishment and development of the Irish settlement in Cardiff shows how an urban immigrant group in nineteenth-century Wales could overcome considerable difficulties and achieve levels of security and prosperity that did not at first seem conceivable. The very small number of immigrants at the start of the nineteenth century were engulfed by the flood of people escaping from the catastrophe of the famine, who had to endure appalling living conditions on their arrival. The odds against creating a successful settlement were very high indeed. The newcomers were penniless and hungry and had no experience of urban living and the new demands it would make upon them. They were also entering an urban setting that was itself changing and developing and that, for an initial period at least, had run out of the control of the municipal authorities. Consequently, houses were being built with no regard for the needs, health or hygiene of their occupants, and were being let at exorbitant rents. Overcrowding and disease were severe and endemic. Work was available but it was hard and the hours were long, and the most readily available source of escape and relaxation was the tavern.

In spite of all this, the settlement was structured from within and achieved an identity that gave its members self-respect and confidence. Churches and schools were built, self-help organisations were set up and flourished through voluntary labour, and the Irish began to move away from the depressed conditions they had endured in the 1840s and 1850s. For a long period during the nineteenth and twentieth centuries they worked together as a group; their objectives were to improve their conditions of life to the point at which they equalled, or exceeded, those of the majority of the indigenous population. This process involved adopting the material standards, attitudes and values of their non-Irish fellow citizens, and so the integration of the Irish into the host society proceeded at an increasing pace throughout the course of the twentieth century.

Notes

1. Paul O'Leary, *Immigration and Integration: The Irish in Wales, 1798–1922,* Cardiff, University of Wales Press, 2000.

2. O'Leary, *Immigration and Integration* pp. 107–33.

3. J.H. Mathews, *Cardiff Records,* I, Cardiff, Cardiff Corporation, 1898.

4. Sources: census volumes for the years concerned.

5. Source: census volumes, 1851.

6. See John Hickey, *Urban Catholics,* London, Geoffrey Chapman, 1967, p. 62.

7. *Cardiff Advertiser and Merthyr Guardian.* Various issues, 1840–1841.

8. PP 1847 XXVII, *Reports of the Commission on the State of Education in Wales,* Vol. I, p. 366.

9. PP 1847 XXVII, *Education in Wales,* pp. 371–72.

10. T.W. Rammell, *Report to the General Board of Health on the Town of Cardiff,* London, 1850.

11. Rammell, *Report,* p. 44.

12. Rammell, *Report,* and the *Annual Reports* of the Medical Officer of Health for Cardiff, 1853 and following.

13. H.J. Paine, *Report of the Medical Officer of Health,* Cardiff, 1855, p. 7.

14. Paine, *Report,* p. 9.

15. Rammell, *Report,* p. 11.

16. Rammell, *Report,* p. 11.

17. Rammell, *Report,* p. 16.

18. Rammell, *Report,* p. 33.

19. PP 1847 XXVII, *Education in Wales,* p. 371.

20. PP 1847 XXVII, *Education in Wales,* pp. 371–72.

21. PP 1847 XXVII, *Education in Wales,* pp. 371–72.

22. Cardiff Diary of the Fathers of Charity, unpublished MS, St Peter's church, Cardiff, 17 December 1859.

23. Cardiff Diary of the Fathers of Charity, 1859.

24. Figures taken from the census volumes for the years concerned and the *Irish Trade Journal and Statistical Bulletin*, Dublin, Central Statistics Office, June 1955, p. 84.

25. *Report of the Commission on Emigration and other Population Problems*, Dublin, Stationery Office, 1955, p. 320, Table 29.

26. Cardiff Diary of the Fathers of Charity, 1866.

27. Cardiff Diary of the Fathers of Charity, March 1867.

28. H.J. Paine, *Report of the Medical Officer of Health*, Cardiff, 1885, p. 59.

29. Cardiff Diary of the Fathers of Charity, 4 August 1865.

30. For details of the establishment and development of the communities, see John Hickey, *Urban Catholics*, London, Geoffrey Chapman, 1967.

31. Hickey, *Urban Catholics*, p. 116.

'Decorous and Creditable': The Irish in Newport[1]

Chris Williams

There were those in the countries of their enforced adoption who looked with doubt and distrust on the present and future of their Irish fellow-citizens. But the condition of Irishmen in great cities was the inevitable result of the past; it had no basis in the real character of the race, and was capable of being blotted out by resolute and properly-directed effort. The Irish situation was painted blacker than it was by race prejudice and want of knowledge . . . The Irishman in the main was patriotic, religious, generous, affectionate, and sympathetic; he could love long and deeply, could hate firmly, could be the tenderest nurse . . . or the fiercest soldier . . . They had no reason to be ashamed of him or of belonging to his race. Those who knew his history of blood and tears, who had studied the conditions under which he had been pitchforked into the hovels and the drudgeries of strange and unsympathetic lands, had the key to a sympathetic and hopeful study of his defects . . .[2]

The coal- and iron-exporting port of Newport, Monmouthshire, grew rapidly in size and economic importance during the nineteenth century. With a population of 1,100 in 1801, it totalled 67,270 by 1901. Many thousands of these turn-of-the-century inhabitants were first-, second- or third-generation migrants who had come from the west of England and Wales to settle in the town. Accompanying them were many migrants born in Ireland, as indicated by Table 1. Notwithstanding that the figures for Irish-born exclude the many second- or even third-generation Irish (those born outside Ireland of Irish parents or grandparents, who may have seen themselves and been seen by others as Irish), Newport may easily be identified as one of the major centres of Irish settlement in Wales. In 1851 Newport had, behind Cardiff, the second largest Irish-born population in Wales (measured as a percentage of the town's total population) and ranked seventh among the large towns and cities of Britain in terms of Irish-born population.[3]

This chapter is the first study to tackle the history of Irish settlement in Newport during the nineteenth century.[4] It is based on an extensive reading of the newspaper press, of archival and other primary sources,

Table 1 *The Irish-born population of Newport, 1841–1901*[5]

Census year	Total population	Irish-born	% Irish-born
1841	12,675	1,171	9.2
1851	19,323	2,069	10.7
1861	23,249	2,163	9.3
1871	27,069	2,282	8.4
1891	54,707	1,624	3.0
1901	67,270	1,422	2.1

and of relevant published work. It incorporates the findings of a study of the 1851 census enumerators' books (CEBs) for the borough of Newport that includes all Irish-born individuals along with many thousands of the total population of the town.[6] The details of 10,312 individuals, representing 52 per cent of Newport's population at that time, have been captured for study, and this sample compares favourably in size and representativeness with similar studies of 1851 undertaken for Cardiff, although obviously smaller than a 100 per cent sample study of Merthyr Tydfil.[7] Manifestly, the study of a single census cannot tell the full story of Irish settlement. However, the great volume of work that is involved in the study of just one set of CEBs acts as an effective deterrent to the ambition of repeated sampling, or at least defers it to either a later article or another scholar. Moreover, there is a good case for settling on 1851: not only was the proportion of Irish-born at its peak in that year, but it also allows a direct insight into the characteristics and conditions of both famine and pre-famine migrants. While it is true that this concentration on the mid-century reinforces the relative neglect in the scholarly literature of the later Victorian age, it is also the case that this focus matches the time when the Irish presence in Newport was at its most visible.

This chapter falls into four parts. Initially, the Irish in Newport before 1847 are surveyed. Not only was there considerable pre-famine settlement but many of the features of the Irish presence that were to last into the second half of the century were established at this time. Subsequently, Newport's experience of the famine (and the famine migrants' experience of Newport) is assessed. This was, in many negative respects, a defining moment that has cast a long shadow over both the history and historiography of Irish settlement in Britain. The third part of the chapter presents and analyses the results of the work undertaken on the 1851 census. Finally, the wide variety of experiences undergone and images generated by Newport's Irish community in the second half of the nineteenth century are considered.

It is likely that there had been an Irish settlement in Newport since the mid-1820s. A considerable trade between the port and Ireland had been established by the beginning of that decade, with 687 vessels taking exports (largely coal) from Newport to Ireland in the year 1819–20, and although the reciprocal trading traffic was much smaller, there was regular passenger traffic between southern Ireland and Newport from 1825.[8] Others arrived in Newport via the Bristol steam packet service, and by 1829 the Newport weekly newspaper the *Monmouthshire Merlin* could state that '[day] after day . . . groups of [Irish] men, women, and children, for the most part without shoes or stockings, are seen parading our streets, begging at tradesmen's shops and houses, and applying to the overseers for relief'.[9] Not all, perhaps not even the majority of these poor Irish would have been residents of the town, for its status as a port ensured that many migrants (permanent, temporary and seasonal) passed through Newport en route to England, or in returning to Ireland. In 1836 Poor Law officials complained that many destitute Irish came to Newport to claim return passage to Ireland at the expense of the local Guardians because whereas 'at Bristol and other places . . . the Irish poor are very strictly searched, this is not done here'. It was suggested that 'were a week's residence in the workhouse made the condition of the passage, many would find their own way without troubling either the County or the parish, as almost all the men have concealed property of some kind'.[10] Three years later, the authorities made a concerted effort to return dependent Irish paupers, totalling 45 adults and 27 children.[11] In three quarters of the cases the adults had left Ireland less than a year earlier, and some had been in Newport only a matter of weeks. However, a few had lived in Britain for upwards of ten years (the longest period being seventeen or eighteen years) but were still being returned (not necessarily against their will) to Ireland.[12] Many suffered from sickness, and not a few were deserted wives or destitute widows. However, tragic though many of these cases undoubtedly are, the image they generate of destitution and want should not be thought typical of the state of most of the Irish resident in Newport at this time.

The existence of Irish friendly societies in the town indicates that there were many of more independent means and higher social status. From 1827 there was a Hibernian Liberal Society based at the Ship on Launch Inn in Skinner Street and by 1837 there was a Newport Hibernian Society based at the Bush Inn in Commercial Street.[13] In 1844 these (male) organisations were complemented by the True Hibernian Sisters Liberal Benefit Society.[14] Such societies tended to attract the greatest public attention on or near St Patrick's Day, at Easter, and on Whit Monday. The earliest record of a St Patrick's Day celebration dates from 1836, when the *Merlin* congratulated the 'Newport Irish' on their high character and good conduct, after they had processed through the streets of the town, headed by a band, before enjoying a dinner at the Bush Inn.[15] Frequently participants would wear emerald green sashes or caps on such occasions, also carrying banners and flags inscribed with suitable mottoes. Thus to mark the opening of the Town Dock in 1842 the Hibernian Club's flag proclaimed 'May justice to Ireland cement love between the sister isles', and the following year the same club displayed one flag embroidered with an Irish harp and a smaller banner with a Union Jack.[16]

From the early 1840s there was the additional element in such celebrations of a service at St Mary's Roman Catholic church. At the beginning of the century it was decided to move the local Catholic Mission from Caerleon to Newport, from where 'occasionally nearly twenty' had come to worship.[17] By 1808 Mass was being said monthly in a room over Miss Pye's gin shop at the corner of High Street and Market Street, the first congregation including Irishman Jerry Driscoll and his wife.[18] Prominent Welsh Catholic John Jones of Llanarth then gave a site on Stow Hill, behind the Westgate Inn, for a chapel, house and garden, and supplied the stone and a £500 endowment.[19] The chapel, supported by a number of local Catholic gentry families, was opened in November 1812, although a permanent priest resided at Newport only from 1828.[20]

By the mid-1830s there were approximately 1,800 Catholics in the town and the existing facilities were considered too small for the potential congregation.[21] It was decided to build a new church and a Catholic school as well, replacing the informal use of a thatched barn opposite St Woolos' church.[22] Fr Edward Metcalfe was instrumental in mobilising the resources of the area's prominent Catholic families, as well as raising money from Irish migrants.[23] In March 1839 the old chapel was demolished and work commenced on the new church, opened in November 1840 and capable of accommodating 900 persons.[24] The consecration was a grand affair with two days of concerts. Eight hundred people attended the opening Pontifical High Mass, including 'many leading individuals in the Protestant religion and respectable dissenters'.[25] This caused no little consternation to the Anglican Bishop of Llandaff, who felt it necessary to hasten to Newport to preach 'against the Roman-catholic errors', fearing their imminent 'ascendancy'.[26] Notwithstanding such Anglican hostility and suspicion the Catholic Church, along with Irish friendly societies, acted as a focus of respectability and civic presence for the Irish population of Newport, and provided one means of integration with the existing indigenous Catholic population, facilitating the development of a sense of mutual interest and common identity.

One of the most prominent Catholic Irishmen in the town was Edward Dowling, proprietor of the *Merlin*, who was elected Newport's

mayor in 1844.[27] Dowling was a keen opponent of the Chartist movement and had been responsible for claiming, in the wake of the failed
1839 Rising, that Newport's Irish population deserved great credit for
allegedly keeping 'completely aloof from the Chartists', a claim that historians have found difficult to uphold.[28] Dowling it was who, in his out-
going speech as mayor, drew the attention of his fellow citizens to the
looming problem of the potato blight in Ireland which, he suggested,
'may ere long call forth the exercise of public charity to a great extent'.[29]

It is unlikely that Dowling foresaw the magnitude of the problem then
developing in Ireland, nor any likelier that he could have anticipated the
impact Ireland's travails would have on Newport itself.[30] However, his
optimism that Newportonians would respond positively to the crisis
began to be fulfilled early in 1847, when at Hope Independent Chapel
between £600 and £700 was raised by the congregation for the relief of
the 'suffering Irish', this being followed by a requisition to the mayor to
set up a subscription from the town as a whole, a request supported vigorously by the *Merlin*.[31]

The public meeting, urging, in Dowling's words, 'the claims of Irish
misery upon British humanity', was attended by a good number of 'the
gentry of the neighbourhood'.[32] A committee of 45 (including the lord
lieutenant, the high sheriff, the mayor, Sir Charles Morgan, Octavius
Morgan MP, Reginald Blewitt MP and ministers from all religious
denominations) was established and began to collect door-to-door sub-
scriptions, to organise charitable theatrical performances, and to coor-
dinate collections in chapels and among workmen at local shipbuilders'
and railway contractors' yards. Within a month over £1,000 had been
raised. Commented the *Merlin*: 'We never remember so hearty a union
between all classes and creeds, for the accomplishment of a great object
of beneficence.'[33] But admirable though this relief effort was, it was
quickly overshadowed by the crisis that landed on the shores of south
Wales itself, early in February 1847.

The *Wanderer*, with its cargo of 113 destitute men, women and children, arrived in Newport in the first week of February 1847 having left
Ireland on 23 December 1846. According to the *Merlin*, 'human con-
ception can scarcely reach the depth of misery in which a large number
of [the migrants] appeared', many close to death.[34] These 'unhappy
creatures' were placed in the thatched barn/school at St Woolos', con-
verted into a temporary hospital, but the *Wanderer* was swiftly followed
by many other vessels with similar cargoes.[35] By late February the *Merlin*
was exclaiming that Newport's streets 'present an alarming and lamentable appearance, being literally crowded with famishing and half-naked
strangers from the most distressed parts of Ireland', and door-to-door
begging and thefts of food were reported.[36] Collections that had been
directed at the Irish in Ireland were now redirected to providing relief for

those arrived in Newport. Private individuals set up impromptu soup kitchens for starving migrants, and working men from the Pill area of the town donated food.[37]

Despite such efforts in civil society, most of the burden of relieving distress fell on the local authorities, and particularly on the Board of Guardians. By 16 February 1847 temporary lodgings and food had had to be found for 1,131 Irish persons in the House of Refuge. Overall, the numbers requiring relief in the first quarter of 1847 represented a sixfold increase of the numbers given relief in the first quarter of 1846 (5,660 as against 857).[38] The workhouse, normally used to accommodating under 100, now housed 160, and up to 200 nightly were found room in the old police station.[39] Severely overworked relieving officers and medical officers had to be granted extra salaries to take account of their increased duties.[40] Many of the new arrivals were ill. According to Boase, 'by far the greater proportion . . . were women with small children, old men apparently feeble, pregnant women, and girls and boys about 10 years old'. Harriet Huxtable, matron of the tramp house, estimated that four of every ten were suffering from infectious fever or dysentery.[41] Many deaths were reported in the coming months, and Neal has estimated that 480 Irish people may have died in Newport between May and November 1847.[42] The authorities, struggling with this situation and in receipt of little additional assistance from central government, attempted to deter the arrival of further shiploads of migrant poor. Hundreds of Irish were immediately turned away at the port, being put back on the ships on which they had just made long and miserable voyages, and a range of financial and legal penalties were deployed against the masters of migrant ships.[43] Shipowners and captains thus took to discharging their cargoes outside the borough limits, further down the river Usk, or at points closer to either Cardiff or Bristol.[44]

Undoubtedly tensions grew between the resident population and the newcomers. The authorities declaimed against both Irish paupers who refused to carry out their duties, and those believed to be fraudulently claiming relief.[45] When denied relief some Irish protested, pelting the workhouse door with stones, dirt and grass, and large crowds gathered outside the relieving officer's home in Hill Street.[46] Local residents complained at the increase in poor rates, and some took to insulting and baiting the migrants in public. According to James Salter, a later relieving officer, the grounds for such hostility were that local people felt they were 'poor enough themselves, and they believe that they will be made poorer than they are through [the migrants'] coming'.[47] Some ratepayers argued that the relatively generous provision being made by the local authorities was encouraging rather than deterring new arrivals.[48] Whatever the justice of these claims (and it is hard to believe that travel to Newport was ever an easy option for impoverished Irish families) the numbers of poor migrants arriving in the port did not slacken through-out the remainder of 1847 or the following year. During 1847 25,319 paupers were relieved in Newport, in comparison with 3,953 in 1846. The Irish may have comprised between three fifths and nine tenths of those relieved in 1847 and 1848, and substantial batches of Irish poor continued to arrive as late as 1853.[49]

By 1849 public concern ran at a high level not just over the volume of the influx, the consequent logistical difficulties and the cost to the rate-payers, but also over the consequences for public health. Although the Irish were not deemed responsible for the wave of cholera sweeping across south Wales in 1848 and 1849, and nor was the rise of the issue of public health solely traceable to their influx, the presence of large numbers of often sick Irish poor in the town led to fear being expressed that 'this great tide of immigration may naturally be expected to bring infection, disease, and death in its wake'.[50] According to the unsympa-thetic Boase, the migrants had been, in the course of their passages, 'huddled together like pigs . . . communicating disease and vermin', and thus they were 'the medium of extending fever and contagion into the heart of the kingdom, into the asylums of the poor'.[51] Chairman of the Board of Guardians Digby Mackworth believed that the Irish 'unhappily . . . have brought not only want with them, but an increased measure of dangerous Typhus fever', and Salter suggested that many of the Irish arriving in Newport were 'generally decrepid or diseased objects', adding 'some of them are full of vermin'.[52] That increasing numbers of such migrants were not just passing through Newport, but settling in the town, intensified official concern. By the end of 1847 magistrates were ordering landlords in Fothergill Street ('this notoriously filthy locality') to whitewash and purify their houses.[53] In 1849 the officers of the Sanitary Board returned to 'the residences, habits and general condi-tions of the hordes of Irish and others who were huddled together in the hovels of Fothergill-street', beds being burned and drains cleaned, and the Registrar later stated that the local cholera epidemic had begun there.[54] When G.T. Clark carried out his inquiry for the General Board of Health in 1850 he also singled out areas of predominantly Irish settle-ment for particular attention. Thus the 'Irish row' in Friars Fields was found to consist of 22 houses 'very much overcrowded' without any drains or a single privy. In Fothergill Street were found 'Irish lodging-houses of the worst class', where the beds were composed of shavings and rags, the windows were closed and the fireplaces stopped up. Similar descriptions were given of Mellon's Bank, Mellon Street, Wedlake's Court, George's Buildings (which Clark thought to 'swarm with low Irish') and Jones's Court, High Street and Castle Street in Pill. Forty-four Irish lodging houses, believed to be 'nests of fever and cholera', were listed as suffering from defects of one sort or another, some housing 'all filthy Irish people'.[55] As Croll has pointed out in relation to Clark's work, '[n]owhere do positive images of the Irish appear'. Rather, for him and his readers, 'Irishness' became 'a convenient shorthand for images of dirt, disease and demoralization'.[56]

Work undertaken on the 1851 CEBs allows qualification of such negative impressions of Irish settlement in Newport, and facilitates direct comparisons with work by scholars on Irish settlement in other British towns and cities. For the purposes of this investigation analysis has concentrated on the following subjects: the regional origins of migrants; the identification of second-generation Irish and the dynamics of migration; the age, sex and marital status of migrants; the occupational distribution of the Irish-born; the assessment of residential segregation in the town; the extent of ethnic exclusivity in patterns of marriage, lodging and the keeping of servants. Excluded from analysis (for reasons of complexity and limited space) are the subjects of household structure and the socio-economic grouping of Irish-born residents.

To begin with the regional origins of the Irish-born, regrettably it is the case that most Newport census enumerators interpreted their duties strictly and did not include additional information on the county, town or parish of birth in Ireland, merely recording most migrants as born in Ireland. Of the 1,981 Irish-born further information is available only for 216 or 11 per cent, a figure that compares unfavourably with the 16.5 per cent found by Chinn for Birmingham in 1851 and the 45 per cent found by Large for Bristol.[57] Of those with further information, 107 (50 per cent) were born in County Cork, and 61 (28 per cent) were born in County Waterford, the predominance of these counties confirming Boase's impression that most of the Irish arriving in Newport in the late 1840s were from County Cork.[58]

Most of the analysis presented in this essay relates to the Irish-born, but some attempt has been made to estimate the numbers of second-generation Irish in Newport. There appears to be no agreement among scholars of the Irish in Britain over how best to identify second-generation migrants.[59] Here it has been decided simply to total the numbers of children co-resident with at least one Irish-born parent. This is problematic in that it includes children with (for example) Welsh-born fathers, who may not have seen themselves as Irish, but it has the advantage that it includes the offspring of widows, widowers, and parents whose spouses were absent on census night, who would otherwise be excluded if the requirement for two Irish-born parents was imposed. This method identified 634 non-Irish-born children (see Table 2), a figure that, if added to the numbers of Irish-born, produces a total of 2,614, representing 13.7 per cent of the total population of the town.

Table 2 also sheds interesting light on the migration dynamics of the Irish resident in Newport, showing that 35.5 per cent of co-resident

Table 2 *Ages and birthplaces of children co-resident with Irish-born parents, Newport, 1851*

Birthplace	0–5	6–10	11–15	Age 16–20	21–25	26+	Total
Newport	272	164	94	30	9	1	570
Ireland	83	115	111	83	29	24	445
Monmouthshire (other than Newport)	5	2	2	1	0	0	10
Wales (other than Monmouthshire)	4	2	4	0	0	0	10
England and Scotland	17	8	7	2	2	2	38
Other	2	1	1	2	0	0	6
Total	383	292	219	118	40	27	1,079

children were aged 0–5 years, and 62.6 per cent aged 0–10 years. 52.8 per cent of all children were born in Newport, and 41.2 per cent were born in Ireland, suggesting that very few Irish had taken up residence elsewhere before reaching Newport (accepting that this measurement excludes childless Irish whose migration paths are not open to assessment). The majority of Irish-born children in the age cohorts 11–15, 16–20, 21–25 and 26+ implies a recently established Irish settlement in Newport, but the number of children aged 11–15 born in Newport also indicates a substantial Irish presence in existence for at least a decade before 1851. Further insight into migratory dynamics can be gained from an evaluation of household relationships (see Table 3). In comparison with the total population, Irish men were more likely to be lodgers, and less likely to be sons. Irish women were also overrepresented among lodgers and among wives, but underrrepresented among daughters. These, again, are characteristics of a relatively recent migrant population, suggesting that many of the Irish migrated before becoming parents, or were (in 1851) still childless, although there was a sizeable minority of families who had migrated from Ireland accompanied by younger children. As one might expect, most Irish households were headed by married men and few by single persons or women, with widows making up by far the largest contingent of female-headed households (see Table 4).[60]

Overall, the age structure of the Irish-born in Newport (see Table 5) was characteristic of a recent migrant population, with low percentages in the age cohorts 0–9 and 10–19, and overrepresentation in the cohorts 20–29, 30–39, 40–49, 50–59 (and for women 60–69).

The study of sex ratios among the Irish (see Table 6) indicates a high

Table 3 *Household relationships: total population and Irish-born population, Newport, 1851*[61]

Category	Male Total population		Irish-born		Female Total population		Irish-born	
	No.	%	No.	%	No.	%	No.	%
Head	1,546	32.1	295	31.3	289	5.8	54	6.0
Wife	–	–	–	–	1,542	31.1	334	37.3
Son	2,045	42.4	242	25.7	–	–	–	–
Daughter	–	–	–	–	1,894	38.2	184	20.5
Other family	145	3.0	21	2.2	252	5.1	38	4.2
Lodger	984	20.4	378	40.1	515	10.4	231	25.8
Servant/employee	100	2.1	6	0.6	442	8.9	55	6.1
Pupil/scholar	0	0.0	0	0.0	20	0.4	0	0.0
Total	4,820	100.0	942	100.0	4,954	100.0	896	100.0

Table 4 *Marital status of household heads, Newport, 1851*

		Total population		Irish-born	
		No.	%	No.	%
Males	Married	1,423	78.3	276	79.1
	Unmarried	53	2.9	9	2.6
	Widowed	62	3.4	9	2.6
Females	Married	51	2.8	10	2.9
	Unmarried	31	1.7	3	0.9
	Widowed	197	10.6	42	12.0
Total		1,817	100.0	349	100.0

level of single male migration from Ireland persisting (with the curious exception of 1861) and even intensifying into the late century.[62]

The CEBs also allow the correlation of birthplace with occupation. The fact that Newport was one of those towns large enough to generate a table devoted to its occupations in the published census report allows one to match Irish occupations against the known picture for the town as a whole, and Table 7 reveals the distribution of Irish occupations across the different employment sectors for both males and females. Although Irish men were found in a wide range of occupational categories, they were underrepresented particularly in machinery and metalworking, in textiles, the food industry, and among seamen. Yet

Table 5 *Age structure: total population and Irish-born population, Newport, 1851*

	Male				Female			
	Total population		Irish-born		Total population		Irish-born	
Age	No.	%	No.	%	No.	%	No.	%
0–9	1,317	25.9	121	12.2	1,218	23.1	86	8.8
10–19	892	17.5	140	14.1	1,056	20.1	176	18.0
20–29	952	18.7	224	22.6	1,145	21.8	243	24.8
30–39	887	17.4	243	24.5	799	15.2	212	21.6
40–49	538	10.6	166	16.8	504	9.6	147	15.0
50–59	294	5.8	69	7.0	285	5.4	56	5.7
60–69	149	2.9	20	2.0	173	3.3	44	4.5
70–79	45	0.9	6	0.6	63	1.2	10	1.0
80–89	17	0.3	0	0.0	20	0.4	6	0.6
90–99	2	0.0	1	0.1	1	0.0	0	0.0
Total	5,093	100.0	990	100.0	5,264	100.0	980	100.0

Table 6 *Sex ratios: total population and Irish-born population, Newport, 1851–1901*[63]

	Males per 100 females	
Census year	Total population	Irish-born
1851	96.8	101.0
1861	97.2	94.0
1871	99.2	116.5
1891	101.9	125.6
1901	98.6	136.6

there were Irish men in middle- or lower-middle-class occupations – agents, brokers, cattle dealers, factors and shopkeepers – and in professional occupations such as civil engineers, doctors and teachers. There were also a few Irish women in lower-middle-class occupations: fishmongers, fruit dealers and greengrocers. Nevertheless, over half of all Irish men were occupied in the category of 'general labour', as revealed in Table 8, with much smaller numbers employed in more skilled artisanal or craft trades. For employed women the service and clothing sectors of the economy provided most employment (see Table 9), although some were also employed in dock labour. Most of those

Table 7 *Distribution of occupations: total population and Irish-born, Newport, 1851*

| | Males | | | | Females | | | |
| | Total population | | Irish-born | | Total population | | Irish-born | |
Field of work	No.	%	No.	%	No.	%	No.	%
Agriculture	158	2.4	19	2.3	22	1.0	4	1.3
Construction	711	10.6	49	6.0	8	0.3	0	0.0
Metalworking	623	9.3	34	4.1	1	0.0	0	0.0
Machinery	97	1.4	2	0.2	0	0.0	0	0.0
Shipbuilding	129	1.9	12	1.5	0	0.0	0	0.0
Chemicals	5	0.1	0	0.0	1	0.0	0	0.0
Coal	192	2.9	15	1.8	0	0.0	0	0.0
Textiles	155	2.3	7	0.9	24	1.0	9	3.0
Clothing	502	7.5	83	10.1	843	36.5	115	38.6
Leather	49	0.7	0	0.0	0	0.0	0	0.0
Wood	194	2.9	9	1.1	7	0.3	1	0.3
Paper	12	0.2	0	0.0	3	0.1	0	0.0
Printing	36	0.5	1	0.1	2	0.1	1	0.3
Food	518	7.7	16	1.9	245	10.6	15	5.0
Transport	1,302	19.4	49	6.0	4	0.2	1	0.3
Service	102	1.5	8	1.0	1,000	43.3	113	37.9
General labour	1,468	21.9	483	58.7	7	0.3	21	7.0
Administration	36	0.5	0	0.0	1	0.0	0	0.0
Commerce and finance	203	3.0	23	2.8	50	2.2	18	6.0
Military and police	58	0.9	4	0.5	0	0.0	0	0.0
Professions	98	1.5	6	0.7	1	0.0	0	0.0
Art, education and entertainment	54	0.8	3	0.4	89	3.9	0	0.0
Total	6,702	100.0	823	100.0	2,308	100.0	298	100.0

engaged in 'commerce and finance' were in fact street traders and hawkers. That the Irish-born formed a higher percentage of those in employment than of the population as a whole is largely attributable to the relatively low numbers of children in their ranks. As Table 10 shows, Irish men were heavily overrepresented among labourers, tailors and hawkers, and Irish women among washerwomen and hawkers. Although domestic service claimed the employment of many Irish women they were not markedly overrepresented in this particular sector.

Table 8 *Ten most common occupations, Irish-born males, Newport, 1851*

Occupation	Number
Labourer	459
Tailor	45
Boot- and shoemaker	22
Hobbler	14
Hawker	13
Cordwainer	12
Mariner	11
Mason	10
Carpenter	9
Blacksmith	8

Table 9 *Ten most common occupations, Irish-born females, Newport, 1851*

Occupation	Number
Domestic servant	92
Laundress	40
Washerwoman	33
Labourer	20
Seamstress	19
Dressmaker	17
Hawker	15
Charwoman	8
Greengrocer	6
Housekeeper	5

One of the most problematic areas of CEB analysis is that of residential segregation. An attempt has been made here to assess the degree to which the Irish-born lived in particular areas of Newport. Evidently every method of assessing residential segregation brings with it its own problems, so here a variety of measurements have been employed. The index of segregation (based on the 25 enumeration districts of the borough) has been calculated at 45.2 for Irish-born residents, very close to the figure of 44 found for the Irish-born in Cardiff in 1861.[64] A more locally varied picture may be obtained by assessing the location quotients of Irish-born for each enumeration district. Location quotients measure the percentage of any particular birthplace group in any given

Table 10 *Proportions of Irish-born in selected occupations, Newport, 1851*

Occupation	% Irish-born
All male employed	12.3
Male labourers	32.9
Male tailors	26.3
Male hawkers	32.5
All female employed	12.9
Female domestic servants	14.0
Washerwomen/laundrywomen	31.5
Female hawkers	88.9

sub-area (here an enumeration district) as against the percentage of the total population in the same sub-area. A value of 1 represents an even distribution of that birthplace group; values below or above represent lesser or greater degrees of concentration or 'clustering'. Map 1 indicates three areas with notably high location quotients. Enumeration districts 2J and 1B were the heart of Irish settlement in Newport, with 42.3 per cent and 37.3 per cent respectively of their inhabitants having been born in Ireland. That single enumeration districts do not necessarily follow actual social or spatial boundaries is evidenced here by the fact that one side of Fothergill Street was enumerated in district 2J and the other in 1B; nevertheless, taking the two together conveys a strong impression of Irish clustering. Excepting a total of 48 schedules in the prosperous Commercial Street, and a few in Commercial Road, Llanarth Street and Dock Street, all other streets included in these two enumeration districts (Fothergill Street, Cross Street, Kear Street, Bream Place, Ebenezer Terrace, Mellon's Bank, Mellon's Square and Mellon Street) reveal high levels of Irish settlement compared with most other districts of the town. Enumeration district 1H, in the Pill district of the town and close to the Town Dock, consisting of 25.1 per cent Irish-born persons, was the only other area to return a location quotient of over 1.5. In 13 of the 25 enumeration districts there was only a minor Irish presence (a location quotient of less than 0.5), but there was no enumeration district without any Irish at all.

The final measurement assesses the numbers of Irish-born living in individual streets in Newport (see Map 2, with total numbers given in Table 11). Although more finely focused than the use of location quotients, even this method is not without its drawbacks: whereas some streets and courts might have been homogeneous social units, others (particularly long main streets) were not. Furthermore, the totals of Irish

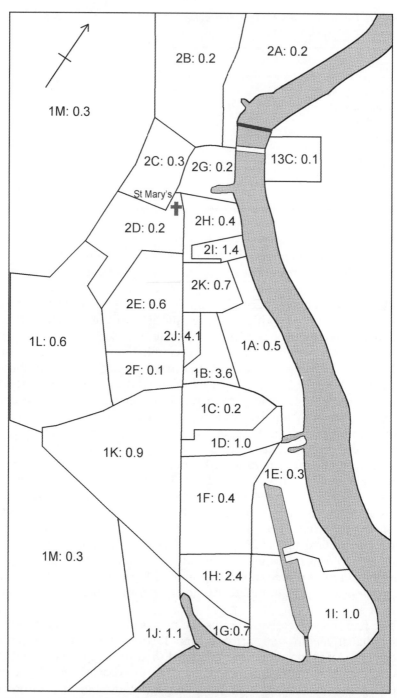

Map 1 *Location quotients by enumeration district: Irish-born, Newport, 1851*

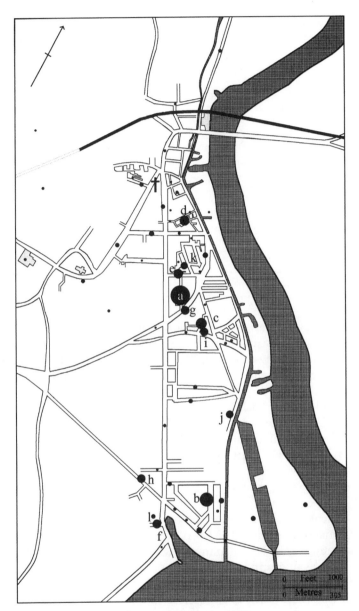

Map 2 *Numbers of Irish-born by street: Newport, 1851*

Note: circles are proportionate in area to the numbers enumerated. The smallest circle represents seven persons.

Key:
a: Fothergill Street, b: Castle Street, c: Mellon Street, d: Friars' Fields, e: Cross Street, f: Globe Cottages, g: Ebenezer Terrace, h: Courtybella Terrace, i: Mellon's Bank, j: Canal Parade, k: Kear Street, l: Wedlake's Court

Table 11 *Concentrations of Irish-born by street, Newport, 1851*

Street	Number of Irish-born	Percentage of Irish-born	Code on Map 2
Fothergill Street	398	70.2	a
Castle Street	199	42.4	b
Mellon Street	128	42.5	c
Friars' Fields	101	16.3	d
Cross Street	92	22.9	e
Globe Cottages	82	59.0	f
Ebenezer Terrace	77	29.6	g
Courtybella Terrace	76	20.9	h
Mellon's Bank	72	59.5	i
Canal Parade	60	7.8	j
Kear Street	56	57.1	k
Wedlake's Court	21	44.7	l

residents in a particular street do not reveal the extent to which the Irish dominated such a street. Accordingly, Table 11 also provides information on the percentage of Irish-born residents per street. Manifestly, Fothergill Street was the densest area of Irish settlement in Newport in 1851. In addition to the 398 Irish-born living there, there were 62 children with at least one Irish-born parent, three spouses of Irish-born individuals, and 11 lodgers or visitors resident in an Irish-headed household. Adding these 76 individuals to the 398 Irish-born yields a figure of 474, representing 83.6 per cent of the total population of the street (567). Although there was certainly no Irish 'ghetto' in Newport, both location quotient and street totalling measurements suggest that this was the closest Newport came to a 'little Ireland'.

Other measurements of segregation by ethnic group are possible. In terms of marriage patterns, 83.5 per cent of marriages involved Irish-born husbands and wives (many of whom, no doubt, had married in Ireland before migrating to Newport). Of the remainder, there were slightly more marriages where the wife was Irish-born than where the husband was Irish-born. It is possible that a number of the apparently 'mixed' marriages were between first- and second-generation Irish migrants. Of Irish-born lodgers, 82.4 per cent lodged in households with Irish-born heads. Finally, 75 per cent of Irish household heads with co-resident servants employed at least one Irish-born servant. But the Irish were not common employers of co-resident servants and 76.8 per cent of Irish-born servants found employment in households with non-Irish heads.

Overall, analysis of the 1851 census reveals an Irish population neither fully integrated into Newport society nor wholly set apart. It also demonstrates that, despite the stereotypes of the male Irish labourer and his similarly proletarian wife, living cheek-by-jowl with many other apparently identical families, the Newport Irish were scattered across the town, many in very different occupations and in a wide variety of family situations. The CEBs do not allow the precise delineation of pre-famine and famine migrants, but the evidence also suggests considerable variation in the experiences of these groups. Clearly more work is required, particularly on later censuses, if an accurate assessment of the changing position of the Irish within Newport's labour market and across its urban landscape is to be made. Such work is, as Neal has pointed out, laborious but 'essential if any attempt is to be made to answer questions not only about spatial distribution but also about family structure, socioeconomic status and age distributions'.[65] In the context of the Newport Irish this essay represents only the first step in such a project.

Negative images of the Irish in Newport persisted for some time in the wake of the famine, generated by concern over public health, criminality and violence, and in turn generating an element of anti-Irish and anti-Catholic sentiment. In 1853 Newport's first medical officer of health, Catholic Robert F. Woollett, argued that 'the poorer Irish . . . have brought with them all their peculiarities in favour of huddling together like so many sheep in a pen, and their prejudices against the ingress of fresh air'.[66] Overcrowded lodging-houses remained under the close scrutiny of the authorities and a close link was believed to exist between areas of Irish settlement and problems of poverty and poor sanitation.[67] Some considered that it was a small step from poor housing and poverty to vice and criminality: the chairman of Monmouthshire Quarter Sessions, Samuel Bosanquet, regularly condemned Irish migrants for what he believed to be their higher propensity for criminal activity.[68] Relieving Officer Salter made a number of highly critical statements about Irish migrants in his evidence to the Select Committee relating to the Removal of the Poor, stating that they were 'very destitute, very ignorant and very unfit persons to come into a town to obtain a livelihood', being 'most improvident in their habits', and with a 'lamentable' tendency to drunkenness.[69] One should be wary of accepting such judgements at face value. Minor cases of drunkenness, theft, burglary and vagrancy among the Irish during the late 1840s were accompanied by only one murder, and much of what passed in the official mind for Irish criminality were actually bouts of public disorder.[70] Drunken brawls, if interrupted by the police, could easily turn to a desire to 'smash the peelers', and the fact that these disturbances often involved Irish women guaranteed sensationalist press reports.[71] In addition, the Irish of Newport were no more exempt than other residents from domestic quarrels that occasionally

escalated into violence.[72] More research is needed into 'Irish criminality' in Newport, but it seems likely that, as Swift has suggested for Britain
as a whole, 'for much of the period in question Irish criminality was overwhelmingly concentrated in less-serious or petty categories'.[73]

Equally, there is relatively little evidence of specifically anti-Irish violence in Newport. Occasionally interpersonal fracas ended in court cases
where a racial dimension appears to have been added rather gratuitously.
Thus, in January 1846 Mary Ann Hughes received one month's imprisonment for having assaulted Mary Welsh (an Irishwoman). After the
assault Hughes had exclaimed, 'I'm sorry I didn't give it a little better to
the Irish —. There's justice to Ireland for ye.'[74] More explicit racism can
be found: in August 1847 navvies attacked 'the poor Irishmen employed
in excavating for the [South Wales] railway', quite possibly stimulated by
the labour market competition they represented.[75] And in December
1848, in the wake of murder and rioting in Cardiff, Irish tinman John
Richardson of Friars' Fields died following assaults by Welsh haulier
John Collins. Collins had approached Richardson at the Globe
Beerhouse and accused him of being 'a bloody Irishman'. Richardson
said he had never denied being so, whereupon Collins attacked him.
Richardson claimed before his death that he had lived in Newport for
eighteen years and had never been so badly treated. Collins was found
guilty only of assault and served one month in gaol for the killing.[76]

Appalling though the death of John Richardson was, it appears to have
been an isolated incident. The closest Newport ever came to an anti-
Irish riot were clashes in 1856 between the Clare Regiment of Militia,
stationed in Newport barracks, and local men. Some of the Irish soldiers
had charged into a brawl shouting 'Ireland for ever' and 'We are the
Clare boys', but such events seem to have been occasioned by what was
common enough tension between soldiers (of whatever ethnic background) and civilians. Magistrates nonetheless felt it necessary to dep-
recate such ill-feeling as existed towards the soldiers on the grounds that
they were Irish, observing that the Crimean War had shown that Irish
soldiers were just as ready as those from England, Scotland or Wales to
fight the battles of 'their country'.[77]

The only other evidence of anti-Irish sentiment concerned the international profile of the Roman Catholic Church. Reaction to what was
considered 'Papal aggression' in 1850 and to 'ritualism' in 1868 saw
anti-Catholic slogans chalked on walls and anti-ritualist meetings held
in the town, but newspaper editors were keen to reassure readers that
such sentiments were not directed against Newport's Irish inhabitants,
the *Star of Gwent* going so far in 1868 as to claim that '[p]robably in no
county in England [sic] has there been a more marked absence of personal and religious animosity than in Monmouthshire'.[78] Of course this
may have been a politically opportune exaggeration, and it would be

unwise to conclude from the fact that only a small number of cases of anti-Irish violence, prejudice or discrimination have been located in the newspapers that such discrimination was minimal, but the available evidence does not support any notion that the Irish were a vigorously persecuted minority much beyond the immediate context of the famine itself.

It is quite possible that the relative absence of such hostility owes more than a little to the positive religious, cultural and associational developments engineered by the Newport Irish themselves. Most important in this respect was the contribution of the Catholic Church. Following the opening of St Mary's the church seems to have made steady progress, amassing an aggregate attendance of 2,200 at the 1851 religious census. By 1892 the town's estimated Catholic population stood at around 6,000.[79] The opening of St Mary's school in 1847 was followed a decade later by an infants' school and convent, and in the 1870s two further schools were opened in other parts of the town. Finally, in 1887, St Michael's church was opened in Pill, catering predominantly for the Catholics working and living in the docks area.[80]

It did not take Newport Catholics long to establish themselves on an equal footing with the Protestant denominations of the town. In 1853 Newport became the first place in Britain to begin the construction of a municipal cemetery, and the question of reserving part of the plot for the burial of Catholics polarised opinions on the newly constituted Burial Board. In 1854 Robert F. Woollett, seconded by fellow Catholic Edward Dowling, proposed such a measure, but this was defeated by eight votes to four, the opposition claiming that such provision would be 'repugnant to the feelings of a large portion of the community'.[81] Undaunted, the Catholics sent a memorial to Lord Palmerston, then home secretary, and his opinion being that provision for Catholics was necessary, the Burial Board eventually had to rescind its earlier decision.[82] Catholicism also robustly rebuffed any efforts that were made to spread the Protestant creed among Newport's Irish population. Both the Newport Town Mission and the curate of Pillgwenlly, Archibald Gault, failed to make any headway in the mid-1850s, town missionary Mr Metcalf being pelted with stones by Catholics whose sensibilities he had offended.[83] Finally in this regard, further evidence of the *political* power of Newport's Catholic community came with the establishment of School Boards in 1871. At the inaugural School Board elections Fr Richardson was elected in fifth position (nine seats being available). The electoral system allowed 213 of his voters to give him all nine of their votes, with only 66 other electors giving him any votes at all.[84] This represented an impressive mobilisation of the Catholic electorate behind their candidate, a phenomenon that was repeated throughout the remainder of the life of the School Board and, later, on Newport's Board of Guardians.

Fr Richardson was a zealous advocate of temperance, and he led the most impressive manifestation of the power of popular Catholicism, in the form of the Catholic Association for the Suppression of Drunkenness (CASD), a prominent organisation in the town from the late 1850s until the mid-1870s, and the pioneer of its type in Britain.[85] Richardson arrived in Newport in 1857, and in December of that year he established the CASD with himself as president.[86] Membership grew quickly: from 420 by the end of 1857 it reached 1,500 by October 1858 and 2,500 by April 1859.[87] For most of the 1860s membership fluctuated between 2,000 and 2,700, but Richardson's departure for Cardiff in 1867 precipitated the movement's decline, and by 1869 it could only boast 300–400 members.[88] Richardson's return in that year revitalised the CASD for a while, but when he left for London in 1875 the Association finally wilted, becoming merged into the League of the Holy Cross.[89] Although Richardson again worked in Newport between 1888 and 1892, starting the 'Holy War' temperance organisation, the CASD's heyday was undoubtedly its first decade of existence.

Richardson was inspired to establish the CASD by what he felt was the great prevalence of drunkenness among the Catholic Irish of Newport, drunkenness that in its turn generated 'heart-rending scenes of wife-beating' and 'disturbances with the police'.[90] Aiming 'not to exact more from the members than they should be able faithfully to comply with', the aim was not to enforce teetotalism but instead to control drunken excess, the 'enemy' being 'not drink, but drunkenness'. Members committed themselves to staying away from public houses and refraining from getting drunk, and were encouraged to renew their resolutions before the altar of St Mary's every quarter.[91] They were also encouraged to supplement this with the 'Truce of God': a three-day abstinence from drink over St Patrick's Day.[92] The Association appointed stewards for each of the districts into which the town was divided, and these were charged with reporting any cases of drunkenness among the membership, and were liable to being fined if they failed to do so. House-to-house visits were carried out with the intention of monitoring even the private consumption of alcohol.[93] Members who avoided the temptations of drunkenness were rewarded with medals, including a 'veteran's bar' for three years' successful temperance.[94] Failures there were: every meeting included a report on the number who had 'fallen under the fangs of the enemy', but frequently it was claimed such delinquents returned to the Association.[95]

Initially the CASD met in the loft of the Tredegar Wharf Company, although at one meeting in 1858 so many people attended that the floor gave way and the building had to be evacuated. By Easter 1860 Catholic railway contractor James Murphy had financed and built premises in Granville Street which became the Catholic Guildhall. Here members could play billiards, draughts, chess and backgammon, join the theatrical society or have a dance or a sing-song: 'in short anything and everything that was not sinful'.[96] Meetings were usually attended by a number of bands, and were family occasions aimed at 'the lower orders of Irish Roman Catholics'.[97] They were complemented by the annual excursion, which usually began with an orderly procession through Newport followed by an annual picnic at a local beauty spot, historic site or estate. By 1862 so renowned was the excursion that thousands of the local townspeople turned out to watch and cheer as the members of the CASD mustered at the cattle market before marching through the town, headed by four bands, to the South Wales Railway station where they caught a chartered train of 30 carriages ('probably one of the largest excursion trains that has ever left the station') to Caldicot Castle. Once there members could enjoy foot racing, a football competition, donkey rides, a shooting gallery and a dancing salon but, of course, no alcohol.[98] The CASD cast its net wider still in its ambition to reform the habits and morals of its members, establishing a penny savings bank, a sickness club and a burial society, as well as a friendly society (the Guild of St Patrick).[99] There was also the Society of St Joseph for young members, aimed at steering them away not just from alcohol but also from tobacco and others of the 'vices of their elders'.[100]

The CASD's wider ideology was Irish, imperial, and patriarchal. Most meetings closed with Richardson calling for 'three cheers for Ireland' and sometimes for a cheer for Daniel O'Connell as well, and then the playing of the National Anthem during which the audience stood 'to show that Catholics were the most loyal subjects the Queen had'.[101] In addition to the strictures against drink, female members of the CASD were also frequently lectured on their responsibilities and failings: particularly to ensure that their men had 'nice and comfortable homes' so that they would not 'be driven to the beerhouse', to 'bestow more care upon their children's clothing and general appearance' and on 'how, when and whom to marry'.[102] Only once, in 1873, did Richardson display a more radical edge, when he lambasted the capitalists of Newport for having forgotten their duty to working men, preached the mutuality of capital and labour and criticised the slum clearance programmes (then in progress in the town) for having increased homelessness and overcrowding.[103]

Most observers were convinced that the CASD made a difference. Within its first year it was noted that there had been a marked improvement in the behaviour of the 'poor Irish' and that the volume of Irish crime (particularly assaults on women and on policemen, and drunken behaviour) had fallen by half. The *Star of Gwent* commented, 'Whitsuntide, St Patrick's Day, and even Stow Fair day changed their aspects and made the police look into the calendar and see if there were not some mistake as to the date upon which these days fell'.[104] The *Merlin* concurred: 'a great reformation has been effected in the life and habits of the lower orders of the Irish population'.[105] However, it was recognised that some remained outside the CASD (believed to be a mix of 'inveterate drinkers and wife-beaters' on the one hand and 'men of sober habits . . . who had not seen the utility' on the other).[106] Furthermore, the CASD's temporary collapse in the late 1860s was dramatic and it never regained the potency it had once enjoyed. It seems very likely that quite apart from its impact on public drunkenness, the CASD also acted to strengthen communal bonds among Catholics (both Irish and non-Irish) in Newport. Catholic businessmen and professionals frequently attended CASD events, or took leading posts in the organisation, and the mayor of the day, Protestant or Catholic, often spoke at major meetings. Leading Protestants in the town gave the Association considerable moral and financial support. The CASD was a society that aimed not simply at temperance, but also at respectability, and, for a while at least, enjoyed considerable success. To it, more than to any other organisation, may go the credit for providing a bridge between the harrowing and alienating experiences of famine migration on the one hand and some measure of acceptance of and self-confidence among the Newport Irish on the other.

Secular developments were also significant in reforming, refining and enhancing the image of the Irish in Newport. Newport's first Irish mayor, Edward Dowling, retired from local politics in 1857 and fellow Catholic and CASD stalwart James Murphy was elected to the town council in 1860, becoming mayor eight years later, and proclaiming this 'a great compliment paid to the Catholic population of Newport'.[107] Other significant Irish local politicians before the end of the century included Alderman D.A. Vaughan and labour pioneer John Twomey. Irish societies continued to demonstrate their presence in public. Regular processions on St Patrick's Day and on Whit Monday by (variously) the Hibernian Club, the United Irishmen Benefit Society and the True United Brothers were occasionally supplemented by involvement in special occasions, such as the cutting of the first sod in the Alexandra Docks in 1868, or the opening of Belle Vue Park in 1894.[108] Other Irish associations in the town included a branch of the Irish National League in the 1890s, and a Newport Hibernians rugby club, which was happy to proclaim its 'loyalty and attachment' to the Crown in 1900, and to send six of its First XV to fight in the Boer War.[109]

In assessing whether or not the Newport Irish were integrated into Newport society during the second half of the nineteenth century it is relevant to observe that while the activities of Irish friendly societies and the CASD were generally received with approval, and while the Catholics enjoyed a successful political presence, none of these developments implied any necessary degree of 'ethnic fade' on the part of the town's Irish inhabitants. On the contrary, they speak of the maintenance of a strong sense of collective identity, and one might argue that, at least until the end of the century, Newport's Irish residents sustained considerable cultural and political distinctiveness, albeit against the background of vigorous participation in the wider society. In a dynamic, expanding town in which notions of national identity (Welsh, British and English) were themselves in substantial flux, the contribution of the Irish in the decades after the famine was increasingly regarded in a positive light. On St Patrick's Day 1894 the *South Wales Argus* gave over its editorial column to a timely consideration of national identity. It commended the Irish for keeping the festival 'of the saint whose name is indissolubly connected with their Fatherland and their race', for such national celebrations tended 'to keep alive an instinct which elevates and refines, and which weakens the artificial barriers of pride and wealth and prejudice'. However, it was evident that, in the opinion of the *Argus*, it was not merely an Irish patriotism that was being created and sustained. On the contrary, 'local patriotism is compatible with, and helpful to, that wider and higher and nobler patriotism which merges the part into the whole and incorporates the country into the Empire'.[110] There is little in the history of the Irish in Newport that seems to contradict such late Victorian optimism.

Notes

1. The *Monmouthshire Merlin* (hereafter *MM*), 21 March 1846, used the phrase 'decorous and creditable' to describe the participants in Newport's St Patrick's Day parade.

2. J. O'Callaghan, responding to the toast of 'the Irish Exiles', at the St Patrick's Day Dinner, 1895, at Thomas's Temperance Hotel, Commercial Street, Newport. *South Wales Argus* (hereafter *SWA*), 19 March 1895.

3. Merthyr Tydfil had more Irish-born than Newport, but they represented a smaller percentage of the town's total population. Cardiff was not included in the table of large towns and cities of Britain. See Colin G. Pooley, 'Segregation or Integration? The Residential Experience of the Irish in Mid-Victorian Britain', in *The Irish in Britain, 1815–1939*, ed. Roger Swift and Sheridan Gilley, London, Pinter, 1989, pp. 60–83 (pp. 66–67).

4. Note, however, the many references to Newport in Paul O'Leary, *Immigration and Integration: The Irish in Wales, 1798–1922*, Cardiff, University of Wales Press, 2000.

5. Source: census enumerators' books (CEBs), 1841; published census reports, 1851–1901. The total population figure for 1841 differs from that given in the 1851 census (10,492) which, the census report noted obliquely, represented 'neither the old nor the present limits' (pp. 18–19); the 1841 report returned 10,815 persons living in the municipal borough of Newport and 2,951 living in the remainder of the parish of St Woollos, with 10,271 living in the parliamentary borough. The figure returned in this table is a total of the numbers recorded in the surviving CEBs, and given their incomplete nature both totals and the percentage of Irish-born are almost certainly underestimates. There was no published census table for Newport in 1881.

    6. Note the discrepancy between the number of Irish-born found in the CEBs (1,980) and the number in the published census report (2,069). Large found a greater discrepancy in Bristol, where only 4,299 Irish were located, as against the published 4,645; see David Large, 'The Irish in Bristol in 1851: A Census Enumeration', in *The Irish in the Victorian City*, ed. Roger Swift and Sheridan Gilley, London, Croom Helm, 1985, pp. 37–58 (p. 38). There were 275 Irish-born individuals enumerated for Newport's military barracks, but the barracks' residents were not included in the published census tables and have not been incorporated in this analysis.

    7. Allan M. Williams, 'Migration and Residential Patterns in Mid-Nineteenth Century Cardiff', *Cambria*, 6 (1979), pp. 1–27; C. Roy Lewis, 'The Irish in Cardiff in the Mid-Nineteenth Century', *Cambria*, 7 (1980), pp. 13–41; Harold Carter and Sandra Wheatley, *Merthyr Tydfil in 1851: A Study of the Spatial Structure of a Welsh Industrial Town*, Cardiff, University of Wales Press, 1982.

    8. James W. Dawson, *Commerce and Customs: A History of the Ports of Newport and Caerleon*, Newport, R.H. Johns, 1932, pp. 51–52, 70; Public Record Office (PRO), CUST 71.

    9. *MM*, 13 June 1829.

    10. PRO MH12/8086, J. Clive, Assistant Poor Law Commissioner, to Frankland Lewis, 4 May 1836.

    11. Gwent Record Office (GRO), Q/OR 71, 0002–0024, 0026–0037.

    12. PRO, HO52/42, 2 November 1839.

    13. GRO, Q/FSR 17.3 (16 October 1830); Parliamentary Papers (PP) 1842 XXVI, *A Return relating to Friendly Societies enrolled in the several Counties of England and Wales*, p. 27; *MM*, 8 October 1842; 'Old St Patrick's Day Celebrations in Newport and Cardiff', *St Peter's Magazine*, April 1924, pp. 110–14.

    14. *MM*, 17 August 1844.

    15. *MM*, 19 March 1836.

    16. *MM*, 15 October 1842, 22 April 1843.

    17. J.H. Canning, *Monmouthshire in the Penal Days*, Newport, 1921, p. 16.

    18. J.H. Canning, *St Mary's, Newport, 1840–1940: A Brief History*, Newport, Mullock & Sons, 1940, p. 7; J.B. Dockery, *Collingridge: A Franciscan Contribution to Catholic Emancipation*, Newport, R.H. Johns, 1954, p. 135.

    19. Canning, *St Mary's*, p. 8; GRO, Llanarth Estate MSS 0034; Fr J. Colbert, 'The Catholic Church in Newport, Mon.', in *The Newport Encyclopaedia*, Bristol, 1937, p. 32.

20. Dockery, *Collingridge*, p. 137; Canning, *Monmouthshire*, p. 17.

21. Canning, *St Mary's*, pp. 8–9; J.M. Scott, *The Ancient and Modern History of Newport, Monmouthshire*, Newport, W. Christophers, 1847, p. 95.

22. Canning, *St Mary's*, pp. 10, 15; *SWA*, 16 August 1892.

23. Canning, *St Mary's*, pp. 11–13.

24. GRO, Q of OD 0003/9 (19 October 1840); 1851 Religious Census, p. 104.

25. *MM*, 14 November 1840.

26. William James Copleston, *Memoir of Edward Copleston, D.D., Bishop of Llandaff, With Selections from his Diary and Correspondence, Etc.*, London, 1851, pp. 171–76.

27. *MM*, 16 November 1844.

28. *MM*, 23 November 1839; O'Leary, *Immigration and Integration*, pp. 66–69.

29. *MM*, 15 November 1845.

30. *MM*, 7 November 1846.

31. *MM*, 9 January 1847.

32. *MM*, 16 January 1847.

33. *MM*, 23, 30 January, 13, 20 February, 17 April 1847.

34. *MM*, 6 February 1847; *Cardiff and Merthyr Guardian*, 13 February 1847.

35. *MM*, 13 February 1847; GRO, Newport Poor Law Union, Board of Guardians Minute Book, 1845–50: 17 April 1847; PRO, MH12/8089: William Downing Evans to the Poor Law Commissioners, 27 April 1847; Report of John T. Graves, Assistant Poor Law Commissioner, 13 June 1847; Dawson, *Commerce and Customs*, p. 71.

36. *MM*, 13, 20 February, 24 April 1847.

37. *MM*, 27 February, 27 March 1847.

38. PP 1847–48 LIII, *Reports and Communications on Vagrancy*, Part II, report by W.D. Boase, p. 29.

39. PRO, MH12/8089: William Brewer and James Hawkins to the Guardians of Newport Union, 3 April 1847, Graves, *Report*.

40. Board of Guardians Minute Book, 20 March, 25 May 1847; PRO, MH12/8089: Evans to the Poor Law Commissioners, 23 March 1847; Digby Mackworth to the Poor Law Commissioners, 3 April 1847; Poor Law Commissioners to Evans, 28 April 1847; W.W. Harris to the Newport Guardians, 21 May 1847.

41. Boase, *Report*, pp. 17, 37–38.

42. *MM*, 10, 17 April, 15 May 1847; PRO, MH12/8089: Poor Law Commissioners to Evans, 26 June 1847; Evans to Poor Law Commissioners, 7 July 1847; Frank Neal, *Black '47: Britain and the Irish Famine*, Basingstoke, Macmillan, 1998, pp. 169–70, 173.

43. *MM*, 17 April 1847, 9, 16 June, 21 July 1849; *The Cambrian*, 3 December 1847; Neal, *Black '47*, p. 71.

44. *MM*, 15 July 1848, 24 February, 10 March, 5 May 1849, 11 June 1852;

PP 1854 XVII, *Report from the Select Committee relating to the Removal of the Poor*, Evidence of James Salter, Relieving Officer of the Newport Union, pp. 492–93; Dawson, *Commerce and Customs*, p. 71.

45. *MM*, 3, 17 April 1847.

46. *MM*, 17, 24 April 1847; PRO, MH12/8089: Harris to the Newport Guardians, 21 May 1847; Salter, *Evidence*, p. 493.

47. *MM*, 30 January 1847; PRO, MH12/8089: Graves, *Report*; Salter, *Evidence*, pp. 492–93.

48. Boase, *Report*, p. 28; *MM*, 29 April 1848.

49. PRO, MH12/8089: *Return of the Number of Vagrants and Trampers Relieved in the Workhouse or Workhouses of the (Newport) Union*, 7 February 1848; *MM*, 15 July 1848, 24 February, 5 May 1849, 15 June 1850, 25 July 1851, 8 April 1853; PP 1849 XLVII, *Returns of the Number of Irish Poor*, p. 2; Neal, *Black '47*, p. 110; PP 1854 LV, *Return of the Number of Irish Poor*, p. 3.

50. *MM*, 2 June, 4 August 1849; Board of Guardians, Meeting 23 June 1849.

51. Boase, *Report*, p. 17.

52. PRO, MH12/8089: Mackworth to the Poor Law Commissioners, 3 April 1847; Salter, *Evidence*, p. 490.

53. *MM*, 25 December 1847.

54. *MM*, 17 November 1849.

55. G.T. Clark, *Report to the General Board of Health on a Preliminary Inquiry into the Sewerage, Drainage, and Supply of Water, and the Sanitary Condition of the Inhabitants of the Borough of Newport*, London, HMSO, 1850, pp. 13, 19–21, 22–28, 40–41.

56. Andy Croll, 'Writing the Insanitary Town: G.T. Clark, Slums and Sanitary Reform', in *G. T. Clark: Scholar Ironmaster in the Victorian Age*, ed. Brian Ll. James, Cardiff, University of Wales Press, 1998, pp. 24–47, 38–39.

57. Carl Chinn, '"Sturdy Catholic Emigrants": The Irish in Early Victorian Birmingham', in *The Irish in Victorian Britain: The Local Dimension*, ed. Roger Swift and Sheridan Gilley, Dublin, Four Courts Press, 1999, pp. 52–74; Large, 'The Irish in Bristol', p. 42.

58. Boase, *Report*, p. 18.

59. See Steven Fielding, *Class and Ethnicity: Irish Catholics in England, 1880–1939*, Buckingham, Open University Press, 1993, pp. 14–15; John Herson, 'Migration, "Community" or Integration? Irish Families in Victorian Stafford', in Swift and Gilley (eds), *The Irish in Victorian Britain*, pp. 156–89; Kristina T. Jeffes, 'The Irish in Early Victorian Chester: An Outcast Community?', in *Victorian Chester: Essays in Social History 1830–1900*, ed. Roger Swift, Liverpool, Liverpool University Press, 1996, pp. 85–117; M.A. Busteed, R.I. Hodgson and T.F. Kennedy, 'The Myth and Reality of Irish Migrants in Mid-Nineteenth Century Manchester: A Preliminary Study', in *The Irish in the New Communities*, ed. Patrick O'Sullivan, Leicester, Leicester University Press, 1992, pp. 26–51; Louise Miskell, 'Irish Immigrants in Cornwall: The Camborne Experience, 1861–82', in Swift and Gilley (eds), *The Irish in Victorian Britain*, pp. 31–51.

60. Similar results were obtained by Lees for her sample of Irish in London: Lynn H. Lees, *Exiles of Erin: Irish Migrants in Victorian London*, Manchester, Manchester University Press, 1979, p. 258.

61. 'Total population' here refers to the 52 per cent CEB sample. Excluded from this and other tables are those residents for whom no information is given.

62. O'Leary, *Immigration and Integration*, pp. 111–12.

63. Source: for 1851, CEB sample; for 1861–1901, published census reports.

64. Richard Dennis, *English Industrial Cities of the Nineteenth Century: A Social Geography*, Cambridge, Cambridge University Press, 1984, p. 224.

65. Frank Neal, 'Irish Settlement in the North-East and North-West of England in the Mid-Nineteenth Century', in Swift and Gilley (eds), *The Irish in Victorian Britain*, pp. 75–100 (p. 83).

66. GRO, Local Board of Health, Newport, Report of the Medical Officer of Health, 27 December 1853; *Star of Gwent* (hereafter *SG*), 30 December 1853.

67. *SG*, 11, 25 July 1857, 11 December 1858.

68. *MM*, 7 July 1849; *South Wales Times* (hereafter *SWT*), 29 August 1857; *SG*, 10 January 1874.

69. Salter, *Evidence*, pp. 490, 494–95, 504–505.

70. *MM*, 7, 28 August, 18 September 1847, 12 May, 21 July 1849, 6, 13 April, 24 August 1850.

71. *MM*, 16 March 1850; *SG* 22 July 1853, 20 June 1857, 28 September 1861, 19 November 1864, 7 July 1866, 3 January 1874, 3 July 1875; *Evening Star*, 11 March 1878.

72. *SG*, 6 July 1861, 1, 15 October 1864.

73. Roger Swift, 'Crime and the Irish in Nineteenth-Century Britain', in Swift and Gilley (eds), *The Irish in Victorian Britain*, pp. 163–82, p. 166.

74. *MM*, 23 January 1846.

75. *MM*, 7 August 1847.

76. *MM*, 9, 16 December 1848, 31 March 1849; O'Leary, *Immigration and Integration*, pp. 95–99.

77. *MM*, 23 February, 3, 24 May 1856.

78. *MM*, 23 November, 7, 28 December 1850; *SG*, 14, 28 March, 4, 25 April, 13 June, 3 October 1868.

79. *SWA*, 16 August 1892.

80. Canning, *St Mary's*, pp. 15–16, 18.

81. *SG*, 6 May 1854; *MM* 19 May 1854; GRO, Minutes of the Newport and St Woollos Burial Board, 17 May 1854.

82. *MM*, 26 May, 2 June, 11 August, 20, 27 October 1854, 6 October 1855; *SG*, 12 August 1854; Burial Board Minutes, 26 July, 9, 23 August, 18 October–13 December 1854 passim.

83. *MM*, 27 September 1856; *SWT*, 31 October 1857; *SG* 16, 23 January 1858.

84. *MM*, 3, 7 February 1871.

85. *MM*, 6 July 1867.

86. *MM*, 20 November 1858.

87. *SG*, 1 January, 30 April 1859.

88. *SG*, 13 April 1861, 18 January 1862, 23 May 1863, 6 July 1867, 10 April 1869.

89. *SG*, 16 January 1875; Revd D.J. Thomas, *The Temperance Movement in Newport, Mon. 1837–1937*, n.d., pp. 34–35; W.D. Lambert, *Drink and Sobriety in Victorian Wales, c.1820–1895*, Cardiff, University of Wales Press, 1983, p. 154.

90. *SG*, 1 January 1859.

91. *SG*, 30 April 1859; *MM*, 1 January 1859.

92. *MM*, 18 January 1862; *SG*, 18 January 1862.

93. *MM*, 10 December 1859, 17 March 1860; *SG*, 17 March 1860.

94. *MM*, 27 November 1858; *SG*, 23 May 1863.

95. *MM*, 17 March 1860.

96. *SG*, 18 January 1862, 1 October 1864, 7 January 1865, 13 October 1866, 7 March 1868, 6 February 1869.

97. *MM*, 1 January 1859.

98. *SG*, 16 August 1862.

99. *MM*, 10 December 1859; *SG* 17 March, 6 October 1860, 25 May, 31 August 1861, 23 July 1864.

100. *SG*, 18 January 1862; *MM*, 23 May 1863.

101. *MM*, 1 January 1859; *SG*, 30 April 1859.

102. *MM*, 30 April 1859, 17 March 1860; *SG*, 20 April 1861.

103. *SG*, 6 December 1873.

104. *SG*, 1 January 1859.

105. *MM*, 18 January 1862.

106. *SG*, 18 January 1862.

107. *SG*, 25 July 1857, 3 November 1860, 10 April 1869.

108. *SG*, 30 May 1868; *SWA*, 6 September 1894. Salter's evidence on the demise of Irish friendly societies (*Evidence*, p. 504) may be prejudiced and unreliable.

109. *SWA*, 14 November 1892, 19 March 1894, 13 February 1895, 27 April, 21, 28 September 1900.

110. *SWA*, 17 March 1894.

The Irish in Wrexham, 1850–1880

Peter Jones

On 15 April 1851, the *Wrexham Advertiser* carried a piece purporting to be a dialogue between a census enumerator and an Irish woman. She was portrayed as excessively fecund, monumentally stupid and very, very 'Oirish'. The paper must have felt that the item would chime with its local readers' experience of the migrants in their midst.

By the middle of the nineteenth century, the town of Wrexham in north-east Wales was beginning to develop the industrial aspect of its economic life. The town's response to the Industrial Revolution had perhaps been delayed by the overwhelming nature of its agricultural activities, but between 1840 and 1880 improved road and rail communications, together with the economic decline of nearby Deeside, enabled Wrexham to become the commercial, administrative and industrial hub of the northern borderland between Wales and England. A variety of craftsmen plied their trades throughout the year in the town's lanes and courtyards and then, for two weeks in March, these artisans were joined at the annual fair by Yorkshire clothiers, Lancashire cotton sellers and Midlands hardware makers. A central business district developed and, concomitant with this process, residential suburbs began to appear. Wrexham would have presented a confident face to an immigrant. Its mixed economy sustained a steady growth in population, its metal industries developed alongside its established role as a market town, its financial services and commercial life grew. Public health and housing were yet to be improved and would have to wait for the full operational powers following incorporation in 1857, plus public and private endeavour later in the century, but there was a hospital and, by 1847, nine schools. Such was the town to which the Irish came in the mid-nineteenth century. Many moved on, some stayed and a few prospered.

By 1851, Wrexham's population was 6,714; thirty years later this had increased by 63.5 per cent to 10,978. Within these totals was an Irish element consisting of those who were born in Ireland and those of the second and third generations who, though not Irish-born, were part of an Irish community. These children, siblings and other relatives of Irish migrants would have absorbed and helped to sustain the values and lore of their Irish households; they would have had this cultural transmission reinforced by the close proximity of Irish neighbours, and would, for demographic purposes, have been effectively Irish. Were they a part of, or apart from, Wrexham society?

Whatever the answer, it should be seen in the context of widening perspectives in historical research. Large-city studies of the Irish, concentrating on the earlier part of the nineteenth century, long dominated historical writing, throwing up two-dimensional and monochrome images of squalid Irish ghettos and fever-ridden 'Little Irelands'. More recently, studies of the Irish in smaller towns and provincial localities, such as Herson's work on Stafford[1] and MacRaild's on Cumbria,[2] have revealed a diversity of Irish experience within their host communities. The Irish were not a homogeneous group and, in so far as they were diverse in religion, occupation, social status and the strength of their sense of identity, they were perceived and received differently in different British towns. To see the question of Irish absorption into Wrexham society as one of simple polarity – integration or segregation – is to miss the changing dynamics of relations between 'host' and 'guest' communities.

David Fitzpatrick has argued that even by 1871 the Irish were neither integrated into British society nor in a clearly defined community of their own: theirs, he says, was 'a curious middle place'.[3] The Irish were indeed perceived as different from their host communities but, on the other hand, if Fitzpatrick is right in saying that they were 'a restless, transient people', a definition of a distinct Irish community is not easily achieved. Mobility, after all, is conducive neither to the growth of a settled community nor to its acceptance by a larger society.

From the census data it may be seen that the dominant feature of the Irish in Wrexham was geographical mobility. Between 1851 and 1861, 341 Irish-born came and 268 left, a net migration of +73. In the following ten years, there was a net migration of +34, 329 Irish-born having arrived and 295 having departed. There was a net loss of 110 from 1871 to 1881, with 118 in and 228 out. This meant that during the period 1850–1881 most of the Wrexham Irish were lately of another place and were shortly to be elsewhere. There were few 'settlers' – only 11 in all – who were present in Wrexham throughout this period, and 86 from 1861 onwards. Between the 1840s and 1871, some 81 per cent of the Irish-born who came to the town had departed; that is, of the 978 who arrived, 791 left. In 1851, there were 308 Irish-born people in Wrexham, representing 4.6 per cent of the town's population; by 1881, there were 348 Irish-born, or approximately 3 per cent of the town's population in that year. While such a rate of turnover in the Irish population may have inhibited a complete integration into local society, nevertheless an Irish presence in the town was maintained. Indeed, in a town with a rapid overall growth, the Irish may have been the only group to have kept its clear identity among a mass of newcomers.

The Irish in Britain at this time were not settled people. Those who arrived before about 1870 may well have been unsuccessful or unwilling migrants, having failed to reach their preferred destination in the New World. Pushed out or pulled out of Ireland for whatever reason, the Irish had a tradition of mobility. The majority had taken a leap into the dark by crossing the Irish Sea. Further leaps from ports of landfall to places such as Wrexham may not have been into such dense darkness, for increasingly information would have been made available by family networks and earlier migrants. This could have contributed to a 'clustering' of people hailing from the same parts of Ireland, local ties being more potent than a common nationality.

In Wrexham, evidence of birthplace as given in census returns suggests a measure of affinity between the town and Connaught, for the counties of Mayo, Sligo, Galway and Roscommon were mentioned frequently as the places of origin of the Irish resident in the town. To take one street as an example: of the 53 Irish-born enumerated in Mount Street in 1851, 45 (85 per cent) came from Connaught, and the remaining eight from Dublin. In 1861, the Connaught connection supplied 53 (73 per cent) of the 73 Irish-born resident there, while the remainder came from Cavan, Dublin, Belfast, Waterford, Wexford and Cork. This pattern was echoed in other parts of Wrexham where the Irish were to be found. Given that time and distance were of prime importance in a migrant's choice of destination, one reason for this apparent connection with Connaught and Leinster could have been proximity to the Dublin–Holyhead ferry. To land in Liverpool meant a longer and more expensive sea crossing but a larger and well-established Irish community at the end of the journey to offer succour; to land at Holyhead meant a slog along the north Wales coast, plus the possibility of work en route, or a trek through the mountains along Telford's road to Llangollen, then north to Wrexham and south Lancashire beyond or south to the Midlands. Both routes would have had their attractions.

However, not all migrants arrived in Wrexham direct from Ireland. From the birthplaces of the children of Irish families it is possible to gain a pointer to the families' wanderings before they reached east Denbighshire. To take Mount Street as an example once more, in 1851 the street had 27 children born neither in Ireland nor in Wrexham whose parents were Irish-born. Ten of these (37 per cent) were born in south Lancashire or Cheshire, nine (33 per cent) in north Wales, five (18.5 per cent) in the Midlands and two (7.5 per cent) in south Wales, while one was born overseas. This means that 63 per cent of Mount Street's Irish children were born in the larger industrial areas of Britain. By 1861, the numbers of such children had more than doubled but south Lancashire and Cheshire still provided the largest number. Such evidence from Mount Street would seem to corroborate the argument of J.G. Williamson that the Irish drifted from the large cities and ports of entry to smaller inland towns.[4] The work of Herson has revealed a similar phenomenon in Stafford, an English town some 40 miles to the east of Wrexham, where there was a comparable turnover among the Irish.[5]

How was this Irish community in Wrexham constituted? The Irish population reached a high point of 631 in 1871 (see Table 1). Married men and widowers were always outnumbered by married women and widows, and only in one year, 1861, were single women fewer than single men. An obvious feature of the group was a changing age profile. Those over 61 years grew in number from 10 to 35 over the 30-year period, improved diet, sanitation and public health no doubt having had their effect. The majority of singletons were in the 0–18 age group for obvious reasons, but it is worth considering whether the marriage patterns among Irish immigrants resembled those in Ireland itself.

The depopulation of Ireland in the late nineteenth and early twentieth centuries – largely a rural phenomenon – had two obvious features: heavy emigration and a decline in marriage. Guinnane has pointed out that by 1911 approximately a quarter of all adults in Ireland in the 40–50 age range had never married.[6] Could the attitudes towards marriage that developed in the home country, with delayed marriage or even celibacy becoming common after the famine, have been reflected in the marriage patterns of the emigrants and their offspring in places such as Wrexham? The younger members of the Irish community did not rush into marriage. Only in one year, 1851, were any under-eighteens married, some five out of a total of 138, or 3.6 per cent. In the same year, 73 per cent of the over-eighteens were married, a figure that had risen to 81 per cent by 1861. The high point for the incidence of matrimony among the adult Irish (85 per cent) was reached in 1871, but by 1881 the figure was back to its 1851 level. The under-eighteens in Wrexham may have been cautious about marriage, but the over-eighteens would seem to have been optimistic enough about local conditions to commit themselves to partnership. Among the Wrexham Irish, any echo of marriage patterns in post-famine Ireland was faint.

As for status conferred by occupation, the livelihood of the town's Irish lay largely in semi-skilled and unskilled jobs. Adopting Armstrong's classification of occupational status,[7] we see that in 1851 just 13 per cent of the Wrexham Irish-born were in the intermediate and skilled categories. In 1861, these combined categories had fallen to 6 per cent, but climbed back to 13 per cent in 1871. The highest figure, 16 per cent, was reached in 1881. Correspondingly, the percentages of Irish-born semi-skilled and unskilled workers were 87 per cent in 1851, 94 per cent

Table 1 *The Irish community in Wrexham, 1851–1881**

(a) 1851

| | Age group | | | | | | | | | |
	0–18	19–30	31–40	41–50	51–60	61–70	71–80	81–90	90+	Total
Married men	3	22	24	19	12	7	0	1	0	88
Single men	77	21	8	3	3	0	0	0	0	112
Total men										200
Married women	2	28	27	24	10	2	0	0	0	93
Single women	56	13	1	2	0	0	0	0	0	72
Total women										165
Total										365

(b) 1861

| | Age group | | | | | | | | | |
	0–18	19–30	31–40	41–50	51–60	61–70	71–80	81–90	90+	Total
Married men	0	15	22	20	13	5	2	0	0	77
Single men	72	20	2	0	0	0	0	0	0	94
Total men										171
Married women	0	30	27	19	18	4	1	0	0	99
Single women	81	8	1	0	0	0	0	0	0	90
Total women										189
Total										360

Table 1 (continued)

(c) 1871

| | Age group | | | | | | | | | |
	0–18	19–30	31–40	41–50	51–60	61–70	71–80	81–90	90+	Total
Married men	0	32	28	39	20	12	8	1	0	140
Single men	150	28	8	3	0	1	0	0	0	190
Total men										330
Married women	0	36	39	34	23	8	4	0	0	144
Single women	140	12	2	1	2	0	0	0	0	157
Total women										301
Total										631

(d) 1881

| | Age group | | | | | | | | | |
	0–18	19–30	31–40	41–50	51–60	61–70	71–80	81–90	90+	Total
Married men	0	16	30	33	19	13	2	0	0	113
Single men	139	36	7	4	3	1	1	1	0	192
Total men										305
Married women	0	20	38	35	19	10	6	0	1	129
Single women	108	7	2	1	1	0	0	0	0	119
Total women										248
Total										553

*Figures include families but not temporary lodgers, visitors, etc.

in 1861, 87 per cent in 1871 and 84 per cent in 1881 – that is, the clear majority in each year. However, these percentages were sometimes lower than those for the town as a whole. For example, Wrexham's male work-force consisted of 96 per cent semi- and unskilled workers in 1871, the figure remaining as high as 91 per cent in 1881. Other changes over the period include fluctuations in the size of the total Irish-born workforce. From 1851 to 1861, the numbers fell by 86 to 71 per cent of their 1851 level. There was an increase of 43 by 1871 although the total was still only 85 per cent of the 1851 numbers. Lastly, from 1871 to 1881, a decrease of 38 Irish-born left the total at only 73 per cent of its 1851 starting point.

Changes also occurred over the period in the numbers of different occupations given for the Irish in the census returns: 37 in 1851, 26 in 1861, 43 in 1871 and 36 in 1881. These changes may have been due to a combination of changes in the town's economy as the century pro-gressed and variations in the criteria for classification on the part of the enumerators and the enumerated. Also, the proportion of women in the Irish-born workforce declined from 30 per cent in 1851 to 16 per cent ten years later, but subsequently increased marginally from 13 per cent in 1871 to 15 per cent in 1881. Why this was so is not obvious. One is led to speculate on how many single women, who had to maintain them-selves financially, arrived in Wrexham after the Great Famine and, in later years, married and had children and thereafter dropped out of the labour market. Again, married women may not have declared their paid occupations to the census enumerators, who, in their turn, may not have accurately interpreted or conscientiously entered the information given to them.

This last point may be illustrated by the classification of labourers. There seems to have been a hierarchy within categories of occupation, a distinction being made between agricultural and other labourers. There could have been uncertainty over job descriptions and, in 1851 at least, confusion over what a person's job had been in Ireland and what it actu-ally was in England and Wales. Consider the figures for Irish-born agri-cultural labourers in Wrexham: they begin in 1851 at 64 and increase to 95 by 1861. Thereafter there is a sudden decline to 15 in 1871 and 9 in 1881. How to explain this change? Could the economy of Wrexham have altered so dramatically as to suck workers in from the farms and estates of the surrounding rural areas? Could 'high farming' and mechanisation on the land have driven the workers away in such large numbers? Similarly, there was a dramatic increase in the numbers of general labourers, from 10 in 1851, through 26 in 1861, to a peak of 123 ten years later and 116 in 1881. Was there some confusion, or at least incon-sistency, in classification? However, bricklayers' labourers appear to have been consistently grouped, there being seven in 1851, nine in 1861, none in 1871 and nine again in 1881. Perhaps in this case there was a clearer understanding of the nature of the job.

At first glance, 1851 seems to be the year of highest employment of the Irish-born in Wrexham, with 296 people listed in 37 occupations. However, the 1851 census was distorted by the event of the town's annual spring fair. Twenty-four strolling players and commercial travellers were included in the count but they were obviously not permanent residents of the town. In addition, there were 71 hawkers of various goods, an atypical figure, as shown by later enumerations. Omitting the strolling players and travelling salesmen and averaging out the hawkers to 22[8] reduces the 1851 total Irish-born workforce to 223 and makes comparison over the years more realistic. Such adjustment makes 1871 the year of highest employment among the town's Irish-born.

A unique pocket of employment within Wrexham's population was the military barracks in Wrexham Fechan, now Hightown. The 23rd Regiment of Foot, which was formed in 1689 by William III and was superseded by the Royal Welch Fusiliers in 1881, maintained links with Wrexham throughout its existence. Irish soldiers were among its numbers. The 1861 and 1871 censuses enumerated only the non-commissioned military officers and their families so that the complete picture is impossible to draw, thus forcing a reliance upon the 1881 data. In the 1881 census, 19 Irish-born enlisted men were enumerated, together with 12 Irish-born wives and 14 Irish-born children, a total of 45 Irish-born in the full complement of 383 resident in the barracks on 3 April. The 19 Irish-born soldiers represented almost 5 per cent of the total in the barracks on that census night, whereas the total Irish-born contingent, including wives and children, equalled almost 12 per cent. Of the 273 enlisted men, the Irish-born represented 7 per cent.

Throughout the 1851–1881 period, there were both changes and continuities in the occupations of Wrexham's Irish-born. Rag gatherers, for instance, numbering 34 in 1851, were not in the count at all in 1861, but returned with seven in 1871 and disappeared entirely in 1881. Shoemakers, on the other hand, remained at six in each year until 1871, but by 1881 were either extinct or included with other craftsmen – the heading 'Other occupations' hides much fine detail. Lodging-house keepers and publicans moved in the four census counts from eight to 16, then 16 to 10, while servants – almost all of whom were women – numbered 25 in 1851, decreasing to eight and then seven in 1861 and 1871, before levelling out to 15 in 1881. The arrival of 'Retailing' in the occupations of the Irish-born in the 1861 census no doubt reflected the changing size and economy of the town. Wrexham's trade was beginning to lose its seasonal rhythm and its annual fair was in decline, to be replaced by permanent shops and market halls. Retailing and office work were alternatives to domestic service, but until about 1870 they were

Table 2 *Irish occupancy of three areas in Wrexham, average percentage, 1851–1881*[9]

Area	Street	Irish occupancy (average %)
Parish church area		27
	Yorkshire Square	56
	Mount Street	28
	Salop Road	20
	Yorke Street	16
	Tuttle Street	16
Pentrefelin		26
Beast Market		21

largely closed to the poor Irish because of the need for further specialist training beyond their inadequate basic schooling.

The earlier mention of 'clustering' raises the question of the distribution of the Irish in Wrexham. Was there a 'Little Ireland' in the town? This is doubtful, for there were never enough Irish to form a self-contained enclave in a town that could be crossed in a few minutes' walk. Again, the Irish may have congregated in certain areas but their qualification for doing so was their poverty, not their Irishness. This said, they were indeed prominent in three main areas: south and east of the parish church of St Giles, an area comprising Mount Street, Yorkshire Square, Yorke Street, Tuttle Street and Salop Road; and some four hundred yards to the west, in the Pentrefelin district. They were also statistically significant in the north-east in the Beast Market. These were the areas of greatest numbers and highest street occupancy by the Irish (see Table 2). In the thirty years after 1851, the streets and alleys clustered near the parish church had an average Irish occupancy of 27 per cent, those in the Pentrefelin and Brook Street district had a figure of 26 per cent, and those in the Beast Market 21 per cent. However, averages disguise the fact that in 1871 Yorkshire Square, immediately south of the parish church, reached a peak of 93 per cent Irish occupancy. Finally, of course, we should not accord too much importance to these differences between streets, because they were, in fact, so close together that they formed one precinct, sharing a common back area in which Irish identity, rather than street loyalties, may have been confirmed.

Even though the numbers of Irish inhabitants declined over the period, they tended to remain in the same locations. Tuttle Street, Yorke Street and Mount Street – all clustered near the parish church – had the strongest claim to be dubbed an Irish quarter, but it is a claim that grew distinctly weaker as time went on. In Yorkshire Square, for instance, numbers dwindled from 94 Irish-born in 1851 to 24 in 1881. Tuttle Street's tally ranged from 18 Irish-born in 1841 to 103 in 1861, falling back to 18 in 1881. Numbers for Yorke Street and Mount Street, on the other hand, showed less volatility and a tendency to increase.

The streets and courtyards around Brook Street and Pentrefelin formed another identifiable 'Irish' quarter. Situated along the River Gwenfro, this dilapidated area was one of the older parts of Wrexham and, as its names imply, was concerned with a water-based economy, especially milling and brewing. In 1851, Brook Street had 51 Irish-born residents, a total that rose to 91 in 1871 and fell to 11 in 1881. By 1871, Bellevue Road appeared in the statistics of the Irish-born. This road ran off Brook Street and Pentrefelin and became an area of relocation for the Irish in the town. In the 1851 census, no Irish-born were enumerated in Bellevue Road and its adjuncts, but in 1881 the road was one of only two that showed an increase from 1871 of their Irish-born populations, Salop Road being the other. It is significant that both Bellevue and Salop Roads were adjacent to Wrexham's two Irish 'heartlands', one found along the Gwenfro and the other around the church. The Irish were spreading into neighbouring streets and this movement, combined with a decline in the total numbers of Irish-born between 1871 and 1881, made the town's Irish areas less Irish. For example, in 1861 the average size of Irish households in Mount Street was 5.6 people, but by 1871 the figure had declined to 4.2. Furthermore, in 1881, when the average size of the street's households was 11.3 people, its Irish houses had an average of 6.2.[10]

The Wrexham Irish in the later nineteenth century may never have existed in sufficient numbers to constitute a ghetto but Irish areas were perceived as places apart. Mount Street was one such area. The local press in the 1850s made frequent references to the 'Irish Brigade', 'an Irish melée' and 'another Tuttle Street row',[11] and even official documents were ready to label areas with a national tag: 'low, damp . . . without privies, and the people chiefly Irish'.[12] Other parts of town endured similar conditions but their Welshness or Englishness was never invoked. Mount Street is suitable for a closer study because it demonstrates, in microcosm, gradual changes in the composition and nature of an Irish community. The numbers involved are large enough to provide a valid sample and the percentage of Irish-born remained relatively constant. Tuttle Street, on the other hand, ranged between 6 per cent and 93 per cent Irish settlement, making it atypical of the Irish experience in Wrexham streets in the second half of the century.

Mount Street was very near to Eagles Meadow where the annual fair was held, a fair that usually coincided with the census. This attracted many temporary residents such as strolling players and hawkers, many of whom took lodgings in Mount Street and adjacent lanes. Many of

Table 3 *1851 census enumeration: No. 2, Mount Sreet, Wrexham*

Name	Birthplace	Status in household	Age	Occupation
Patrick Marran	Ireland	Household head	50	Hawker of trinkets
Margaret Marran	Ireland	Wife	38	Hawker of confectionery
John Marran	Manchester	Son	18	Dyer
Peter Marran	Wrexham	Son	10	Scholar
Patrick Marran	Oswestry	Son	7	Scholar
Thomas Marran	Wrexham	Son	2	–
Ellen McGuire	Ireland	Unmarried	20	Servant

these itinerants were of Irish origin and their numbers could distort an analysis of the Irish-born in Wrexham. Therefore, care must be taken to distinguish between permanent and temporary residents. On the night of the census in 1851, Mount Street had 374 occupants. Of these, 53 were permanent Irish-born residents and 91 were effectively Irish, that is, not Irish-born but members of Irish families. The 53 represented almost 14 per cent of the street's population, but if the 91 are included the percentage rises to 38.5. The last point owes something to W.J. Lowe's 'Widnes factor' for calculating the 'realistic' (or reliable) number of Irish in a small town: that is, a household is counted as Irish if a minimum of two of its members – including the household head – were Irish-born.[13] In short, Lowe's 'Widnes factor' recognises that 'Irishness' was not entirely dependent on an Irish birthplace but could be nourished by an Irish family ethos. For instance, in the 1851 census, No. 2, Mount Street had a total occupancy of 32 people, only seven of whom were permanent residents (see Table 3). It is true that only three of the seven permanent occupants were Irish-born but the strength of the Irish influence may be assumed to have been tangible. The remainder of the occupants of No. 2 were 'temporary lodgers'. Of these 25 transients, nine were Irish-born. They were described as hawkers of fruits (13), confectioners (2), itinerant musician (1), pedlar in small wares (1), housemaids (2), collier (1), baker (1), dealer in pictures (1), and three unclassified. Eight of the 14 hawkers were Irish-born.

No. 4, Mount Street had 22 occupants, only four family members plus a servant being permanent residents. These were Irish-born Patrick McDermott, a 32-year-old marine store dealer, and his 28-year-old wife Ann, also born in Ireland, together with their two daughters, two years old and six months old respectively, both of whom were Wrexham-born. Their unmarried 19-year-old servant girl was Irish-born. Of the other occupants, seven were born in Ireland, giving an Irish-born element of 45 per cent. The lodgers in this household, however, were not directly connected with the annual fair. In 1851, there were 10 Irish households in Mount Street out of a total of 61 (16 per cent), but by 1861 this number had grown to 21 out of a total of 93 (22.5 per cent). Furthermore, there was only one household in the street in 1851 with 100 per cent Irish occupancy, whereas, by 1861, there were 14 such households.

By 1871, the Irish population of Mount Street numbered 104 out of a total of 537 (19.3 per cent). While the street's population was also 537 in 1881, its Irish population had risen to 172. There had been a declining Irish presence in the street since 1851, but the period from 1871 to 1881 saw an arrest of this trend, probably as a result of an increase in the birthrate and improvements in public health and housing conditions.

Most of the Mount Street Irish were labourers, but others were dealers, miners, makers or assemblers of such products as umbrellas and shoes. As the period progressed there were more frequent mentions in the census returns of skilled or semi-skilled occupations, such as carvers, gilders, masons and surveyors. Indeed, by 1871, there was a close correspondence between the occupational classifications of Irish males in Mount Street and in Wrexham as a whole, semi-skilled accounting for 24 per cent and unskilled 72 per cent. By 1881, these figures were 20 per cent skilled and 73 per cent unskilled.[14] This progressive alignment of Mount Street's workforce with that of the town may have been a measure of the gradual integration of the Irish, together with an overall economic and technological change.

While the majority of Irish during this period were impoverished and in low-status occupations, there were exceptions. Patrick McDermott of Mount Street and, later, Yorke Street, was one. Over the years since his arrival in Wrexham before 1845, his business diversified into horse dealing and iron founding. He bought and rented out houses and built a substantial property which bore his family name, McDermott's Buildings. 1871 was a high point in Patrick McDermott's fortunes, when Oswestry, a town to the south, opened its new reservoir in May. The original contractor had become bankrupt and McDermott, as his guarantor, completed the work. The opening ceremony was held on the bed of the reservoir with the town's mayor and council present and McDermott himself proposing the health of the Queen. It was all a long way from Galway, his blighted native land. In all, McDermott lived in the town for over fifty years and fathered ten children, all Wrexham-born. He became a man of property whose death necessitated grants of probate and letters of administration.[15] In him is to be seen an aspect of the Irish experience in nineteenth-century Britain that was not always visible, a reminder that stereotypes can be dangerously misleading.

However, as we saw earlier with reference to the dilapidation of the Pentrefelin area, the Irish in Wrexham, as elsewhere, did not usually live in the most salubrious parts of town. The 1850 *Report of the Health of Towns Commission* spoke of Pentrefelin's typically 'ill-paved courts, pigsties, donkey stables, close or no back premises, windows not made to open'.[16] There were more fortunate parts where 15 houses shared one privy, and all for sixpence a week. The town's civic pride was, it seems, limited to its façades, for the *Report* commented that 'the good appearance of Wrexham . . . is confined to its main streets and to the fronts of the houses composing them'.[17] Mount Street also had 'a total absence of proper drainage, accumulations of dung . . . and collections of stagnant, filthy water'. Yorkshire Square, with its ratio of 35 tenements to one privy, was 'in a state quite unapproachable'. The adjacent churchyard was 'crowded with dead bodies', 'giving off a most oppressive smell', and 'being used principally for the Irish people and paupers, of whom I have seen three interments at once'. Poor, noxious and Irish!

However, as we have seen, the Irish did not monopolise sub-standard housing in these areas. In this respect, there was a parallel with Stafford at a similar period. Herson found that the Irish in Stafford were 'scattered throughout the town, mostly in pockets of slum housing which existed before the bulk of the Irish arrived'.[18] In short, in both Wrexham and Stafford there was no Irish squalor, merely squalor. And with poor housing went a high death rate. The *Report to the General Board of Health*, of 1850, gave the average mortality rate for Wrexham between 1841 and 1848 as 28.6 per thousand per annum and, for 1848 to 1849, as 29.2 per thousand.[19] This, said the report, was 'excessive'. In 1841, Wrexham, after Newtown, had the highest mortality rate in north Wales, namely 23.7 per thousand, while Anglesey appeared to be the healthiest place with 15.6 deaths per thousand, that is 3.2 per thousand fewer than the north Wales average. The 'excessive' average death rate for Wrexham over the period 1841–1849 was 28.9 per thousand and, compared with such a figure, that for the poor – and significantly 'Irish' – quarter around the parish church was indeed high: 43.6 per thousand. In short, for those seeking culprits, death and the Irish could have seemed close companions. And yet the Irish-born at the time constituted only 22 per cent of the area's population. Meanwhile, in another 'Irish' enclave, Pentrefelin, the death rate was 25.6 per thousand, below the town's average. The highest death rate in town, 56.2 per thousand, was found in Abbot Street where there were virtually no Irish inhabitants.

The same report to the Board of Health gave the deaths from epidemic diseases between 1845 and 1849. Cholera and typhus were the chief predators, carrying off 13.8 per cent of the town's 145 victims, with scarlatina a close second with 11.7 per cent. Seven 'poor' streets associated with the Irish suffered a third of the town's total of deaths, with scarlatina and diarrhoea being confined almost entirely to these places. Again, however, the percentages were not so high as to make the diseases exclusive to the Irish; contiguity of location was a more likely cause of the spread of infection. For instance, Yorke, Mount and Salop Streets, all adjacent to one another, had 24 deaths in the four years; areas alongside the River Gwenfro also had 24 deaths. Yorkshire Square, which in 1851 was to have 57 per cent Irish-born, suffered only two deaths, from typhus and from smallpox. Death and disease did indeed discriminate – against the poor of whatever ethnic origin.

Further insights into the health of the town were provided by Dr Hubert Airy in his investigation into the outbreak of diphtheria in 1877.[20] The *Wrexham Advertiser* reported on 15 December 1877 that a public house had acted as an 'incubator' for the infection which attacked, in the main, children attending a Roman Catholic school in Bridge Street. This public house, the White Lion in Mount Street, was kept by Thomas and Mary O'Brien, who were recorded in the 1871 census as both 28 years old, Irish-born, with four children and two lodgers. One of the children, five-year-old Winifred, was taken ill on 23 November 1877 and died two days later. The doctor found the alehouse to be 'cleanly kept but confined and ill-ventilated'. The O'Brien family was friendly with another family in the street, the Kellys; all were present at Winifred's funeral. A Kelly child contracted diphtheria and died on 12 December. The children of these families attended a Catholic school about which Dr Airy said 'there appeared to be nothing unwholesome'.[21] In early December more cases appeared among the pupils but this time they were from 'a crowded nest of low-class tenements called Pierce's Square' in the Pentrefelin area.[22] Dr Airy concluded that the outbreak was spread 'by means of school congregation' but he made no link between the disease and the town's Irish. Indeed, he was at pains to point out that all the schools had become 'centres of infection'.

Dr Airy's apparent blindness to ethnic differences may be one indication of Irish integration into Wrexham society as the century progressed: the 1845 Health of Towns Commission had mentioned the Irish, but by 1878 for Dr Airy they had become 'invisible'. An established Irish presence, coupled with an identification with the indigenous poor, had, in this regard, blurred Irish separateness in Wrexham and altered the earlier point of view, which connected disease and Irishness in a simple equation composed of disease, poverty and bad housing.

One of the reasons for studying the experience of the Irish in Wrexham in the late nineteenth century is their uniqueness. A settled, calm society holds little interest and often its underlying character can be seen only when its surface is disturbed. The Irish were a distinct group in this north-east Wales town at this time and, as elsewhere in Britain, they had many of the qualities of aliens. For some, the Irish were a beleaguered minority who remained outcasts from the mainstream of British society in the nineteenth and early twentieth centuries; they were seen as staunchly maintaining their separate identity and therefore as suffering no 'ethnic fade'.[23] For others, the Irish had by 1900 shaken off their past and adopted British values and social practices, exchanging their rural tradition for an urban culture.[24] David Fitzpatrick has been more circumspect, arguing that the Irish occupied a 'curious middle place'.

Such evaluations are largely based on the study of cities such as Liverpool, where the dynamics of Irish migrant life were very different from those in smaller towns such as Wrexham. Numbers are significant here: clear and sustained segregation from a host society requires a group with a substantial membership. What may have been fashioned in Liverpool in 1851 with its Irish-born population of 83,813[25] could have been done only in miniature or not at all in Wrexham with its 341 Irish-born. Here, in a reduced context, the Irish would have had to react to small, local stimuli, for they would not have been numerous enough to dominate spheres of activity. The Irish may have gained control over dock labour in Liverpool but two or three of their country cousins in a Wrexham brewery could hardly have established an Irish-only closed shop. Furthermore, there would have had to be clear benefits to be gained for continued segregation to have been worthwhile and sufficient numbers to sustain it. Integration was the more likely phenomenon – if only because it required less energy – and, given such a small and highly mobile migrant population, absorption into the larger and culturally dominant community was virtually inevitable. It may be that a state of inherence was achieved, with the Irish distinguishable but inseparable from the host society. Consequently, while there may have been Irish 'quarters' in Wrexham, based on a variety of factors such as common birthplace and family connections, they were small and, as we saw in Pentrefelin, fluid in their boundaries. Besides, as slum clearance proceeded, people of all origins were dispersed and their populations were thus culturally diluted.

There could, therefore, have been a tug between the impulse towards integration and that towards segregation, the strength of which changed as the century moved on. At a point in mid-century, the local paper, the *Wrexham Advertiser*, could carry items that assumed not the melding but the cohabitation of two cultures; by the 1880s there was less need for such differentiation. On 13 August 1859, it reported the arrest of a monoglot Welshman by an Irish policeman who obviously could not understand his prisoner's utterances. Six months later the paper reported the admonition of a recalcitrant Irish witness in a local magistrates' court 'in the language of the Green Isle'. Seventeen years later, on 11 November 1876, the paper's editorial commented on the election of Irish-born John Beirne to the mayorship of Wrexham. The election vote had not been unanimous, it seemed, the sticking-point not being his worthiness for the office or his standing in the community, and not his Irish origins. Instead, it was his Roman Catholicism, which forbade his attendance in the parish church for civic services. The days of the newspaper's interest in the 'Irish melée' and the 'Tuttle Street row' seemed to be over, and even the Irish joke was passé.

The Irish may have had certain distinguishing qualities in Wrexham, but how typical was their experience? Comparisons between Irish settlement in the larger urban areas and in smaller provincial towns have highlighted differences born of scale and geographical distribution. Herson has shown that the Irish in small-town Stafford were residentially dispersed, pointing out that both the economy of the area and the liberal attitude of the Poor Law Guardians were important attractions for the Irish migrant.[26] He has also shown that an overemphasis on the mobility of the Irish, as individuals and groups, can disguise the stability to be found within families, stability that promoted integration with the host society.[27] Pooley has also argued that even in large towns such as Liverpool the Irish were not totally geographically isolated.[28] On the other hand, MacRaild, in his study of the Irish in Victorian Cumbria, demonstrated that allegiances formed mainly in Ireland were perpetuated after migration, so that intra-communal conflicts between Green and Orange were translated to such places as Cleator Moor.[29] Internecine strife of this kind would have militated against integration, delimiting the Irish from the main community. This was a point noted by John Davies about Merthyr Tydfil and Cardiff where most Irish migrants came from southern Ireland, bringing with them no Green–Orange animosity. Merthyr and Cardiff were thus free of such Irish factional conflict.[30] Wrexham, too, whose Irish derived mainly from Connaught, had little or no political conflict. Small numbers may have prevented such friction, but at the same time nearby Flint, a town with similar numbers of Irish migrants, developed what was described by the *Chester Chronicle* on the occasion of a visit in 1886 by Michael Davitt, the Land Leaguer, as a politically aware 'Irish colony'.[31] Reports of Fenian activity in the 1860s appeared in the local press, especially about the time of the nearby Chester Castle raid in 1867, but most reports were concerned with rumours and sightings of suspicious characters. In January 1868, the Reverend Canon Browne, the Catholic priest of St Mary's in Wrexham, whose flock was almost all Irish, wrote to the local Bench of magistrates, assuring them of his congregation's loyalty to the Queen.[32] It is significant that, in his letter, he pledged Catholic loyalty, without specifically mentioning the Irish. This may have been diplomacy on the canon's part, or it may have been that in Wrexham, even by 1868, the process of integration was in train.

Notes

1. John Herson, 'Irish Migration and Settlement in Victorian Britain: A Small Town Perspective', in *The Irish in Britain, 1815–1839*, ed. Roger Swift and Sheridan Gilley, London, Pinter, 1989, pp. 84–103.

2. Donald M. MacRaild, *Culture, Conflict and Migration: The Irish in Victorian Cumbria*, Liverpool, Liverpool University Press, 1998.

3. David Fitzpatrick, 'A Curious Middle Place: The Irish in Britain, 1871–1921', in Swift and Gilley (eds), *The Irish in Britain*, p. 11.

4. J.G. Williamson, 'The Impact of the Irish on British Labour Markets during the Industrial Revolution', in Swift and Gilley (eds), *The Irish in Britain*, p. 140.

5. Herson, 'Irish Migration', pp. 84–103.

6. T.W. Guinnane, 'The Vanishing Irish: Ireland's Population from the Great Famine to the Great War', *History Ireland*, 5 (1997), p. 33.

7. W.A. Armstrong, 'The Use of Information about Occupation', in *Nineteenth Century Society: Essays in the Use of Quantitative Methods for the Study of Social Data*, ed. E.A. Wrigley, Cambridge, Cambridge University Press, 1972, Chapter 6. In 1851, in St John's parish in Chester, there were 2,032 Irish-born in a total city population of 27,835. The occupational status of the Irish-born was as follows: Class I, 1.8 per cent; Class II, 13 per cent; Class III, 14.7 per cent; Class IV, 43.3 per cent; Class V, 27.2 per cent (Class I: professional, e.g. solicitor; Class II: semi-professional, e.g. teacher; Class III: skilled, e.g. carpenter; Class IV: semi-skilled, e.g. gardener; Class V: unskilled, e.g. labourer). See Kristina T. Jeffes, 'The Irish in Early Victorian Chester: An Outcast Society?', in *Victorian Chester: Essays in Social History, 1830–1900*, ed. Roger Swift, Liverpool, Liverpool University Press, 1996.

8. Over the period 1861–1881, 66 hawkers were enumerated.

9. Source: census enumerators' returns for 1851, 1861, 1871, 1881.

10. Source: census enumerators' returns for 1861, 1871, 1881.

11. *Wrexham Advertiser*, 24 April, 14 August 1858, 4 June 1859.

12. PP I 1845, *Second Report of the Health of Towns Commission*, p. 217.

13. W.J. Lowe, *The Irish in Mid-Victorian Lancashire: The Shaping of a Working-Class Community*, New York, Peter Lang, 1989, Chapter 3.

14. Source: census enumerators' returns, 1871, 1881.

15. Sources: *Wrexham Advertiser*; Probate Registers of the High Court of Justice, 1900, County Record Office, Ruthin, BD/C/371; Slater's Directories.

16. PP I, 1845, *Second Report of the Health of Towns Commission*.

17. G.T. Clark, *Report to the General Board of Health on a Preliminary Inquiry into the Sewerage, Drainage, and Supply of Water, and the Sanitary Conditions of Town, Borough, or Place of Wrexham*, pp. 4–5.

18. Herson, 'Irish Migration', p. 95.

19. PP 1850, *Report to the General Board of Health*.

20. Dr Airy's *Report to the Local Government Board on Diphtheria in Parts of the Wrexham Registration District*, p. 1.

21. Airy, *Report*, p. 2, para. 7.

22. Airy, *Report*, p. 2, para. 8.

23. John Belchem, 'Freedom and Friendship to Ireland', *International Review of Social History*, 39 (1994), pp. 33–56. See also MacRaild, *Culture, Conflict and Migration*, passim, where the 'assimilation perspective' is questioned by reference to the sectarian flavour of Cumbrian Irish life.

24. James Walvin, *Passage to Britain: Immigrants in British History and Politics*, London, Penguin 1984, p. 58.

25. Colin G. Pooley, 'Segregation or Integration? The Residential Experience of the Irish in Mid-Victorian Britain', in Swift and Gilley (eds), *The Irish in Britain*, p. 66.

26. Herson, 'Irish Migration', pp. 89, 93.

27. John Herson, 'Migration, "Community" or Integration? Irish Families in Victorian Stafford', in *The Irish in Victorian Britain: The Local Dimension*, ed. Roger Swift and Sheridan Gilley, Dublin, Four Courts Press, 1999, pp. 156–89.

28. Pooley, 'Segregation or Integration?', p. 80.

29. MacRaild, *Culture, Conflict and Migration*, p. xv, Chapter 6.

30. John Davies, *A History of Wales*, London, Penguin, 1990, p. 385.

31. *Chester Chronicle*, 13 February 1886.

32. *Wrexham Advertiser*, 4 January 1868.

Reassessing the Anti-Irish Riot: Popular Protest and the Irish in South Wales, c. 1826–1882

Louise Miskell

The presence of hostility towards the Irish has, to a greater or lesser degree, been of interest to historians engaged in work on a variety of aspects of modern British history, from the development of the British state[1] through to the history of the working classes[2] and the question of post-war multiculturalism and race relations.[3] As well as this wider significance, however, anti-Irish disturbances, which tended to be extensively reported in the press, offer a particularly useful insight into the nature of the Irish immigrant experience. Historians of the Irish in Britain have thus devoted increasing attention in recent years to the study of anti-Irish disturbances and their causes. Despite this level of interest, however, there has been little variety in approach to the study of anti-Irish rioting. To date, our knowledge of anti-Irish sentiment in Britain has been dominated either by broad surveys examining the reception of the Irish in a British-wide context,[4] or by evidence based on studies of the large Irish populations in the big English and Scottish cities.[5] Recent developments in Irish immigrant historiography, however, have seen a move to more local or regionally based studies, which have revealed greater diversity and variety in the Irish immigrant experience in Britain.[6] By applying the same methods to the analysis of anti-Irish hostility, a more accurate and regionally sensitive picture of the different causes and manifestations of anti-Irish disturbances in Britain can be produced.

Until recently, Wales has been largely absent from the study of anti-Irish hostility in Britain.[7] The numbers of the Irish in Welsh industrial towns, with the exception perhaps of mid-nineteenth-century Merthyr, never rivalled those found in the big English and Scottish cities. Among the 20 British towns with the largest Irish populations in 1851, Merthyr was the only Welsh representative, in nineteenth place with a little over 3,000 Irish-born inhabitants.[8] These comparatively small numbers have meant that Wales has not featured prominently in general surveys of the Irish immigrant presence in Britain.[9] Neither has it been seen as an area where anti-Irish tensions were strong, mainly because of the widely held assumption that anti-Irish hostility was more pronounced in areas where the Irish were most numerous. In a recent study of Irish immigrants in Coventry, for example, Pauline Mulkern suggested that English–Irish tensions in the town never boiled over because the Irish population was relatively small, and consequently 'the inhabitants never felt overrun by immigrants'.[10] As well as linking anti-Irish disturbances to the size of the Irish presence, this kind of interpretation has also led to the characterisation, by default, of smaller centres of Irish population as more passive and tolerant. In precisely this way, the industrial towns of south Wales, with their small Irish immigrant contingents, have been perceived as particularly tolerant towards the Irish. One historian has even suggested that the reception of the Irish in Wales was the most passive anywhere in Britain.[11] Since then, this impression of Welsh–Irish relations has been convincingly refuted. Recent research has led to the identification of 20 separate incidents of anti-Irish violence in Wales between 1826 and 1882, some of which were serious and prolonged.[12]

As well as its low profile in Irish immigrant historiography, the study of anti-Irish disturbances in Wales has also been absent from the the the otherwise well-documented history of popular protest in nineteenth-century Wales. South Wales, in particular, was noted for the frequency and scale of both rural and urban disturbances in the first half of the nineteenth century, including the Merthyr Rising in 1831, the Chartist march on Newport in 1839 and the protracted and often violent campaigns of the Rebecca rioters in the Welsh countryside throughout the 1840s.[13] Such incidents combined to characterise Wales as a hotbed of unrest and agitation and prompted government investigations into the causes of disorder.[14] Despite the prominence ascribed to these events in the writing of Welsh social history, there has been no attempt to integrate the phenomenon of anti-Irish rioting into this picture of popular protest and disturbance in nineteenth-century Wales. Instead, historians have tended to focus on two phases of high tension and unrest: the first linked to the radicalism of the late eighteenth and early nineteenth centuries, culminating in the Chartist activity of the 1840s, and the second associated with industrial unrest, strike action and the growth of trade unionism and socialism in the late nineteenth and early twentieth centuries.[15] Anti-Irish disturbances in Wales, stretching from the 1820s through to the 1880s, and thus spanning the decades of apparent stability between 1850 and 1880, have not been accommodated into this chronological framework. Yet the patterns of anti-Irish rioting witnessed in Wales owed much to traditional forms of popular protest familiar in both rural and industrial areas, and can only really be understood in this context.

As well as its significance for this area of Welsh social history, the study of anti-Irish disturbances in Wales also presents some important challenges to the traditional image of anti-Irish rioting in Britain, which has emerged from general surveys and big-city studies. So far, although the myth of peaceful Welsh–Irish relations has been revised, little has been done to assess the implications of the Welsh evidence of anti-Irish rioting for the historiography of the Irish in Britain as a whole. In this chapter, the aim is to show that traditional interpretations of anti-Irish rioting in Britain, based substantially on British-wide surveys and big-city studies, cannot be applied generally to explain the causes and patterns of disturbances in smaller towns or in particular regions. Anti-Irish violence in south Wales did not conform to many of the traditional interpretations and general assumptions about the reception of the Irish British-wide. Instead, the pattern and chronology of disturbances in south Wales require examination in the context of Welsh popular protest. In this way, a clearer understanding of the causes and patterns of anti-Irish rioting in Wales can be achieved which contributes to a more diverse and regionally sensitive picture of anti-Irish disturbances in Britain.

The conventional approach to the study of anti-Irish hostility in Britain has been to adopt a fairly limited chronological framework. Studies of anti-Irish rioting have been virtually confined to a brief period around the middle decades of the nineteenth century. Graham Davis, for example, found that '[in] assessing the level of conflict and hostility experienced by Irish labour in Britain, the overwhelming impression is that the frequency and ferocity of disturbances over employment had subsided from the peaks of sporadic violence that occurred between the 1830s and 1860s'.[16] This chronology suggests that the lifespan of anti-Irish rioting in Britain was fairly short, with the frequency and intensity of attacks declining after the 1860s, as the rate of Irish immigration into Britain began to fall. The highest number of Irish-born people living in nineteenth-century Britain was recorded in the 1861 census, when 601,634 were enumerated in England and Wales.[17] After that, the rate of immigration declined and the original Irish-born immigrants were gradually outnumbered by their British-born descendants. Anti-Irish hostility is traditionally seen as peaking at the height of the post-famine influx, and then gradually declining thereafter along with the rate of immigration. This interpretation corresponds neatly with recent portrayals of Britain's Irish immigrants as a group that gradually achieved assimilation and integration with the host population over time.[18]

Historians have only recently begun to revise this view, with the help of evidence from south Wales.[19] Incidents of anti-Irish rioting in Wales can be traced back to the pre-famine years, when attacks were made on Irish workers imported into south Wales to help with the construction of the new ironworks in the Monmouthshire and Glamorgan valleys. In Rhymney in 1826, for example, hostilities flared up between locals employed at the Bute ironworks and a group of Irish workers imported to carry out the construction of three new blast-furnaces.[20] In the 1830s and 1840s there were further incidents of anti-Irish rioting. In 1834 the Varteg ironworks in Pontypool was the venue for a clash between local workers and Irish inhabitants who were accused of undercutting the wages of the native workforce,[21] while less than a decade later attacks on Irish houses in Blaina were sufficiently serious to require the presence of police reinforcements and the alerting of troops.[22]

Anti-Irish protests showed no signs of abating in the second half of the nineteenth century. In 1853 there were attacks on Irish inhabitants in Ebbw Vale and Brynmawr,[23] and the trend intensified in the 1860s as anti-Irish tensions grew in response to increased Fenian terrorist activity in Britain. Fears of Fenianism were widely disseminated by the press, causing anxiety among the public and increasing anti-Irish sentiment throughout south Wales. Among members of the public there was a genuine belief that the majority of Irish immigrants were Fenians. The industrialist George Clark said of his Irish employees at the Dowlais ironworks: 'I believe they are one and all Fenian sympathisers, and I daresay they all subscribe.'[24] In Merthyr in December 1867, a number of arrests were made of local Irish immigrants who were suspected members of the brotherhood. Fears of Fenianism also prompted hostilities later in the decade, such as at Pontlottyn in Glamorgan where anti-Irish rioting broke out in 1869.[25] Although Fenian activity subsided in the 1870s, disturbances continued to occur in south Wales towns. Ebbw Vale in Monmouthshire, which had already played host to anti-Irish attacks, was again the scene of rioting against the local Irish population on Christmas Day, 1879.[26] Three years later, however, it was the nearby town of Tredegar that witnessed Wales' most serious incident of anti-Irish rioting. There, Irish residents were the target of disturbances that engulfed the town for a whole weekend in July 1882, and threatened to spread to the neighbouring towns of Blaina and Brynmawr.[27]

The persistence of anti-Irish rioting in Wales through to the 1880s illustrates the difficulty of attempting to apply conventional interpretations of anti-Irish disturbances to the situation in south Wales. There, despite the decline in the rate of Irish immigration after 1861 and the presence of relatively small numbers of migrants, anti-Irish rioting continued to occur with undiminished intensity through to the latter decades of the nineteenth century. Attacks were often violent, resulting in extensive damage to property and serious, sometimes even fatal injury to persons. Rarely spreading from their areas of origin to other towns, they relied heavily on local enmities and an intimate knowledge of the local Irish population and where they lived and worked. The Christmas Day disturbance at Ebbw Vale in 1879 was typical of the format the riots tended to follow. The most common form of attack was against property. Rioters targeted Irish homes, damaging windows, doors and door-frames. A policeman giving evidence against the Ebbw Vale rioters described the extent of the damage they caused to property in the Irish district of Newtown:

> I went to Newtown after a time and found houses broken down, but the mob had dispersed. The windows in Crooked Row in which the Irish live were all broken in, frames and all. I visited several of the cottages and saw stones, bricks and parts of the window frames scattered about the floors.[28]

Similarly at Blaina in 1843, rioters 'demolished the doors and windows', not only of Irish houses, but also of the homes of local people suspected of harbouring their Irish neighbours.[29] The Tredegar riot, in July 1882, was the most serious of all anti-Irish attacks in Wales. There, an estimated 50 Irish homes were wrecked during a weekend of violence. Rioters also made bonfires from the furniture and possessions seized from the houses. The *South Wales Daily News* reported that '[b]eds, chairs, chests of drawers and every conceivable article to be found in the houses were heaped on the flames'.[30]

As well as violence against the homes and property of the Irish, physical attacks against individuals were also common. At Blaina in May 1843 it was reported that '[m]asses of people armed with heavy bludgeons and other weapons . . . traversed the neighbourhood of Blaina in pursuit of the Irish labourers, attacking the houses in which they were known to dwell, and obliging every person obnoxious to them, to fly for his life'.[31] The degree of injury inflicted varied from minor to life-threatening. During the riot at Pontlottyn in August 1869, an Irishman was kicked, stoned and beaten with a shovel and died from his injuries.[32] At Tredegar in 1882, an estimated 15 Irish people were seriously injured during the riot. One of them was Thomas Fitzgerald, a wealthy Irish contractor, who was attacked at his home in the town. A policeman at the scene described the assault:

> I helped keep the mob from entering Fitzgerald's house. I had a blow on the head with a stone. I saw them break in and drag Fitzgerald out into the yard and kick him on the ground. He was hardly conscious when we got him to the station.[33]

At Ebbw Vale in 1879, several Irish, both male and female, were attacked and injured. John Cocklin was one of the Irish casualties who later identified his attackers in court:

> That man, Lewis Nicholas, struck me. I told him not to strike me because I was already under the peace. There was a crowd on the bridge, these came at me . . . I was upset on the footpath, and one of the three followed and kicked me . . . I know Nicholas, who is a boilermaker and we were brought up together from boyhood.[34]

Such accounts indicate the degree of familiarity between the Irish and their attackers. Local knowledge was essential in the location of Irish houses and the identification of individuals as targets for attack. In this way, the pattern of anti-Irish rioting in Wales was strongly community-based, and reliant on local knowledge of the Irish population and their residential settlement.

The extent to which these riots were shaped by personal knowledge and local issues raises important questions for the identification of the causes of anti-Irish hostility in Wales. Studies of anti-Irish hostility elsewhere in Britain have often focused on religious animosity or, more specifically, anti-Catholic sentiment as one of the most common causes of tension in Irish–British relations. In her recent work on the education of the Irish in Britain, Mary Hickman argued that the role of traditional anti-Catholicism in Britain was central to the shaping of negative attitudes to Irish immigrants.[35] Indeed, the 'religious riot' has proved to be perhaps the most popular context in which to study the causes and patterns of anti-Irish protest. In Pauline Millward's analysis of the 1852 Stockport riot, for example, the violent response to the town's Roman Catholic Sunday School march was interpreted as part of a long tradition of anti-Catholicism and 'no-popery' stretching back to the Reformation.[36] Other historians have also emphasised the role of religious hostility as a catalyst for disorder. Alan O'Day found that '[d]uring the 75 years after 1846, the usual flashpoint for an outburst of anti-Irish violence was a religious dispute'.[37] Likewise, Donald MacRaild identified religion as '[the] greatest factor in fostering negative attitudes towards the Irish among the indigenous population'.[38] He has also argued that the continuation of anti-Irish hostilities into the Edwardian period was, to a large extent, a consequence of the strengthening of Orangeism and Protestantism.[39]

In Wales, the majority of Irish immigrants came from Ireland's south-western counties, predominantly Cork and to a lesser extent Limerick and Waterford. The immigrants from these areas were overwhelmingly Catholic and, as a result, they did not bring with them the deep-seated religious rivalries found among the Irish populations of some English and Scottish cities, where immigrants from Ireland's northern counties were more numerous.[40] Although Wales did not experience the undercurrent of sectarianism that proved so volatile in cities such as Liverpool and Glasgow, there were religious tensions of a different kind. Throughout the nineteenth century the growth of Independent (Congregationalist), Methodist and Baptist congregations in Wales was such that, by the last quarter of the century, religious nonconformity and Welsh identity were fused as never before.[41] It has been suggested that the strength of nonconformity, coupled with traditional anti-Catholic sentiment in Wales, created a climate of hostility towards the Irish in which they were subjected to harassment and animosity.[42]

Despite the existence of traditional anti-Catholic suspicions and the dominance of Protestant nonconformity, however, anti-Catholicism was not a major catalyst of anti-Irish disturbances in south Wales. Although Catholic targets were attacked during anti-Irish rioting, religious tensions were seldom at the root of hostilities. Fr William Williams, Catholic priest at Tredegar, wrote a letter to the home secretary after the anti-Irish disturbances in the town in July 1882. In his analysis of the rioting he stated that '[my] school has been wrecked and my house and church . . . would have been wrecked on Sunday but for the victory of the police'. At no point in his lengthy analysis of the causes of the riot, however, did he mention anti-Catholic sentiment as a factor prompting the attack. In fact, far from experiencing religious animosity in the town he claimed that, 'personally I have always stood well with every class of the community here'.[43] Under his ministrations the Catholic Church had proved a point of contact rather than a source of division between the Irish and the host population of Tredegar. During periods of hardship such as the coal stoppage of 1878, for example, charitable relief was dispensed from the Catholic hall to Catholics and non-Catholics alike.[44]

Of greater significance in precipitating the riots, as far as Fr Williams was concerned, was the issue of work and wages. The idea that the Irish were responsible for taking jobs that rightfully belonged to local people, and working for lower pay, thereby forcing down wage rates, was commonly expressed in the wake of anti-Irish rioting in Wales. Following the Tredegar riots, Fr Williams observed that '[t]here has always been a grudge rankling in the minds of the Welsh all over the iron and coal district in consequence of the influx of Irish people which has lessened the amount of work reserved for them and perhaps lessened the rate of wages'.[45] The same grievances were voiced almost everywhere that anti-Irish disturbances occurred. Rioting in the iron towns of Rhymney and Pontypool in the 1820s and 1830s was accompanied by similar complaints of the effects of Irish labour on the jobs and wages of locals.[46] Elsewhere, too, historians have found that labour rivalries were likely to spark hostility. In his study of the Irish in Manchester and Salford, for example, Steven Fielding claimed that '[h]ostilities followed the ebb and flow of demand for labour and were determined by the nature of the local job market'.[47]

Although the expression of such grievances against the Irish was common, there are difficulties with accepting at face value the allegations of wage undercutting and competition for jobs. The evidence from south Wales suggests that unskilled Irish labourers made few inroads into skilled employment in the iron industry. As George Clark, the trustee of the Dowlais ironworks, explained, the Welsh and Irish filled different positions in the workplace: 'The place of an Irish emigrant is filled no doubt by an Irish immigrant, but the space of the skilled Welshman cannot be filled by an Irishman. The men we get for that purpose are the men who have been bred up in the rural districts.'[48] Numerous informal work practices operated to ensure that newcomers were not given the opportunity to learn skills that would give them access to less menial and better paid jobs in the coal and iron industries of south Wales. The Monmouthshire Friendly Society of Coalmining, established in 1831, stipulated that its members refrain from taking newcomers underground so as to ensure that access to the skills required for the best mining jobs was restricted to native workers.[49] Iron puddling was another carefully protected occupation. Described by one historian of the south Wales iron industry as 'an aristocrat of the skilled working class',[50] the puddler was responsible for the process of converting pig iron into wrought iron and was one of the most highly skilled and well paid of workers in the iron industry. Knowledge of the puddling process, however, was acquired gradually and required a close association with the iron industry from an early age. One contemporary explained that '[in] England and Wales, puddling is begun to be learnt by the boys around the mills, and they grow up into this knowledge from early boyhood, and hence by the time they get a furnace they are really accomplished and experienced puddlers'.[51] Immigrants from primarily rural backgrounds in Ireland thus had little opportunity to acquire such skills and, as a result, few made their way into this kind of employment. In Tredegar, where some 300 Irish-born workers were employed in the iron industry in 1861, only 16 were puddlers.[52] This was not untypical of the situation in other towns. The *Morning Chronicle*'s correspondent in Merthyr in 1850 claimed that '[s]uch a wonder as an Irish Puddler was never heard of'.[53]

Although the Irish rarely competed for the most skilled industrial jobs, they were still perceived as a threat to local workers. In fact, their prevalence in unskilled and lower paid occupations fuelled the belief that they were responsible for lowering the rate of pay in the local economy. Only in recent years has work by economic historians seriously challenged the validity of this view of Irish labour and its effect on the wage rates of the British working class. Jeffrey Williamson, in particular, has asserted that in fact the Irish were not a numerically significant enough presence in the workforce to have had any tangible effect upon wage levels.[54] In the light of these findings it is unlikely that the relatively modest numbers of Irish immigrants in south Wales towns in the second half of the nineteenth century brought about a general lowering of wage levels across all employment sectors. In fact, they were considered by some to be an indispensable element of the industrial workforce in south Wales. After the Tredegar riot, for example, when it became clear that large numbers of Irish had fled the town, concerns were voiced about the problems that this loss of labour would cause for the local iron industry. A meeting held at the town's Temperance Hall concluded that '[it] will be impossible to keep the furnaces in blast much longer unless something is done to assist the company in getting men'.[55]

Although the threat posed by the Irish to the jobs and wages of south Wales workers was thus more perceived than real, this is not to say that anti-Irish riots in Wales had nothing to do with economic issues. On the contrary, disturbances such as those at Ebbw Vale in 1879 and Tredegar in 1882 did coincide with periods of industrial depression and economic insecurity. By the late 1870s the iron industry, to which both towns owed their prosperity, was suffering from falling demand as the market for iron in the rail industry declined. The impact of these conditions on the south Wales iron industry was significant. Many small works were subject to temporary stoppages or to outright closure. In 1878 a number of south Wales works fell victim to the depression including Llynfi, Ogmore and Tondu.[56] Larger works such as Tredegar faced a similar fate unless they were prepared to adapt to a future man-ufacturing steel. The introduction of new Bessemer converters, which processed pig iron into steel instead of wrought iron, threatened the extinction of traditional skills such as iron puddling in south Wales.[57] Such threats caused considerable insecurity among the native working populations of the iron towns. Significantly, the anti-Irish disturbances in Tredegar occurred at a time when the town's ironworks was tempo-rarily closed for a period of re-equipment to manufacture steel. As a result, there was not only temporary hardship in the town but also widespread uncertainty about the future. Fr Williams explained the effect of these conditions upon the local population:

> Unfortunately Tredegar is in state of transition, since our works are being changed from iron to steel works. This has caused a stoppage of the usual work, it has pinched both the Irish and Welsh, and I think it has something to do with the recent disturbances. Men are naturally restless when their fam-ilies are ill-provided for.[58]

These conditions provided a background of tension and insecurity in Tredegar to which other factors of wider political resonance also con-tributed. Lawlessness and violence in Ireland were at the forefront of the political agenda in the early 1880s. Violent land agitation and the out-lawing of the Land League in 1881 helped foster images of lawlessness and anarchy in Ireland, which were widely disseminated by the British press. Further confirmation of this negative image, however, was pro-vided in the early summer of 1882, just two months before the eruption of anti-Irish disturbances at Tredegar. On 6 May in Dublin, Lord Frederick Cavendish, the newly appointed government secretary for

Ireland, and his under-secretary T.H. Burke, were murdered in Phoenix Park. Although the killings were vigorously condemned by Parnell and other Irish nationalist MPs, the reaction in Britain was one of outrage, which had a bad effect on the Irish immigrant population as a whole. Evan Powell, Methodist minister and historian of Tredegar, described 'a feeling of horror mingled with indignation' at the news of Irish outrages and murders.[59] Fr Williams, in his letter to the home secretary after the riots, claimed that hostility towards the Irish in Tredegar had been intensified by 'events that have taken place during the last twelve months in Ireland'.[60]

These circumstances, along with the uncertain economic conditions, undoubtedly created an undercurrent of hostility towards the Irish in Tredegar, but were not in themselves responsible for the outbreak of disturbances. What tipped the balance towards the eruption of rioting in this case was an apparently minor incident in which some local Irish residents attacked a procession of the Tredegar corps of the Salvation Army. Clashes between the Irish and members of the Salvation Army were not unusual in this period. As far as the Salvationists were concerned, the Irish formed a prime target of their evangelising mission work among the urban working classes.[61] In general, their efforts to win converts from among the Irish were unsuccessful. In Tredegar in July 1882, however, the local Salvation Army corps achieved a significant success with this otherwise resistant section of the population, when it gained its first Irish convert. This provoked anger among local Irish residents which was further compounded by 'the use the Salvationists made of the fact, in as much as they were expressing in the streets their pleasure at having got some Irish blood amongst them at last'.[62] As a result, groups of Irish residents gathered to jeer Salvation Army processions in the town and a number of women threw flour in the faces of the female Salvationists at the head of the processions.[63] It was this incident, according to Fr Williams, that provided 'the immediate reason and pretext for the riots'.[64]

Similar small-scale incidents were also responsible for sparking off anti-Irish rioting in other south Wales towns. In Ebbw Vale in 1879, it was the sight of Irish customers drinking in the 'wrong' pub that unleashed the disturbances. PC Kendal of the local police force later gave an account of the events surrounding the outbreak of the riots to the town magistrates:

> On Christmas Day about three o'clock, I was called to a disturbance outside the Drysiog Inn. I went with PC Davies and saw a mob around the Inn, about 200 or more; many appeared to be under the influence of drink. They were shouting and clamouring to Mr Lewis who stood at the door . . . I asked Lewis what was the matter. He said the crowd was going to pull the house down because he had some Irishmen in the house.[65]

Public houses were common venues for hostilities between the Welsh and the Irish. In Blaina in May 1843 the Red Lion pub was the scene of an attack by a group of local men on two Irish workers.[66] That disturbances were often sparked off in pubs was not surprising. They were the main focus for the leisure activities of the large working populations of south Wales towns. In Tredegar, for instance, one historian has estimated that there were some 83 alcohol-selling establishments in 1882.[67] There, as in other towns, certain pubs and inns became associated with the Irish to the extent that attempts to drink elsewhere were likely to meet with an unwelcome response of the kind witnessed in Ebbw Vale in 1879.

In this context, the outbursts of anti-Irish rioting at Tredegar and Ebbw Vale, which followed the apparently minor incidents of the Salvation Army attack and the confrontation at the Drysiog Inn, can be viewed as attempts by local people to 'police' Irish behaviour in their towns. Against a background of economic insecurity, provocative Irish behaviour was unacceptable and collective measures to restore normal behavioural codes appeared justified. In order to understand more clearly anti-Irish disturbances in south Wales as examples of community regulation, it is necessary to examine them in the wider context of popular protest and traditional forms of collective action in this period. Wales had a long tradition of violent protest aimed at community regulation. In rural areas this manifested itself in the activities of the Rebecca rioters, who saw themselves as the defenders of popular rights against unfair restrictions. In the 1830s and 1840s they protested against the limitations placed on rights of movement around the Welsh countryside by the introduction of toll gates and, in the second half of the nineteenth century, a second wave of activity aimed at the restoration of traditional rights to salmon fishing was initiated.[68] The *Ceffyl Pren* (wooden horse) was an older example of this tradition of popular policing.[69] Used to punish what was perceived as immoral behaviour, the targets of the *Ceffyl Pren* included adulterers and unmarried mothers as well as police informers, bailiffs and others seen to be acting against the community interest. Protesters carrying the makeshift wooden horse would go in procession late at night to the home of the unfortunate victim where brutal beatings were often administered.[70]

These rural protest traditions also found expression in Welsh industrial towns from the early decades of the nineteenth century, primarily through the activities of a clandestine group known as the Scotch Cattle. Described by one historian as 'the Rebecca of the coalfield',[71] the Scotch Cattle were active in the valley towns of south-east Wales, where they aimed to preserve what were perceived to be normal and fair working practices. Common targets of their attacks were people seen as posing a threat to the traditional balance of skill and authority, such as employers who tried to introduce new recruitment procedures, or workers who were thought to have risen unfairly to a position of skill or responsibility in the workplace. Immigrant workers in skilled jobs were particularly vulnerable to attack.[72] John Corbet, an Irish mason employed at the Bute ironworks, for instance, received a midnight visit from Scotch Cattle in Blaen Rhymney: 'A great crowd of people were making a noise outside, some of them roaring and bellowing as if imitating the noise of cattle . . . both the door and windows were forced open and several people burst in at the same time through the door and window, which had been smashed to pieces'.[73]

The activities of the Cattle usually took place against a background of economic insecurity. The enforcement of strike action in protest at wage reductions was one of their most common activities. Workers who failed to observe the strike and continued to work at the reduced wages would be singled out for attack. Richard Jerry, an employee at Nantyglo ironworks, was targeted in this way in April 1832:

> A number of men (supposed to be about 200 in company) entered the dwelling house of Richard Jerry . . . and broke the windows, doors, door-framings, and the principal part of the furniture in a most wicked and wanton way. The wife of Jerry came down stairs to remonstrate with them, but she was told, if she did not instantly go back, she would be destroyed. Richard Jerry had been at work at Mr Brown's of Nantyglo at the *reduced* wages, which is supposed to be the cause of this outrageous proceeding.[74]

Threatening letters and warning notices were also used by the Cattle to warn people of the consequences of strike-breaking or other unacceptable forms of behaviour. To a large extent, these methods of regulating community life in the industrial towns were successful. Calls to strike action were generally adhered to and police appeals for help in identifying Cattle members rarely elicited any response.[75]

These customary forms of community regulation formed part of the shared knowledge of the populations of the industrial communities where the Irish settled. The use of threatened or actual violence against persons or property as a means of regulating community life and punishing behaviour that appeared to threaten established norms was thus a familiar feature of life in the densely populated towns of the south Wales industrial belt. Seen in this context, the causes and patterns of anti-Irish rioting in the region can be understood as a strand of this tradition of popular policing. Often conducted in a climate of economic insecurity in which any departure from normal forms of behaviour appeared especially provocative, anti-Irish riots were essentially attempts to keep the immigrant population in check and to reassert control. Attacks on the Irish, their homes and property were also a way of identifying the Irish as outsiders who could conveniently be blamed for economic problems and insecurities in the wider community. The grievances cited as the cause of these attacks, namely the undercutting of wages and the importation of migrant labour, reflected insecurities in industrial towns about wage levels and job opportunities. Moreover, the association of the Irish with these insecurities strengthened with the frequency of attacks, creating a familiar and 'justifiable' explanation for anti-Irish rioting. In south Wales, anti-Irish disturbances were thus an extension of wider protest patterns familiar to rural and industrial populations as a means of regulating codes of behaviour and authority within communities.

Responses to anti-Irish rioting in south Wales were also influenced by these older protest traditions. Attacks on the Irish in the towns of south Wales rarely prompted popular condemnation or expressions of remorse among local people. On the contrary, there was often evidence of firm support for anti-Irish attacks among the wider community. After the Tredegar disturbances, for example, the appearances of the accused rioters at the town magistrates' court were attended by large crowds of well-wishers who, according to newspaper reports, 'shouted and hurrahed as if royalty had honoured the district with a visit'.[76] Donations from members of the public proved sufficient to ensure that the prisoners could be given 'substantial dinners every day whilst they were under remand'.[77] In addition, a 'Defence Fund' was set up to help finance the payment of solicitors to represent the accused rioters, along with any other legal and practical costs that might be incurred. The appeal attracted an impressive response and by November £185 11s 7d had been raised from public donations.[78] This degree of community sanction was not always evident in the aftermath of anti-Irish rioting elsewhere in Britain.[79] In Wales, however, the tacit acceptance of the violent activities of groups such as the Scotch Cattle helped legitimise the use of similar attacks on Irish residents and their property.

These observations on the nature of anti-Irish hostility in south Wales in the nineteenth century have some important general implications for the study of the Irish in Britain. Primarily, they reinforce the value and importance of adopting a regional approach to the study of Irish immigrant history. By looking at south Wales in particular, it has been possible to dispel the myth that the area was one in which the Irish received a particularly tolerant reception. Though they were fewer in number than the Irish populations of larger English and Scottish towns and cities, the Irish in Wales made an impact upon the communities in which they settled that was significant enough to prompt the development of informal work patterns and 'policing' practices designed to guard traditional ways of life against interference from the newcomers. The failure of the Irish to comply with expected codes of behaviour defined by the host community was most often the cause of the rioting that erupted with surprising frequency in the towns of industrial south Wales.

The evidence of anti-Irish hostility in Wales, however, does not fit neatly into conventional interpretations of the phenomenon in Britain as a whole. Attacks were not confined to the middle decades of the nineteenth century, as a number of general surveys have suggested. Instead they occurred with regularity from the 1820s through to the 1880s, long after the rate of Irish immigration into Britain had begun to decline. In turn this undermines the assumption, which has underpinned the study of anti-Irish hostility in Britain, that riots were more likely to occur where the Irish were at their most numerous. The evidence from Wales illustrates instead that small, well-established populations of immigrants could incur hostility which manifested itself in violent attacks on individuals and property. It also reveals that the declining rate of Irish immigration into Britain after 1861 was not accompanied in all parts of the country by a diminution of anti-Irish rioting. In south Wales, local tensions and provocative incidents continued to ignite anti-Irish sentiments among the working populations of the industrial towns.

Moreover, the factors traditionally used to explain the causes of anti-Irish disturbances in Britain are of limited use in interpreting the outbursts of rioting witnessed in Wales. Elsewhere in Britain, religious tensions had a more direct role in fuelling anti-Irish hostilities, but in Wales anti-Catholic sentiment was not a major factor in precipitating riots. Nor was the usual grievance of labour rivalries between native and immigrant workers more than a backdrop for disturbances. Instead, the wider context of nineteenth-century Welsh protest patterns provides a more useful and instructive framework in which to analyse the anti-Irish attacks in Wales. In this context, the study illustrates the new insight that can be derived from examining anti-Irish rioting within a framework of local protest patterns and, in doing so, offers a possible model for new research in this field.

As well as diversifying the picture of anti-Irish behaviour in Britain, this study also has an important contribution to make to the history of popular protest in nineteenth-century Wales. Drawing on customary rural and industrial protest patterns dating back to the early decades of the century, anti-Irish attacks in Wales came to form a significant strand of the traditional, popular policing methods used in Welsh communities to regulate behaviour and punish deviancy. Used as a corrective measure to restore normal codes of behaviour, anti-Irish rioting became part of the shared knowledge of the populations of south Wales towns, where attacks on homes and individuals in defence of perceived collective interests had long been practised by groups such as the Scotch Cattle. In this way, the study of anti-Irish rioting in Wales adds an extra dimension to the history of Welsh popular protest, which has traditionally focused on the pre-1850 and post-1880 periods as the main phases of protest activity. The previously under-researched decades omitted from this picture in fact formed part of an extended period of anti-Irish rioting that spanned much of the nineteenth century. The study of these disturbances thus fills an important chronological gap and consequently provides a new perspective on the history of Welsh social protest.

Notes

1. See, for example, Linda Colley, *Britons: Forging the Nation, 1707–1837*, London, Yale University Press, 1992, pp. 329–30.

2. See, for example, E.P. Thompson, *The Making of the English Working Class*, London, Penguin, 4th edn, 1991, pp. 469–81.

3. See, for example, Colin Holmes, *A Tolerant Country? Immigrants, Refugees and Minorities in Britain*, London, Faber & Faber, 1991, pp. 73–75.

4. See, for example, J.A. Jackson, *The Irish in Britain*, London, Routlege & Kegan Paul, 1963; Graham Davis, *The Irish in Britain*, Dublin, Gill and Macmillan, 1991.

5. See, for example, Frank Neal, *Sectarian Violence: The Liverpool Experience, 1819–1914*, Manchester, Manchester University Press, 1988.

6. See, for example, John Herson, 'Irish Migration and Settlement in Victorian Britain: A Small Town Perspective', in *The Irish in Britain, 1815–1939*, ed. Roger Swift and Sheridan Gilley, London, Pinter, 1989, pp. 84–103; Roger Swift and Sheridan Gilley (eds), *The Irish in Victorian Britain: The Local Dimension*, Dublin, Four Courts Press, 1999.

7. Two notable exceptions to this are Jon Parry, 'The Tredegar Anti-Irish Riots of 1882', *Llafur*, 3.4 (1983), pp. 20–33; and Paul O'Leary, 'Anti-Irish Riots in Wales', *Llafur*, 5.4 (1991), pp. 27–36.

8. See Colin G. Pooley, 'Segregation or Integration? The Residential Experience of the Irish in Mid-Victorian Britain', in Swift and Gilley (eds), *The Irish in Britain*, p. 66.

9. See, for example, Jackson, *The Irish in Britain*; Davis, *The Irish in Britain*.

10. Pauline Mulkern, 'Irish Immigrants and Public Disorder in Coventry, 1845–1879', *Midland History*, 21 (1996), pp. 119–35.

11. Kevin O'Connor, *The Irish in Britain*, Dublin, Torc Books, 1974, p. 121.

12. Nineteen of these incidents are identified by O'Leary, 'Anti-Irish Riots in Wales', p. 27. See also Louise Miskell, 'Custom, Conflict and Community: A Study of the Irish in South Wales and Cornwall, 1861–1891', unpublished PhD thesis, University of Wales, 1996, pp. 182–86, for details of a further outbreak in Ebbw Vale in 1879.

13. For details see Gwyn A. Williams, *The Merthyr Rising*, Cardiff, University of Wales Press, 1988; D.J.V. Jones, 'Crime, Protest and Community in Nineteenth-Century Wales', *Llafur*, 1.3 (1974), pp. 5–15.

14. PP 1844 XVI, *Report of the Commissioners of Inquiry into Civil Disorder (South Wales)*.

15. See, for example, Phillip Jenkins, *A History of Modern Wales, 1536–1990*, London, Longman, 1992, pp. 257–58.

16. Davis, *The Irish in Britain*, p. 121.

17. Census of England and Wales 1861, *Preliminary and General Report*, London, 1863, p. lxxiii.

18. See, for example, Pooley, 'Segregation or Integration?', pp. 60–83.

19. See Donald M. MacRaild, *Irish Migrants in Modern Britain, 1750–1922*, London, Macmillan, 1999, pp. 166–67.

20. O'Leary, 'Anti-Irish Riots in Wales', p. 28.

21. *Monmouthshire Merlin* (hereafter *MM*), 10 May 1834, p. 3.

22. *MM*, 13 May 1843, p. 3.

23. O'Leary, 'Anti-Irish Riots in Wales', p. 32.

24. PP 1867–68 XXXIX, *Royal Commission on Trade Unions, Minutes of Evidence*, p. 87.

25. *MM*, 4 September 1869, p. 3.

26. For details see *MM*, 2 January 1880, p. 8.

27. For details see *South Wales Daily News* (hereafter *SWDN*), 15 July 1882, p. 3.

28. *MM*, 2 January 1880, p. 8.

29. *MM*, 13 May 1843, p. 3.

30. *SWDN*, 10 July 1882, p. 3.

31. *MM*, 13 May 1843, p. 3.

32. *MM*, 4 September 1869, p. 3.

33. *Western Mail* (hereafter *WM*), 18 July 1882, p. 4.

34. *MM*, 2 January 1880, p. 8.

35. See Mary J. Hickman, *Religion, Class and Identity: The State, the Catholic Church and the Education of the Irish in Britain*, Aldershot, Avebury, 1995.

36. Pauline Millward, 'The Stockport Riots, 1852', in *The Irish in the Victorian City*, ed. Roger Swift and Sheridan Gilley, London, Croom Helm, 1985, pp. 207–24.

37. Alan O'Day, 'Varieties of Anti-Irish Behaviour in Britain, 1846–1922', in *Racial Violence in Britain 1849–1950*, ed. Panikos Panayi, Leicester, Leicester University Press, 1993, p. 32.

38. Donald MacRaild, 'William Murphy, the Orange Order and Communal Violence: The Irish in West Cumberland, 1871–1884', in Panayi (ed.), *Racial Violence in Britain*, pp. 44–64.

39. MacRaild, *Irish Migrants in Modern Britain*, p.183.

40. See David Fitzpatrick, 'A Curious Middle Place: The Irish in Britain, 1871–1921', in Swift and Gilley (eds), *The Irish in Britain*, p. 19.

41. See K.O. Morgan, *Rebirth of a Nation: Wales 1880–1980*, Oxford, Clarendon Press, 1981, p. 90; and Jenkins, *A History of Modern Wales*, pp. 180–210.

42. See John Davies, *A History of Wales*, London, Allen Lane, 1993, p. 385.

43. PRO HO144/100/A18355, 13 July 1882, letter from Fr W. Williams to Sir W. Harcourt.

44. See *MM*, 18 January 1878, p. 8.

45. PRO HO/144/100/A18355, letter from Williams to Harcourt.

46. O'Leary, 'Anti-Irish Riots in Wales', pp. 27–28.

47. Steven J. Fielding, *Class and Ethnicity: Irish Catholics in England, 1880–1939*, Buckingham, Open University Press, 1993, p. 35.

48. PP 1867–68 XXXIX, *Royal Commission on Trade Unions, Minutes of Evidence*, p. 92.

49. W. Scandrett, *Old Tredegar, Vol. 2*, London, P.W. Scandrett, 1992, p. 149.

50. J.A. Owen, *The History of the Dowlais Iron Works, 1759–1970*, Newport, Starling Press, 1977, p. 82.

51. PP 1867–68 XXXIX, *Royal Commission on Trade Unions, Minutes of Evidence*, p. 92.

52. For details of the occupations of the Irish in Tredegar, see Miskell, 'Custom, Conflict, and Community', pp. 71–76.

53. Jules Ginswick (ed.), *Labour and the Poor in England and Wales, 1849–1851*, III, *South Wales–North Wales*, London, Cass, 1983, p. 36.

54. Jeffrey G. Williamson, *Coping with City Growth During the British Industrial Revolution*, Cambridge, Cambridge University Press, 1990, p. 160.

55. *WM*, 24 July 1882, p. 3.

56. See J.P. Addis, 'The Heavy Iron and Steel Industry in South Wales, 1870–1950', unpublished PhD thesis, University of Wales, 1957, pp. 30–37.

57. See L. Ince, *The South Wales Iron Industry, 1750–1885*, Merton, Ferric, 1993, p. 7.

58. *SWDN*, 21 July 1882, p. 2.

59. Evan Powell, *History of Tredegar*, Cardiff, 1885, p. 103.

60. PRO HO144/100/A18355, letter from Williams to Harcourt.

61. See N.H. Murdoch, 'From Militancy to Social Mission: The Salvation Army and Street Disturbances in Liverpool, 1879–1887', in *Popular Politics, Riot and Labour: Essays in Liverpool History, 1790–1940*, ed. John Belchem, Liverpool, Liverpool University Press, 1992, pp. 160–71.

62. PRO HO144/100/A18355, letter from Williams to Harcourt.

63. See *SWDN*, 8 July 1882, p. 3.

64. PRO HO144/100/A18355, letter from Williams to Harcourt.

65. *MM*, 2 January 1880, p. 8.

66. *MM*, 13 May 1843, p. 3.

67. W. Powell, *Our Town: Law and Order in Times Past*, Aspects of Local History, No. 2, Tredegar, W. Powell, 1992, p. 19.

68. D.J.V. Jones, 'The Second Rebecca Riots: A Study of Salmon Poaching on the Upper Wye', *Llafur*, 2.1 (1976), pp. 33–54.

69. The Rebecca riots and the *Ceffyl Pren* tradition were closely associated. See Rosemary A.N. Jones, 'The Disappearance of the *Ceffyl Pren* in Cardiganshire', *Ceredigion*, 11 (1988–89), p. 26.

70. Jones, 'Disappearance of the *Ceffyn Pren*', pp. 19–38.

71. D.J.V. Jones, *Before Rebecca: Popular Protests in Wales, 1793–1835*, London, Allen Lane, 1973, p. 105.

72. Jones, *Before Rebecca*, p. 106.

73. *MM*, 27 September 1834, p. 3.

74. *MM*, 14 April 1832, p. 3.

75. See M.E. Bidder, 'The Scotch Cattle in Monmouthshire, *c.*1820–25', *Gwent Local History*, 63 (Autumn 1978), p. 11.

76. *WM*, 25 July 1882, p. 4.

77. *WM*, 14 July 1882, p. 4.

78. For a reproduction of the Defence Fund document, see F.E.A. Yates (ed.), *Tredegar's Yesterdays: Collected Jottings of W.C. Smith*, Newport, Starling Press, 1979, pp. 24–25.

79. See, for example, Louise Miskell, 'Irish Immigrants in Cornwall: The Camborne Experience, 1861–82', in Swift and Gilley (eds), *The Irish in Victorian Britain*, p. 44.

The Cult of Respectability and the Irish in Mid-Nineteenth-Century Wales

Paul O'Leary

In the burgeoning literature on the Irish in nineteenth-century Britain, little attention has so far been paid to those Irish men and women who subscribed to the mid-Victorian cult of respectability. In some ways, this is a surprising omission. Increasingly it is recognised that hackneyed generalisations about Irish migrants being 'hewers of wood and drawers of water', a group bunched exclusively at the base of society, are inaccurate descriptions of the social composition of the group as a whole. Recent analyses of the census enumerators' books have revealed that, although the majority of the Irish who settled in British towns in the mid-nineteenth century were poor and endured some of the worst housing available, a substantial minority enjoyed higher-status occupations and were dispersed throughout areas of better quality housing.[1] An acceptance of this view must be accompanied by a consideration of the extent to which some Irish men and women expressed their ethnic identity in terms comparable with a grouping in the host society that has been described as the 'aristocracy of labour'.[2] Yet, in a 1990 survey of the state of the debate on the history of work in modern Britain, Patrick Joyce argued that the peasant background of Irish immigrants put them 'at one remove from an ethic of material advancement and individual self-help'.[3] This essay questions the validity of this generalisation and argues that plurality is the key theme of Irish settlement in mid-nineteenth-century Wales.

Research on the socio-economic composition of Irish migrant settlements has been part of a gradual shift in the preoccupations of social historians towards the statistical and quantifiable as opposed to relying on the more impressionistic evidence provided by contemporary observers, whose assumptions about Irishness determined what they saw. However, as Robert Gray has reminded us, the cultural process is not susceptible to precise measurement and it has to be reconstructed from a qualitative analysis of language and social imagery. The principal source for such an analysis is observation of working-class life from above.[4] This raises a number of methodological problems, particularly about the use of literary sources about the Irish in mid-nineteenth-century Britain, because those sources are so deeply influenced by considerations (whether conscious or unconscious) of the moral worth of the Irish. In the case of Wales, there is the added dimension of the construction of national identity by means of describing the Irish as the antithesis of Welshness, at least until the 1880s. Such factors ensured that lines of difference were drawn sharply in an attempt to construct and reinforce cultural boundaries. Thus, a consideration of Irish respectability is inescapably relational; that is, it entails a discussion of the relationship between the Irish and ideas prevalent in the host society.

Respectability was the leitmotif of public life in mid-nineteenth-century Wales.[5] The aim of self-reliance and the doctrine of self-help dominated the pulpit and the press and informed discussions of social issues such as the Poor Law, crime and temperance. The formation of a national self-image of the Welsh as a uniquely religious and moral people, free from serious crime and loyal to the state, took place during the mid-century decades in reaction to the serious political unrest of the 1830s and 1840s. It was also a response to the attack on Welsh morals and religion by the government's Education Commissioners in 1847 and by publications such as *The Times* in 1866.[6] As with all such identities, it was strengthened by repeated contrast with an opposite, or 'Other', a role that was filled to a large extent by Ireland and the Irish. Following the experience of the famine years, a view of the 'low Irish' as a destitute and drunken people was written into an emerging narrative of urban and industrial Wales, in which outsiders were perceived as a destabilising element in society. Mid-nineteenth-century writers described Irish immigrants to Wales as an alienated group with their own customs and beliefs. For many contemporaries, the Irish were drunken, lawless papists, prone to wild and indecorous behaviour – all traits that disqualified an individual from membership of respectable society.[7]

At the heart of the concern with morality in mid-nineteenth-century Wales was an anxiety about the role of women in society. The accusations of the Education Commissioners about Welsh women's low standards of morality provoked widespread outrage and precipitated a reaction in the form of an idealisation of Welsh womanhood as pure and virtuous, a characterisation that chimed conveniently with notions of domesticity and separate spheres for men and women.[8] Against this background, Irish women were perceived as feckless Catholics, liable to be sent begging by their husbands and prone to succumbing to the temptations of drink.[9] As with all encounters with 'the Other', the picture is more complex than it might at first appear. There was a distinction between those social commentators who saw the Irish as an alien minority, separated from the host community by racial differences that were compounded by religion and socio-economic position, and those who believed that the differences between the Welsh and the Irish stemmed from different environments alone. Exponents of the latter view believed that Irish immigrants were open to 'improvement' under what were considered to be the more favourable conditions of a Protestant society.

At first glance, therefore, it might appear that Irish immigrants were marginal to the cult of respectability. The Irish have often been seen as forming a kind of lumpenproletariat outside the status system of Welsh society, distanced from its values by social position and by an adherence to Catholicism. Associated with all those characteristics deemed to be the very antithesis of respectability, the immigrants who arrived during the famine years provided a convenient yardstick against which the Welsh could measure their own social progress.

The principal medium for disseminating this view of the Irish was the press, in both English and Welsh languages. At the same time as the press preached the merits of self-help and temperance, it reported the behaviour of those who transgressed the acceptable norms of society with a sensationalist enthusiasm veering from the hysterical to the humorous. Yet, as we shall see, the press was also confronted with the need to report on public expressions of respectable Irish behaviour, a fact that led to declarations of surprise mingled with paternal pride at the improvement in the material and moral condition of the Irish. Given the absence of an Irish immigrant or Catholic press in Wales until the last quarter of the nineteenth century, the reportage of the Welsh press was of special importance.

What did respectability mean to contemporaries? At its simplest, it entailed making the effort to 'maintain certain standards and the determination not to let things slide'.[10] However, looked at as the coping stone of a wider social ideology, the cult of respectability encapsulates some of the central concepts of class, gender and ethnicity as they emerged during the nineteenth century. Each of these forms of social identity was subject to redefinition during the mid-century decades. One of the central questions for historians of these years is the degree to which the working class was subjected to control from the middle classes and the extent to which it developed an autonomous culture. Although rarely discussed, a parallel can be found in the construction of Irish immigrant ethnicity: to what extent was its content determined by the Catholic Church and to what extent was it a product of an autonomous culture?

While historians are broadly in agreement about the centrality of the cult of respectability to the bourgeois image of social stability projected during the mid-nineteenth century, there are conflicting views about its precise significance as a demarcator of social identities. According to Geoffrey Best, there was no sharper dividing line in mid-Victorian Britain than that which demarcated those who were respectable from those who were not; in his view, the distinction between 'rough' and 'respectable' overshadowed that between rich and poor or employer and employee.[11] According to this view, class divisions between the lower middle class and the upper working class were blurred by adherence to a set of common values. This interpretation has not gone uncontested. As Hugh Cunningham has argued, the rough/respectable dichotomy is 'an extraordinarily crude tool for the description of social reality', adding that historians should be wary of making a clear distinction between those who belonged to the 'rough' element and those who belonged to the 'respectable' element when people at the time experienced great difficulty in drawing that boundary. He rejects the implication of Best's thesis that those who espoused the cult of respectability in all classes had more in common with one another than they did with members of their own class who did not. Cunningham believes that contemporaries' attempts to make this distinction are of considerable interest, but by adopting it themselves as a basis for analysing social relationships historians have confused the history of moral fears with the history of lived experience.[12]

The debate about the cult of respectability centres on the question of the extent to which the working class retained its independence from other social classes during this period. In the view of some historians, the class divide was not displaced but merely glossed over by the moral and intellectual hegemony of the middle class and the dominant ideology espoused by that class in the post-Chartist decades. According to Trygve R. Tholfsen, the consensual values of this period were redefined in class terms in a manner that underlined and justified middle-class hegemony, while at the same time emphasising the inferiority of the working class. Respectability, then, was a quintessentially middle-class ideology, representing a system of values that expressed what it meant to belong to that class, whereas working people were assumed not to share those values – they had to earn respectability by their efforts and good conduct.[13] From this perspective, respectability was the polar opposite of 'genuine' working-class independence – 'conceived as an all-embracing moral, intellectual and social ideal' – because it was conferred from above, requiring working people to seek acceptance from members of another class.[14]

Setting aside the enormous difficulties entailed in defining the notion of 'genuine' working-class independence, there has been an attempt to reassess the meaning of personal independence in terms of gender relations in mid-Victorian society. From this perspective, personal independence is a goal associated with men's aspirations, whereas the triumph of respectability requires the reduction of women's status to that of dependants in a household in which the male is breadwinner. Thus, for Sonya O. Rose, respectability was 'a gendered language of family status premised on steady and sufficient family wage, earned by the male head of household'.[15] In such a context, a working wife was perceived as degrading to the male. Historians concerned with the cult of respectability have always paid attention to the significance of the household and family life in the pronouncements of those concerned with promoting the respectable ideal, but historians of gender have taken this further by foregrounding the relationship between women's position in the household and their place in the sexual division of labour, emphasising also that working men's position in society rested on women's exclusion from capitalist relations of production as well as on their own subjection in the labour market.[16] By placing gender relations at the centre of attempts to explain the cult of respectability, such historians have collapsed the distinction between work and home that was increasingly being made by Victorian social commentators.[17]

By contrast, studies of the cult of respectability have little to say about ethnicity as a way of organising social difference. Nevertheless, an ethnic identity was central to the emergence of a distinctive leisure culture among those Irish men and women who espoused respectable ideals. Hibernian friendly societies and other provident organisations provided an institutional focus for the cultivation of the values of self-help, temperance and thrift. In so doing, they challenged received notions in the host society about Irish dependence on the Poor Law. For a minority – but a substantial minority – of immigrants and their descendants, they also redefined what it might mean to be Irish in migrant settlements. A close analysis of the celebrations of Irish societies demonstrates that there was no homogeneous ethnic identity, but rather a variety of different ways of being Irish, which certain commentators experienced some difficulty in differentiating. Irishness was continually constructed and reconstructed, defined and redefined, by different groups of migrants and their putative community leaders in an attempt to pin down what was in reality a fluid identity, one that was capable of adapting to new situations as circumstances required.

Although the individual was privileged in all discussions of respectability, there is a real sense in which working-class respectability also implied a collective dimension. Particular areas of towns, and sometimes individual streets or even parts of streets, were generally understood to be 'respectable' and, conversely, there were other areas that were known to exhibit the opposite characteristics. Although families living in less salubrious areas might strive to achieve a degree of respectability in their own lives and homes, there was always the fear that the 'contagion' of neighbours might undermine their efforts.

This aspect of respectability has a particular significance for Irish migrants, who were widely believed to inhabit the worst areas of nineteenth-century towns. That the epithet 'Little Irelands' was adopted to describe such areas should be a reminder that contemporaries were quick to demonise whole areas and social groups. The notion of 'Little Irelands' has been rightly criticised by historians for failing to take full cognizance of the complex ethnic reality of these areas and of the fact that many of the Irish lived outside them, yet the force of the perception for contemporaries cannot be gainsaid.[18] It was widely accepted at the time of the Great Famine that the inhabitants of these areas lacked the qualities of personal independence that could elevate them to a respectable existence. Dependence on parish relief was seen as the most compelling evidence of this deficiency.

Frank Neal estimates that the total financial cost of the famine refugees to England and Wales in 1847 – the worst year of the Great Famine – was £155,000, or 2 per cent of total expenditure on poor relief.[19] However, this figure disguises the uneven incidence of the burden across the country. As far as local authorities in places such as Liverpool, Glasgow, Cardiff and Newport were concerned, this was a national problem paid for by the ratepayers of a few localities. Was this a crippling burden to those towns, such as Liverpool, that were worst affected? On balance, Frank Neal believes that it was not. Even so, a concern with Irish dependence on the Poor Law continued to exercise local politicians and officials long after the immediate panic had passed.

One of the most pervasive criticisms of the Irish, which persisted long after the crisis years of the 1840s and early 1850s, was that they relied heavily on the Poor Law for financial support when times were bad instead of cultivating financial independence by saving when times were good. This supposed contrast between the Irish and Welsh was voiced regularly by social commentators. As late as 1879 complaints were heard that the Irish in Cardiff were disproportionately dependent on the parish.[20] Official statistics showed that they accounted for less than one eighth of the town's population but contributed nearly one third of the paupers. In the context of other towns in Britain these were exceptional figures and there was no obvious explanation for the large discrepancy, though official opinion ascribed it to a simple lack of personal independence in financial matters. This theme resurfaced regularly during the following decades, with commentators frequently drawing attention to the insobriety of the Irish poor and the desirability of cutting back on financial assistance to them.[21] The role of public officials in demonising the Irish should not be underestimated. In this respect, Dr H.J. Paine combined his positions as medical officer of health and chairman of the Board of Guardians at Cardiff to devastating effect. It was he who depicted the Irish as a particularly insanitary section of the population in his long series of annual reports extending from the 1850s to the 1880s, and it was he who suggested in 1887 that financial assistance to the Irish poor should be severely cut back because, he believed, they squandered money on drink. In his opinion, assistance should be offered on the basis of a loan, to be repaid when the labourer eventually found work.

Such views were challenged in an official forum during the 1890s when a Royal Commission collected evidence on the effects of the Welsh Sunday Closing Act of 1881, when Catholic clergy and lay spokesmen for the Irish insisted that the Irish were not the only group who inhabited an underworld of shebeen-keeping and poverty.[22] Even so, entrenched attitudes were difficult to dislodge. In 1908 a commentator at the iron-producing settlement of Dowlais pointed up the contrast between the 'hatred' of parish relief among the Welsh locally and the readiness of the Irish to take advantage of such relief: 'Although they live, as a rule, very peacefully amongst their Welsh fellow citizens, yet they will not suffer much hardship, before they cry out.'[23] As these comments make clear, as far as officialdom was concerned it was not poverty as such that prevented the Irish from cultivating respectability, it was their alleged lack of personal independence in the face of adversity.

Some Irish commentators insisted that their people had their own informal networks of assistance for dealing with the effects of poverty. Working-class neighbourhoods, it was claimed, developed their own unofficial mechanisms for self-help, which did not require the formation of special associations or a personal investment in the values associated with respectable culture. 'Neighbourliness' was a feature of Irish working-class life highlighted by Joseph Keating, the son of Irish migrants. His recollections of life among the Irish in the coalmining village of Mountain Ash describe a close-knit web of ethnic relationships that provided succour and a degree of security for neighbours. 'If illness or poverty happened to be in one house,' he recalled, 'nearly every other house proffered help.'[24] Such networks of assistance operated outside the ambit of institutional responses to poverty and were maintained particularly strongly by women. The evidence for the way they operated is patchy, but the importance of such networks cannot be gainsaid.[25]

There is much more evidence about the institutional response to the problem of dependence on parish relief, the formation of friendly societies. These voluntary organisations were based on members' regular contributions as a way of insuring against ill health, unemployment or other misfortunes. More than that, they embodied a set of assumptions about social life that included temperance and respectability. In the case of the Irish they also tended to promote a constitutional form of patriotism based on the image and legacy of Daniel O'Connell and sometimes of the Grattan parliament of the late eighteenth century.[26] These organisations placed great store by an individual's public appearance as evidence of his or her respectability.

Friendly societies were actively encouraged by the Catholic Church, which saw in them an opportunity for raising the respectable profile of the church as a whole as well as improving the well-being of individuals in the flock. They understood that the Irish were perceived as lacking the personal qualities esteemed by the wider society and that that failing was attributed in part to the religion they professed. Hibernian friendly societies were not under the control of the church, but the clergy nevertheless played a prominent part in their ceremonial activities, including officiating at special ceremonies. In the case of societies such as the Roman Catholic Association for the Suppression of Drunkenness, established at Newport by Fr Richardson and exported to other towns in the region, the clergy performed a more interventionist and decisive role.[27] As the following letter to Bishop Hedley demonstrates, organisations such as the Ancient Order of Hibernians accorded the clergy an institutionalised regulatory role in their affairs:

> The society [the Ancient Order of Hibernians] in these Islands is numerically strong and powerful. In Ireland there are 130,000 members; in Scotland 50,000; in England 20,000; and in your own diocese [Newport] there are over 5,000. It is powerful also considering the members who are at its head. In this diocese we have men such as Harold Turnbull & Thomas J. Callaghan, and elsewhere men of the same standing are connected with it. No division or branch of the society is perfect without a chaplain, from whom no secrets can be withheld, and who has access to all the books and accounts of the branch or division to which he belongs.
>
> Personally, I consider the establishment of a branch in a parish as good as a mission for many of our careless and indifferent Irish people. It stimulates them to come to the sacraments, and they find in the Order that *public opinion* which at home in Ireland sweetly leads our people to mass and to the sacraments. It also affords our people a blend of religion and patriotism, which is most helpful to them.[28]

The 'public opinion' referred to here was more problematic than the writer cared to admit. To begin with, there were other influences on the life of the Irish in Britain that pulled them in different directions. Equally importantly, this public opinion was often based on contested notions of how society should be organised, including the proper place of men and women in society. It was also rooted in an idealisation of how personal affairs should be ordered, not least the home and family economy.

A concern with domestic arrangements was an important part of the cult of respectability. Constructions of gender were central to this development. Just as there is nothing primordial about ethnicity, so ideas of masculinity and femininity are products of their time and place, and they reveal a great deal about the ways in which power and authority are articulated in society. By ascribing different roles to men and women, the cult of respectability helped to define the accepted ideals of what it meant to be masculine and feminine in mid-Victorian Britain. The belief that women were ideally suited to operate in the domestic sphere had its corollary in the public profile adopted by men in the parades of friendly societies. Women were intended to develop housekeeping skills and a predilection for cleanliness designed to transform the character of the domestic environment. As in the epigram that graced thousands of parlour walls, 'Cleanliness is next to godliness', the moral dimension to the domestic set-up was never in doubt.

Although respectable Irish men and women shared the same basic values underpinning the cult of respectability as their Protestant neighbours, a specifically Catholic version of respectability emerged also. It shared the same idealisation of womanhood as was found in Protestant tracts but added to it an additional responsibility, that of the mother's duty of ensuring that her children remained true to the Faith. Thus, Irish women's domesticity was meant to be a bulwark against 'leakage' from the church as well as maintaining the morality of the home. Investing women with this responsibility meant that they were accorded a central, if subordinate, role in immigrant communities.[29]

At the same time as the home was being idealised and romanticised by middle-class commentators as a 'haven in a heartless world', a bulwark against the excesses of the wider world, so it was that the interdependence of the two supposedly separate spheres became ever more apparent. Maintaining a wife who was not engaged in waged work necessitated industriousness and application in the workplace together with thrifty behaviour at home. Time after time commentators exhorted men to avoid the public house and enjoined women to make the home sufficiently attractive and welcoming for the husband. The role of women in developing domestic skills, such as sewing and mending, was underlined.

One crucial mark of respectable status was that a married woman should not seek employment outside the home. The ideology of respectability prescribed that a man should be capable of earning a 'living wage' sufficient to maintain his wife without her having to coarsen herself through the experience of waged employment. A rejection of waged employment was not synonymous with not working, for the home was a workplace in its own right and one that required dedicated application to ensure that a conducive environment was created in which the husband and father could relax from the pressures of the outside world.

A full implementation of the ideology of domesticity was impractical for many Irish immigrants and their families in the mid-nineteenth century, for the simple reason that large numbers of them shared accommodation with other families.[30] However, there is a considerable amount of evidence to suggest that the ideal of the home was sufficiently attractive for a significant number of Irish men and women to aspire to it. The romanticisation of the domestic environment underlines a strongly felt need to draw an emphatic boundary between home life and the world of work, a boundary that was drawn because of the alienating conditions of male employment in an industrial economy. For obvious reasons, it is the restrictive character of this ideology for women that has attracted the greatest attention from historians, and it is the idealisation of the family economy based on a male breadwinner's income that has been most roundly criticised as fettering women's aspirations. The extent to which such ideals were consistently realised in working-class communities is open to question, but the centrality of the ideology in public debates is beyond doubt.

The extent to which respectability entailed the rejection of older forms of women's socialising and interaction in the community is open to discussion. In a subtle analysis of the significance of women's use of language and its relationship to respectable behaviour, Rosemary A. Jones has argued that during the mid-Victorian years of relative social stability the female gossip was seen as a threat to domestic and marital harmony.[31] Gossip was a form of social regulation within the community that had the ability to corroborate or damage an individual's reputation. As such, it had a certain degree of informal power that could be wielded to devastating effect. Direct evidence relating to gossip is fragmentary and inconclusive but it is clear that it was a phenomenon of great importance in maintaining women's reputations in working-class communities.

For men, public appearance was a far more important key to respectability. Yet the cult of respectability made explicit the relationship between the public and private spheres at the same time as it insisted on their complete separation. The centrality of the ideology of domesticity to the respectable ideal placed a special emphasis on the notion of separate spheres for men and women. The public/private dichotomy was intended to match the masculine/feminine divide, and so in confronting what it meant to be Irish in the Victorian town, proponents of the cult of respectability were forced to address the question of gender roles. For many commentators in mid-nineteenth-century Britain to be an Irishman was to be fit for heavy manual work; masculinity in this case was defined in terms of physicality and the productive effort. For respectable working men, the parameters of this definition were different, encompassing restraint and regular behaviour and finding their most high-profile public expression in the parades and processions of friendly societies.

These events took place on public holidays and annual national and religious festivals such as St Patrick's Day and the festival of Corpus Christi. As such, they were occasions when participants demonstrated a public commitment to their ethnic identity in terms of a specific set of values. By so doing, they projected an orderly and respectable image of Irish migrants that contradicted and questioned a key feature of the dominant discourse of social commentary, which constructed a view of the Irish as an outcast minority alienated from the values of respectable society.

By parading through the streets in an orderly fashion, participants raised important questions about the use of public space and about the relationship between the public and private domains. Parades can be seen as ritual acts of integration into urban culture, which carried particular meanings for participants and observers alike. By temporarily appropriating public space for an orderly demonstration of Irishness, participants were implicitly challenging the characterisations of Irish life in urban Britain as consisting of a ghetto existence. The notion of 'Little Irelands', with their overtones of residential segregation and enforced apartness, has been discredited.[32] Such areas were never populated entirely by the Irish, nor were all of the Irish in the towns found within the boundaries of such areas. But the pervasiveness of the view among contemporaries that there existed Irish ghettos is evidence of a moral fear gripping the imaginations of those in authority. Against this background, a determination to use public thoroughfares for a distinctively Irish celebration could cause some anxiety. In such a context, it was essential that Hibernian societies not only preached conformity to the values of respectable society but ensured that their conduct and dress were also unimpeachable.

Public thoroughfares were an important arena for contesting meaning in urban society, places where unregulated trading, unauthorised congregations of people, and public 'nuisances' such as begging and prostitution might be encountered. One of the tasks entrusted to the local police forces established in some places in the 1840s, and the comprehensive network of county police forces from 1856, was to regulate this urban environment and suppress disorderly behaviour. It should also be borne in mind that the superintendents of police in many towns shouldered some responsibilities for public health and Poor Law relief. This was the case with Superintendent Wrenn at Merthyr Tydfil and Superintendent Stockdale at Cardiff. Their experience in these roles, which brought them into contact with the poorest element in the Irish community, undoubtedly influenced their attitudes to policing. It contributed to a view of certain districts associated with Irish immigrants as problem areas. Irish disorder was part of the received wisdom of mid-nineteenth-century Wales, as it was in other British towns and cities. Evidence to support this view was found in the crime statistics and in the propensity of the Irish to commit offences stemming directly from drunkenness, such as being drunk and disorderly or assaulting a police officer.[33] Together with reports on the poor sanitary conditions of areas associated with Irish settlement, these factors had a strong influence on how the Irish were perceived.

It was against this background that the enactment of respectable street rituals, such as processions, acquired particular meanings. Processions and parades were colourful events, characterised by the distinctive clothing of the participants and the emblems and mottoes on the banners they carried. They also drew attention to themselves by the use of music, often performed by a uniformed fife and drum band or brass band. Newspaper reports ensured that impressions of the sights and sounds of such happenings were carried to a wider community of readers, most of whom would not have been among the company of participants or onlookers. For those who had been present, perusal of reports and editorial comment served to amplify their personal experience, fixing it in print, or alternatively it might provoke a questioning of the symbolic significance of the event reported.

According to Gareth Stedman Jones, respectability did not mean church attendance, teetotalism, or the possession of a Post Office savings account (i.e. the attributes of middle-classness), 'it meant the possession of a presentable Sunday suit and the ability to be seen wearing it'.[34] The social history of clothing has as much to tell us about the cult of respectability as does an analysis of the drum-banging message of the temperance movement or a study of the writings of ideologues such as Samuel Smiles. The way an individual dressed in public was a crucial symbolic marker of his or her position in society.

One historian of leisure in the nineteenth century has adopted a particularly arresting metaphor derived from clothing to encapsulate the very essence of respectability. In arguing that respectability was a 'role' that the working people adopted and enacted on certain occasions when they saw fit, Peter Bailey suggests that 'respectability was assumed or discarded, like a collar, as the situation demanded'.[35] Even if this striking metaphor underplays the full significance of respectability in the everyday lives of many individuals, the idea of people participating in a social drama with allotted roles is a compelling one. Wearing Sunday best was, by definition, an exceptional rather than a daily event for working people, and organised parades and processions were even more infrequent occurrences, thus making the sense of theatricality all the more palpable. It is also worth noting that Bailey's metaphor is gender-specific: it was the working man who attached and removed a shirt-collar, while his wife was entrusted with washing and starching it. The performative aspects of respectability entailed the input of both men and women, even if men were the most prominent public faces of this joint endeavour.

It was men's dress rather than women's that received most attention from contemporary commentators, probably because it was mainly men who paraded. In a real sense it was considered part of the 'civilising process'. It is no coincidence that navvies – a group of workers popularly associated with the Irish – were distinguished from other workers not only by the highly mobile nature of their work and by their notoriously unruly behaviour, but also by the way they dressed, particularly the wearing of moleskins. Dress and social behaviour reinforced one another.

Dress is a symbolic marker of selfhood.[36] It is surely significant that when the *Morning Chronicle* reported on Merthyr Tydfil in 1850 its correspondent sought to convey the cultural distance between the Irish and the Welsh inhabitants of the town by contrasting the 'clean and warmly clothed' children of the Welsh with the appearance of 'stark naked' Irish children standing at the doors of their houses: 'though the frost was severe they seemed happy in their nudity, and equally to disregard decency and the sharpness of the cold'.[37] The comparison succeeds in establishing the apparently un-self-conscious contentedness of the Irish with their lack of clothes, a point made more forceful by the fact that it is Irish *children* who appear in this account as blissfully uncivilised figures, whereas their Welsh counterparts are not. Even at this early age, when children had yet to mature into their adult roles, cultural difference was apparently established.

A transformation in this view of Irish children was partly a product of the proliferation of Catholic schools and partly a consequence of the prominent role accorded children in the Corpus Christi celebrations at Cardiff. This annual Catholic feast-day grew in support and prestige from its inception in the early 1870s. An integral part of it was the public parade, which attracted widespread attention from non-Catholics and the local press. By the 1890s the event had grown in size and significance to become the most notable ceremonial event in the town's civic calendar and, unlike Catholic parades in some other towns and cities in Britain, it encountered scarcely any local opposition from the majority Protestant community.[38]

Corpus Christi occurred annually in May or June on the Thursday after Trinity Sunday and consisted of a procession led by children from the Catholic schools of the town to Cardiff Castle, the residence of the Catholic Marquess of Bute. The procession traversed the town's main thoroughfares, interrupting the traffic for several hours and attracting large crowds of spectators. Young girls dressed in white and sporting colourful sashes were the focus of the procession, while choir boys and male altar servers also attracted attention because of their distinctive dress. On arrival at the castle grounds, thousands of adults and children attended an open-air service. Local newspapers reported this exotic event enthusiastically and made determined attempts to explain the significance of the ritual to their predominantly Protestant readership. The respectable appearance of participants was the subject of much comment.[39]

The most striking clothing on display during Corpus Christi was that of the children. It was emphasised that women made the children's dresses, thereby reinforcing the connection between domestic skills and respectability. The point is illustrated by a report of 1906. In that year it was noted that the great majority of the children who participated in the procession were drawn from the poorest parts of the city but that their appearance belied their poverty. When questioned about this aspect of the celebrations, a priest maintained that parents were ready to undergo considerable self-sacrifice to ensure that their children turned out in new clothes for the festival:

> Hundreds of the pretty dresses you saw to-day are the result of weeks, if not months, of careful sewing. Shall I give you an illustration – not a good one, perhaps – but it reveals the influence of Corpus Christi. I endeavoured to per-suade a man to abandon his drinking habits. 'You ought to save your money to get clothes for your children', I said; 'Corpus Christi will soon be here.' The man replied, 'This is one of my bouts, but before I started on it I bought my kiddies clothing and boots for the festival, and now I'm happy.[40]

The transformation in image of Irish children from the unreflective nudity recorded at Merthyr by the *Morning Chronicle* reporter at the time of the famine influx could not have been more complete. The association of cleanliness and purity implied by the white dresses had elevated these children, whether poor or not, into the ranks of civilised society. Given the positive response to the procession by the press and inhabitants of Cardiff, it should be little wonder that by the beginning of the twentieth century other Catholic congregations in south Wales had begun to send groups of children to participate in the Cardiff procession.

Similar contrasts were observed among adults. It was the ragged appearance of Irish men and women at the time of the Great Famine that reinforced an image of the indigent immigrant. Against this background, the parades of friendly societies confounded the expectations of observers. One reporter could not conceal his astonishment at the appearance of participants in a Hibernian parade in Newport in April 1850. Recent events had led him to expect 'a ragged regiment of tatterdemalions', whereas he was actually confronted with the sight of 'a company of young and middle-aged men, who in point of dress and propriety of demeanour would bear comparison with any body of gentlemen in the country'.[41] Celebrations of St Patrick's Day in Merthyr Tydfil in 1858 produced a similar response from the press, with reporters expressing 'agreeable surprise' at the respectable dress of the Irish.[42] One report of a Hibernian procession at Whitsuntide in 1879 drew attention to the appearance of the 250 Irish participants, who marched through the streets behind their bands and banners 'making a gallant show'. As well as being dressed in dark cloth coats and white trousers, the processionists made a show of green silk decorations. To onlookers, they exuded an air of comfort and prosperity.[43]

Thus, dress has a normative dimension and in the mid-nineteenth century it was intimately connected with – even sustained – rigid codes of behaviour. Recalling his first visit to south Wales in 1873, Fr Hayde was impressed by the respect accorded the Hibernian Society. He found it exhilarating to see 'these stalwart men – 600 or 700 strong – all dressed in the same way and walking with wonderful order and precision'.[44] These two features – the manner of dressing and the orderliness and discipline of behaviour – were linked. The wearing of a respectable suit, especially in procession, had an impact on the bodily comportment of participants.

The possession of a Sunday suit was a symbol of independence from the dirty and polluting world of work, a statement that an individual had the financial wherewithal and moral determination to rise above the baser demands of industrial capitalism, if only for one day of the week. Even though religion was not necessarily a defining characteristic of respectability, attending church on a Sunday was one of the few occasions for displaying the fact that one possessed a suit. And it should be remembered that social distinctions were not entirely abandoned inside the doors of the Catholic Church, despite that institution's famed mission to the urban poor in the nineteenth century. As in the Established Church, it was possible to purchase a sitting by payment of a pew-rent. This practice was used in the larger Catholic churches, such as St David's church at Swansea, though it is unlikely to have been as common in the smaller churches and chapels, which catered for a largely homogeneous working-class congregation. The division between the sittings for rich and poor forcibly struck one non-Catholic visitor to St Peter's church at Roath, Cardiff, in 1886. 'On entering the building one can always see at service time a large body of devout worshippers,' he observed. 'In the centre sit the wealthier portions, and on the left the poorer. A collection is always demanded from strangers on entry if they desire to occupy the central seats.'[45]

Thus, maintaining respectability had an extremely public and social dimension, and the correct or acceptable personal appearance was central to it. It presupposed that an individual and his or her family were anxious to be considered by their neighbours and by society at large as embodiments of a particular set of values and that they possessed recognisable aspirations.

Although women contributed to the cult of respectability, their presence in processions and other public ceremonies was rarely mentioned. Irish women's friendly societies existed in south Wales before the famine, though they do not appear to have survived beyond the 1840s.[46] It is likely that the rather poor opportunities for women's waged work in the region were partly responsible for this, though the same constraints did not prevent the formation of friendly societies by Welsh women.[47]

There was a central tension between natives and immigrants in the ideology of respectability as articulated in Victorian Wales. This tension was expressed in terms of a series of dualities that ascribed specific and contrasting values to each group. Thus the Welsh celebrated their personal independence in financial matters, while condemning the Irish for excessive dependence on the Poor Law. Similarly, the overrepresentation of the Irish in criminal statistics reinforced a view of them as lacking respect for the law, whereas the Welsh prided themselves on being particularly law-abiding. This was interpreted as a reflection of the two groups' relative moral worth, a distinction that was overlaid by the Protestant/Catholic dichotomy. Other oppositions were built on this series of dualities, such as a view of the Irish as a disloyal group (especially during the 1860s when Fenianism was in full swing), whereas the Welsh emphasised their loyalty to the State. As with the idea of Little Irelands, enough evidence could be found to convince contemporaries that the characterisation was an accurate one, though again as with Little Irelands, the notion of the Welsh and Irish as two homogeneous and contrasting groups is an inadequate and an inaccurate representation of social and cultural reality.

The force of the contrast between Irish and Welsh attitudes to parish relief resided in the way in which the cult of respectability was internalised by Welsh culture during the mid-nineteenth century. A notion of the respectable and religiously observant nation took root and replaced the political turbulence of earlier decades. This point can be overdrawn, but it retains a great deal of value as a description of how the increasingly dominant expression of Welsh nationality was perceived by its exponents.[48] In this narrative of Welshness the Irish invariably featured as the 'low Irish', the polar opposite of the respectable values espoused by the Nonconformist Welsh. In many ways, the 'low Irish' were the equivalent of the 'roughs' who featured in the generic divide between rough and respectable.

However, implicit in the term '*low* Irish' was the assumption that there was another sort of Irish person, or at least that another sort of Irish person was possible, one who embodied the antithesis of the values associated with the poor and destitute refugees who thronged the streets and lodging-houses of British ports during the terrible years of the Great Famine. In this space grew an alternative social identity. It is the ability of contemporaries to transcend, or transgress, established social categories such as 'rough', 'respectable' and 'low Irish' that is striking, rather than the existence of hermetically sealed categories. This was seen most visibly in the friendly society movement.

A study of respectable Irish labour provides an avenue of enquiry for elucidating the process of integration in the wider society. Adherents of the cult of respectability effectively created an idealised, or imagined, Irish community that contradicted the received wisdom of social commentators and forced some observers to rethink their evaluation of the character of Irish migrants. It is difficult to gauge how representative this is of the Irish in Britain as a whole. In cities such as Liverpool and Manchester, the parades of Irish Catholic societies may simply have enhanced the sense of Irish apartness and cultural difference. The recent emphasis of historians on the revival of Orangeism in the north of England and in Scotland in the late nineteenth century may point to a significant factor here. Where there existed social and cultural pressures to deepen ethnic boundaries, participation in the friendly society movement may not have had such a pronounced integrative effect as it manifestly did in south Wales. By achieving integration, the ethnic rituals of this group in the longer term engendered their own obsolescence.

Notes

1. See Colin G. Pooley, 'Segregation or Integration? The Residential Experience of the Irish in Mid-Victorian Britain', in *The Irish in Britain, 1815–1939*, ed. Roger Swift and Sheridan Gilley, London, Pinter, 1989, pp. 60–83.

2. For an introduction to the literature on the aristocracy of labour, see Robert Gray, *The Aristocracy of Labour in Nineteenth-Century Britain, c. 1850–1914*, London, Macmillan, 1981.

3. Patrick Joyce, 'Work', in *The Cambridge Social History of Britain, 1750–1950*, II, *People and their Environment*, ed. F.M.L. Thompson, Cambridge, Cambridge University Press, 1990, p. 142. This is a reflection of contemporary views, summed up by E.P. Thompson as follows: 'By the 1830s and 1840s it was commonly observed that the English industrial worker was marked off from his fellow Irish worker, not by a greater capacity for hard work, but by his respectability, his methodical paying-out of energy, and perhaps also by a repression, not of enjoyments, but of the capacity to relax in the old uninhibited ways'; E.P. Thompson, *Customs in Common*, London, Penguin, 1993, p. 396. The same was true of Welsh attitudes.

4. Gray, *The Aristocracy of Labour*, p. 37. See also I.G. Jones, *Mid-Victorian Wales: The Observers and the Observed*, Cardiff, University of Wales Press, 1992, pp. 1–23.

5. I.G. Jones has described the public face of mid-Victorian Wales as being 'respectable, religious, [and] petty bourgeois in style and aspiration'; I.G. Jones, *Explorations and Explanations: Essays in the Social History of Victorian Wales*, Llandysul, Gomer, 1981, p. 270.

6. See Ryland Wallace, *Organise! Organise! Organise! A Study of Reform*

Agitations in Wales, 1840–1886, Cardiff, University of Wales Press, 1991; David Jones, *Rebecca's Children: A Study of Rural Society, Crime and Protest,* Oxford, Oxford University Press, 1989, ch. 7; I.G. Jones, *Mid-Victorian Wales,* ch. 5; Prys Morgan (ed.), *Brad y Llyfrau Gleision,* Llandysul, Gomer, 1991; *idem,* 'From Long Knives to Blue Books', in *Welsh Society and Nationhood: Historical Essays Presented to Glanmor Williams,* ed. R.R. Davies et. al., Cardiff, University of Wales Press, 1984, pp. 199–215; Gwyneth Tyson Roberts, '"Under the Hatches": English Parliamentary Commissioners' Views of the People and Language of Mid-Nineteenth-Century Wales', in *The Expansion of England: Race, Ethnicity and Cultural History,* ed. Bill Schwarz, London, Routledge, 1996, pp. 171–97; Paul O'Leary, 'The Languages of Patriotism in Wales, 1840–1880', in *The Welsh Language and its Social Domains in the Nineteenth Century, 1801–1911,* ed. G.H. Jenkins, Cardiff, University of Wales Press, 2000, pp. 533–60.

7. This portrayal of the Irish was not an entirely new confection in so far as it was grafted onto a much older perception of the Irish as lawless papists that had evolved over many centuries.

8. Sian Rhiannon Williams, 'The True "Cymraes": Images of Women in Nineteenth-Century Periodicals', in *Our Mothers' Land: Chapters in Welsh Women's History 1830–1939,* ed. Angela V. John, Cardiff, University of Wales Press, 1991, pp. 69–92; Jane Aaron, *Pur fel y Dur: Y Gymraes yn Llên Menywod y Bedwaredd Ganrif ar Bymtheg,* Cardiff, University of Wales Press, 1999.

9. See, for example, 'Drwg a Da Cenedl y Cymry', *Y Gwron Cymreig,* 7 January 1852, reprinted in *Gweithiau Barddonol a Rhyddieithol Ieuan Gwynedd,* ed. W. Williams, Dolgellau, 1876, pp. 470–72.

10. Standish Meacham, *A Life Apart: The English Working Class, 1890–1914,* London, Thames and Hudson, 1977, p. 26.

11. Geoffrey Best, *Mid-Victorian Britain, 1851–75,* London, Fontana, 1979, p. 282.

12. Hugh Cunningham, 'Leisure and Culture', in Thompson (ed.), *The Cambridge Social History of Britain,* II, pp. 289–90.

13. Trygve R. Tholfsen, *Working Class Radicalism in Mid-Victorian England,* London, Croom Helm, 1976, pp. 216–21. See also E.J. Hobsbawm, *Worlds of Labour: Further Studies in the History of Labour,* London, Weidenfeld and Nicolson, 1984, pp. 242–43.

14. Tholfsen, *Working Class Radicalism,* p. 217.

15. Sonya O. Rose, *Limited Livelihoods: Gender and Class in Nineteenth-Century England,* Los Angeles, University of California Press, 1992, p. 151.

16. Keith McClelland, 'Masculinity and the "Representative Artisan"', in *Manful Assertions: Masculinities in Britain since 1800,* ed. M. Roper and J. Tosh, London, Routledge, 1991, pp. 74–91. See also John Tosh, 'What Should Historians Do with Masculinity? Reflections on Nineteenth-Century Britain', *History Workshop Journal,* 38 (1994), pp. 179–202.

17. See, for example, Rosemary A. Jones, 'Separate Spheres? Women,

Language and Respectability in Victorian Wales', in Jenkins (ed.), *The Welsh Language and its Social Domains*, pp. 177–213.

18. Graham Davis, *The Irish in Britain, 1815–1939*, Dublin, Gill and Macmillan, 1991.

19. Frank Neal, *Black '47: Britain and the Famine Irish*, London, Macmillan, 1998, p. 279.

20. *Cardiff Times*, 22 March 1879.

21. See, for example, the *Western Mail*, 6 June 1887, and correspondence published on 9 June 1887.

22. PP XL 1890, *Report of the Royal Commission appointed to Inquire into the Operation of the Sunday Closing (Wales) Act, 1881.*

23. *South Wales Daily News*, 21 October 1908, quoted in Neil Evans, 'Immigrants and Minorities in Wales, 1840–1990: A Comparative Perspective', *Llafur*, 5.4 (1991), p. 7.

24. Joseph Keating, *My Struggle for Life*, London, Simpkin, 1916, p. 13.

25. For an insight into this culture, see John Belchem, 'The Immigrant Alternative: Ethnic and Sectarian Mutuality among the Liverpool Irish during the Nineteenth Century', in *The Duty of Discontent: Essays for Dorothy Thompson*, ed. O. Ashton, R. Fyson and S. Roberts, London, Mansell, 1995, pp. 231–50.

26. I have discussed this elsewhere. See Paul O'Leary, *Immigration and Integration: The Irish in Wales, 1798–1922*, Cardiff, University of Wales Press, pp. 186–212.

27. O'Leary, *Immigration and Integration*, pp. 203–208, 211; and Chris Williams' article in this volume.

28. Fr Fennell to Bishop Hedley, 24 March 1913, Archdiocese of Cardiff Archives, box marked 'Friendly Societies'. These archives have now been deposited at the National Library of Wales.

29. Martha Kanya-Forstner, 'Irish Women and the Catholic Church in Victorian Liverpool', in *The Great Famine and Beyond: Irish Migrants in Britain in the Nineteenth and Twentieth Centuries*, ed. Donald M. MacRaild, Dublin, Irish Academic Press, 2000, pp. 180–81.

30. O'Leary, *Immigration and Integration*, pp. 117–19.

31. R.A. Jones, 'Separate Spheres', p. 181.

32. Davis, *The Irish in Britain*, pp. 51–82.

33. On the Irish and crime in Wales, see O'Leary, *Immigration and Integration*, ch. 6. For a different interpretation, see Veronica M. Summers, 'Irish Life and Criminality: A Study of Cardiff, *c.* 1840–1920', unpublished Open University MA dissertation, 1999.

34. Gareth Stedman Jones, 'Working-Class Culture and Working-Class Politics', *Journal of Social History*, 7 (1974), p. 475.

35. Peter Bailey, *Leisure and Class in Victorian England*, London, Methuen, 1987 edn, p. 184.

36. Dress links the biological body to the social being. It is one of the symbolic markers that strengthen and reinforce boundaries: 'Dress is the frontier between self and not-self'; Elizabeth Wilson, *Adorned in Dreams: Fashion and Modernity*, London, Virago, 1985, p. 3.

37. Jules Ginswick (ed.), *Labour and the Poor in England and Wales, 1849–51*, London, Frank Cass, p. 65.

38. For sectarianism in other British towns, see Frank Neal, *Sectarian Violence: The Liverpool Experience 1819–1914*, Manchester, Manchester University Press, 1988; John Belchem (ed.), *Popular Politics, Riot and Labour: Essays in Liverpool History, 1790–1940*, Liverpool, Liverpool University Press, 1992; Tom Gallagher, *Glasgow, the Uneasy Peace: Religious Tension in Modern Scotland, 1819–1914*, Manchester, Manchester University Press, 1987; Tom Gallagher, 'A Tale of Two Cities: Communal Strife in Glasgow and Liverpool before 1914', in *The Irish in the Victorian City*, ed. Roger Swift and Sheridan Gilley, London, Croom Helm, 1985, pp. 106–29.

39. These comments are based on a close reading of the *Cardiff Times*, *Western Mail*, *South Wales Daily News* and *Welsh Catholic Herald* from the 1870s to 1914.

40. The anecdote was reproduced in two local newspapers: the *South Wales Daily News*, 15 June 1906 and the *Cardiff Times*, 16 June 1906. Cardiff was granted city status in 1905.

41. *Cardiff and Merthyr Guardian*, 6 April 1850.

42. *Cardiff and Merthyr Guardian*, 20 March 1858.

43. *Cardiff Times*, 7 June 1879. The Society had 400 members and a capital of £2,000. During the preceding six months it had made relief payments of £350 to members and their families.

44. *Welsh Catholic Herald*, 13 June 1908.

45. *Cardiff Times*, 19 June 1886. He added that the service was 'no more ritualistic than [that of] High Anglicans'.

46. See O'Leary, *Immigration and Integration*, ch. 2.

47. Dot Jones, 'Self-Help in Nineteenth-Century Wales: The Rise and Fall of the Female Friendly Society', *Llafur*, 6.1 (1984), pp. 14–26.

48. See, for example, Neil Evans, '"As Rich as California . . .": Opening and Closing the Frontier, Wales 1780–1870', in *The People of Wales*, ed. Gareth Elwyn Jones and Dai Smith, Llandysul, Gomer, 2000, pp. 111–44.

'The Black Hand': 1916 and Irish Republican Prisoners in North Wales

Jon Parry

Whether the Irish who came to Wales in the nineteenth and early twentieth centuries came willingly or unwillingly is a matter for debate. There can be no doubt, however, that the 1,800 men who passed through Frongoch, a small, isolated village in the mountains of Snowdonia, from May to December 1916 were far from happy to be leaving Ireland. These were the men who were interned as a result of their participation in the Easter Rising. Their brief sojourn in rural Wales nurtured the seeds of modern Ireland. The name Frongoch has resonated through the decades as one of the symbols of the revolutionary period in Ireland. It was one of the few Welsh names with which Irish people were familiar, even if they found it unpronounceable. Similarly, as we shall see, to some Welsh men and women it became a symbol of national struggle, but like so many symbols it was given a significance that was not really there.[1]

One of the tragedies of modern Irish and Welsh historiography is how little knowledge and understanding the two countries have of each other's modern past.[2] The conspiracy myths surrounding Frongoch that have attracted Welsh people have also done much to detract from an understanding of Ireland. Similarly, terse references to Frongoch in the Irish media or in history books do not lead to further interest in Wales and its history. The view of Dominic Behan that '[t]heir poets are paid about ten pence a week provided no ill of England they speak/Thank God we're surrounded by water' aptly sums up the view of many Irish nationalists towards the 'principality'. Ernie O'Malley, one of the most active republican fighters of both the War of Independence and the Civil War, described his early upbringing at home as being so devoid of interest in his country that he might just as well have been living in Wales.[3]

In 1916 Wales was a loyal pillar of the British Empire: its mines were fuelling the war effort and its greatest son, Lloyd George, would soon be in the seat of power as prime minister. Although its old, Edwardian confidence was under threat from the strain of war and the modernising of society, it was staunchly unionist in terms of its position within the

United Kingdom. Preparations for Welsh Home Rule were in hand but they were becoming increasingly redundant.[4]

In the past, Irish Home Rule had aroused a great deal of interest and was inspirational for many Welsh politicians, but the 'extreme nationalism' of Sinn Fein and the violent rebellion of 1916 found little support in Liberal Wales.[5] In the south Wales valleys, the political epicentre of Wales, what support there was for the Irish cause within the labour movement was largely out of common cause with James Larkin and the Irish Transport and General Workers' Union and sympathy with the suffering endured in the 1913 Dublin strike. In many cases, however, the ethnic division of labour embittered relationships between Irish and Welsh workers, and this conflict would persist wherever the two Celtic groups met and worked.[6] There were indeed pockets of support for James Connolly and his Irish Citizens' Army, and a very few Welshmen were to follow Larkin to America, while others would be involved in the War of Independence.[7] These, however, were exceptions. In 1916, Captain Jack White, who had trained the Citizens' Army, visited Cardiff and the Rhondda and Aberdare valleys seeking support for Connolly. At Aberdare on 25 May 1916 he was given two sentences of three months each for trying to 'sow the seeds of sedition in an area which had nothing to do with the grievances of Ireland either real or imaginary' and at a time when 'a peaceful settlement was being arrived at'.[8] The initial reaction of Welsh people to the 1916 rising when they eventually found out about it was little different from that of the people of Dublin, albeit less vociferous. The latter had subjected the captured insurgents to a cacophony of taunts and insults as they were marched off for court martial and deportation or execution.[9]

Some of the leaders of political and industrial labour in Wales had entered the political establishment at Westminster and were part of the wartime government. They, too, had little sympathy with those who had rebelled against the Crown. In his capacity as a junior minister at the Home Office, William Brace, one of the pioneering leaders of the South Wales Miners' Federation and now turned elegant parliamentarian, had the task of reporting on and defending the conditions in Frongoch camp to the House of Commons. Welsh Labour MPs may have joined in with Arthur Henderson when he allegedly applauded the execution of the Rising's leaders, including James Connolly.[10] Other men with personal or commercial Welsh connections would one day be trying to maintain British authority from Dublin Castle.[11]

The actual rising and its associated events are so meticulously detailed elsewhere they need not detain us here.[12] The immediate outcome was a series of executions and draconian life sentences; all the latter were commuted and a line was drawn under the executions after James Connolly's name. There were also mass arrests of republicans and those suspected of republican activities. Hundreds were rounded up not only in Dublin, but also in Cork, Galway, Limerick and other towns throughout Ireland.[13] Internment, an issue that was to dog Irish and British politics for decades, had reared its head on a massive scale. Once the rising had been crushed both the civil and military authorities were faced with major logistical as well as political problems.

Although it had been relatively easy to deal with the leaders of the rising, so well known were they to the G Division of the Dublin Metropolitan Police who were responsible for gathering intelligence on seditious oganisations, the rank and file were a different matter. So many had been arrested that there seemed to be nowhere in Ireland that they could be securely imprisoned and in any case such imprisonment would only serve to aggravate an already difficult situation. Two thousand rebels could not remain on the soil of their native land. They could not be conscripted into the forces in Europe, as had happened to common criminals elsewhere, so the obvious and simplest solution was to deport them to England where the gaols were relatively empty. The problem and the solution were to exercise the minds of civil servants in the War Office and in the Home Office.

On 9 May 1916, General Maxwell, adjutant-general of the British forces in Ireland, wrote to the attorney-general requesting clarification of the legal position of prisoners being sent to gaols in England. It was, he said, clearly impossible for such prisoners to stand trial in Ireland; although condemnation of the rising had been widespread, the closeness of the Irish and their protective spirit towards friends and families, coupled with the nature of the conflict, would make identification of the culprits difficult if not impossible and charges might not stick.[14] Moreover, he was concerned as to their constitutional rights under habeas corpus. The cabinet agreed that as British subjects the men had a right to trial by a civil court, and it was decided to set up an advisory committee to review each individual case.[15] Furthermore, despite assiduous intelligence-gathering by the G Division, there was still much uncertainty as to who, apart from the senior figures, had been involved in the rising. There is no doubt that many innocent people had been arrested and that some of the police had taken the opportunity to settle old scores. General instructions had been given for a round-up of Sinn Fein members, but it had been stressed that this should not include 'Strong Nationalists' and that where there was doubt the police should err on the side of the nationalists. The deputy adjutant noted that many innocents had been arrested and that his office had been swamped with letters from 'respectable members of the community, including clergymen, demanding the release of individuals on the grounds of respectability'. The question of whether they were directly or indirectly involved in the rising was conveniently glossed over.[16]

Consequently, the British government had on its hands a substantial number of articulate, educated, political men and women and little clear idea about what to do with them. As a short-term measure it was agreed that they be temporarily detained and confined to camps that had hitherto been used to incarcerate German prisoners of war. Such a place was Frongoch. Originally the site of a Welsh whiskey distillery that went bankrupt, Frongoch was bleak, barren, very wet and relatively isolated. The small market towns of Bala and Dolgellau were not too far away and the larger settlements of Wrexham and Chester were easily contactable. The latter was especially important from a military point of view. There was also a military camp at Tonfannau on the Cardigan Bay coastline. With its railway station Frongoch was an ideal spot for a POW camp. There were some 120 soldiers already stationed there, and up until 1916 the German inmates had made the best of life, with concert parties and entertainments, and had tried to come to terms with the fact that some of them spoke better English than the local inhabitants. A very few never left Merioneth, for they succumbed to influenza and were buried locally.[17]

The camp itself was large, and it was for this reason as well as its location that it had been selected to house the Irish.[18] They were transported from Holyhead, but also, in time, from other prisons in Britain. Some were to be released fairly quickly, others would remain until Christmas 1916.[19] They lived in two camps, North and South, and were under military jurisdiction. Each camp had its own mess and the men were housed in large sheds. Each shed had its own 'policeman' chosen by the men. There were no women in the camp: female Irish prisoners had been detained in gaols in England.[20] Smoking was permitted, spitting was not. There was to be no noise of singing, but conversation was allowed provided it stopped at the sound of the camp whistle. Running was permitted only in the event of a fire.[21]

Such rules were almost impossible to enforce. Just like their German predecessors, the Irish held concert parties and put on amateur dramatics. Michael Collins, the most famous graduate of this 'University of Revolution', was good at recitation, and it was possibly at Frongoch that a future actor in the Oscar-winning film *How Green Was My Valley* demonstrated talents that would later be revealed to Hollywood as they had been to audiences in Dublin's Abbey Theatre.[22] The practice of adopting nicknames and group names initially began in jest but it would soon provide a sense of unity and identity in opposition to the camp's authoritarian regime. Hence the Black Hand Gang and the Rajah of Frongoch enter history. They were also useful code names.[23] As one inmate put it, the entertainment for a time helped them to forget what the bare walls and barbed wire and all the other things stood for. Some men admitted to having enjoyed themselves during their incarceration and compared the picturesque scenery to their own parts of Ireland.[24] But camp life was not meant to be enjoyed. The food was generally poor, and there were rats in the huts. No more than three people were allowed to go to the latrines after lights out. During the day the prisoners had to maintain a distance of at least eight feet from the perimeter fence or they would be fired upon. Needless to say, anyone trying to escape would be shot.[25] There were few creature comforts for the men, nor indeed for their guards. As well as taking up craft work some men formed work parties to cut the grass in the camp, for which they received $1\frac{1}{2}d$ per hour until the veteran labour leader William O'Brien persuaded them to strike for better pay.[26] Others took the opportunity to learn Irish and even Welsh, but life was generally tedious. Darrel Figgis referred to the camp as a place from which no good reports came. Local tradesmen from Bala and Dolgellau visited the camp bringing provisions, cutting hair and supplying news. Tim Healy, one of the prisoners' champions in the House of Commons, believed that if it had not been for what he called the quality of heart of the local population, the men would have starved.[27]

Two essential services had to be sought from the outside world, namely medical support and religious succour. As might be expected, almost all of the men were Catholics and they chose to make much of their piety. In most cases this was a genuine expression of feeling, but for some it was merely a stick with which to beat the camp commandant. As there was no priest in the immediate vicinity, arrangements were made for one to journey from Wrexham, which came under the Catholic diocese of Menevia. The route was by no means easy for a penurious priest who occasionally had to stay overnight at the camp. Should he return to Wrexham he was often summoned back at a moment's notice. He was impatient with the camp authorities and became even more so when, several months after the release of the prisoners, he was still writing to the Home Office on the thorny question of his expenses.[28]

There was also a need to minister to Protestant sensibilities. The Home Office had naturally been aware of the prevalence of Catholicism in the camp and had made arrangements as a matter of course. No such thought had been given to non-Catholics. In fact, the very idea that there should be Protestants within the ranks of Sinn Fein or the Irish Republican Brotherhood (IRB) came as something of a surprise to London civil servants, even though Dublin Castle had spent many hours watching the likes of Ernest Blythe and Bulmer Hobson. Therefore, the absence of a minister to tend to the needs of the Protestant internees – all three of them – became another cause célèbre in the camp; deputation after deputation attended the camp commandant stressing that the spiritual needs of fellow Christians could not be ignored. The whole issue was blown out of proportion to cause maximum embarrassment to the camp authorities and to score propaganda points against them.[29]

Publicity and propaganda were of great importance to the internees. Members of the Irish Parliamentary Party, such as Tim Healey, Laurence Ginnell and others, continually raised questions in the House of Commons about conditions in the camp and agitated for the release of the prisoners, though sometimes this was a thankless task, as Tom O'Donnell, the MP for West Kerry, found to his cost.[30] Laurence Ginnell MP had problems with the authorities. Well known for his strong views, he was always a maverick politician and after making an inflammatory speech at Stafford gaol he was refused permission to visit Frongoch.[31] Although subject to wartime rules of censorship, newspapers on both sides of the Irish Sea carried reports of conditions in the camp. In England, the *Manchester Guardian* published detailed accounts of the living conditions, particularly of the food and the rats, while in Ireland the provincial papers contained both articles and letters from prisoners detailing their experiences.[32]

The apparent lack of medical care was particularly noted and led to widespread protests both inside and outside the camp. There is no doubt that conditions were primitive. Later in the year it was extremely cold, prisoners were undernourished and some did suffer acute problems, both physical and mental.[33] Again, the prisoners took advantage of these conditions. So vociferous did the protestations become that the local doctor who had been employed as a medical officer found the strain too great and committed suicide by drowning. There was much recrimination over this incident, with blame being placed squarely on the shoulders of the prisoners. It was necessary for one of the camp leaders to write to the commandant and to the Home Office insisting that no deliberate harm had been intended and that the death of the man was deeply regretted. The author of the letter was Michael Collins.[34]

Meanwhile, in Ireland, affairs in Frongoch were being carefully monitored. Family and friends of prisoners were incensed at what they thought were the harsh conditions endured by their loved ones. Protest groups were organised throughout Ireland, but particularly in Dublin and areas of Munster, to bring to the public view the position of the men not only in Frongoch but also in English gaols. One of the most ardent protesters was the redoubtable Mary McSweeney, whose brother, Terrence, would later become a republican martyr and who at this time was languishing in Frongoch. McSweeney wrote to the home secretary seeking details and explanations about conditions in the camp and she peremptorily informed the minister that she intended visiting the Home Office to obtain the information.[35] In November 1916 the *Cork Free Press* printed a story describing the mass hunger strike and was penalised for doing so.[36]

Hunger strikes were a fairly common occurrence, though rarely on such a large scale as the one described by the Cork paper. That particular protest had come about when the authorities attempted to conscript three of the prisoners to fight at the Front. All the prisoners refused to answer at a roll call and 300 of them were transferred to the unpopular South Camp. The subsequent hunger strike involved 109 men, many of whom became very weak, and it ended only with the intervention of the priest. The event caught the imagination of the relatives in Ireland and fuelled public debate on internment and on conscription. Conscription was an extremely emotive issue. In Ireland there was constant fear that the system might be introduced or imposed on the Irish as it had been earlier that year in Britain, and opposition to it united all shades of public and political opinion. More space in the press was devoted to the threat of conscription than was devoted to the rising.[37] In later months the authorities even feared that another rising would occur as a result of the conscription crisis. There is much to be said for the argument that it was conscription, more than any other factor, that led to the electoral success of Sinn Fein and the popularity of the new nationalist movement in the final years of the First World War.[38]

Quite a few Irish men had left Britain specifically to avoid conscription. Furthermore, several men who had been born and bred in Britain had gone to Dublin to join the rising. Most of them had been members of the London branch of the Irish Volunteers or the London GAA or Gaelic League. In the eyes of the authorities they were legitimate conscripts and their evasion of service was regarded as a heinous crime. In Frongoch they were noticeable because of their accents, and so could be singled out fairly easily. It was felt that if and when any internees were to be released such men should be the last to leave, or preferably should not be released at all.[39] The efforts made by the prisoners to prevent their comrades being conscripted added to the sense of unity that developed in the camp and strengthened the men's sense of identity.

Although the authorities did their best to play down contentious issues, it was almost impossible to prevent news from leaking out or in. Events in Europe generally and in Ireland were moving fast, and the men were able to keep in regular contact despite the efforts of the censor. Initially they could write letters only once a week, though soon they were allowed two a week.[40] Many of them wrote in Irish. In turn, they received 160 packets and over 1,000 letters a day. The camp commandant bemoaned the fact that there was only one censor at Frongoch, and he simply could not keep up with the volume of mail received. The use of Irish further exacerbated his problem.[41]

Irish classes (and Welsh classes) were held at Frongoch, and, as is well known, the inmates also began to develop their political education. But most of them had little understanding of political issues. The majority of them had never been outside Ireland in their lives and knew few people outside their immediate locality; most were young and devout.

They were regarded as dupes of a few intelligent men or simply as criminals. Some, it was claimed, 'are thoroughly bad characters who have done time for civil offences. The effect of these men and of the agitation in the camp on youngsters from Galway and other benighted districts cannot fail to be disastrous . . . the latter follow their leaders like sheep'. At Frongoch, it was claimed, '[the] most disloyal are the educated middle class, clerks, government officials and schoolteachers'. To this occupational analysis Dublin Castle added the younger sons of farmers and shopkeepers, while the press drew attention to the image of a tall, clean-cut elite whose 'association in life was probably to be found in the professional classes'.[42]

The camp authorities and military intelligence were in no doubt as to the pervasive influence of the Irish Republican Brotherhood within the camp, even though this was later denied. But it was impossible to establish a list of members because of its secretive nature, and so, it was admitted, 'those whom we assume to be in it may not be members at all'. Identification of individuals within the camp was a major problem. Records were inadequate and men could lose themselves for days if not weeks by simply moving from North Camp to South Camp and back again. Undercover help was requested in the hope that if Irish detectives could be brought over to play the role of prisoners there might be some chance of identifying the troublemakers.[43] There was little time for sophisticated intelligence-gathering. The advisory committee that had been set up to consider the release of prisoners did its work smoothly, although without cooperation from the prisoners and gradually most internees were freed. The rapturous welcome they received in their home towns on return is well recorded.[44] Those who returned retained much of their personal naivety, but now they were more aware of the political world. Nevertheless most of them remained the foot soldiers of the new movement, the young rank and file who were the inheritors of the legacy of Easter 1916 rather than the leaders of the rising. They had not been important enough to be sent to gaols at Hereford, Portland, Knutsford or Dartmoor: it was while in the Frongoch camp itself that they had become important.[45]

Sinn Fein had been a small, nondescript political party and the IRB an elite, secret society led by people of whom few had heard and who were more renowned for their eccentricity than for their political skills. But by the time the men returned from Frongoch to their own towns and villages, they had become household names. It seemed as if everyone in Ireland now knew somebody who had been in Frongoch and who had therefore helped to create a new, popular political culture that had little time for the musty Liberal doctrines of Home Rule. The release of the men, coupled with the conscription crisis, energised Irish politics.

Yet even a populist movement has to have hierarchies, and these were established at Frongoch. The executions in 1916 had removed the leaders, and what was left was the second level; De Valera had risen to the top because of the fact of his political survival. There was now an opportunity to seize their chance in a new political world, an opportunity that they would never have had before 1916. The cult of leadership was established and the political dynasties that came to dominate Irish political life for decades were begun.[46]

By 23 December 1916 all the internees were back in Ireland. In 1918 many of them were back in prison, this time in England rather than in Wales (though a few were sent to Usk). The mood was different now: the prisoners were more political, more confident, more aware of being Irish. The governor of Reading Gaol thought them to be 'a rough lot', unlike the prisoners in 1916 who had been 'real gentlemen'. Already the myths of 1916 and the status of its heroes had begun to grow. The prisoners now gloried in their Gaelic identity. As one 1918 internee wrote to his daughter, 'I am glad you are studying the Gaelic language . . . when a country's language dies its people become slaves with the tongue of the conqueror in their mouths'.[47] These men were a tougher force, and the guerilla war from 1919 was far harder-fought than the brief episode of 1916.[48] Some Frongoch men did not involve themselves in the new struggle, while others were reluctant participants in the early assassinations ordered by Michael Collins.[49]

Frongoch would now enter Irish mythology and the men who had languished there became part of a hierarchy of the revolutionary tradition. To have been interned at the camp was central to their position in that hierarchy. Several members of the government and the general staff of the new Free State had been there, including Joe Sweeney, J.J. O'Connell and Richard Mulcahy. Similarly, members of De Valera's future cabinets had also been interned. For Fianna Fail, Frongoch became its greatest *Ard Fheis*, having nurtured the party's ultimate victory, even though most of the internees had followed Collins and moved towards Cumann na nGaedheal and later Fine Gael. At a more prosaic but nonetheless significant level, Jimmy Mulkearns, who had been the Rajah of Frongoch, continued to use the title on his release and performed at fund-raising concerts for the volunteer movement. Frongoch had become a symbol. A house was named after it in Ranalagh; in Henry Street, Dublin, there was a Frongoch barber's shop and a Frongoch newsagent's.[50]

For Irish people in more modern times Frongoch is no more than a couple of pages in the memoirs of old men. At the same time it became of interest to Welsh people. Originally the Welsh had been condemnatory of the rising, or of what little they knew of it. News filtered back to Holyhead from the Welsh who worked in and around the city and its port. Many of Dublin's Welsh residents were prosperous and professional people who lived in the suburbs and outlying districts. They would later recall the difficulties they had in reaching the city during the days of fighting. In Wales Sinn Fein had little if any support apart from the 'notorious' article by D.J. Williams in *Y Wawr*, the student magazine of University College of Wales Aberystwyth.[51] When the internees arrived in Merioneth, local people saw them marching to the camp and encountered them when food deliveries were made to the camp and when prisoners had their hair cut. The prisoners engendered sympathy for their plight rather than for their actions. Ironically, some monoglot Welsh people from the Frongoch area who saw the prisoners were later to serve in the hated Black and Tans in the forthcoming war in Ireland. Indeed, Welshmen served in both the Black and Tans and in the Auxiliaries, and some were active in the secret service work in Dublin Castle.[52]

Again, in recent times, Frongoch took hold of the Welsh imagination, particularly, of course, among the nationalist community. The fact that many hundreds of so-called republicans were incarcerated in that most Welsh of areas intrigued many young, and not so young, members of language protest societies such as Cymdeithas yr Iaith Gymraeg (the Welsh Language Society) and Adfer. The idea of martyrs fighting for Y Weriniaeth (the Republic) was opium to a few. As a section of the Welsh people began to discover Ireland in their quest to lose England, so they looked to the history of the Irish struggle, of which Frongoch was their nearest symbol. At the time of the 1950s campaign to prevent the Tryweryn valley in Merioneth from being flooded to supply Liverpool with water, protesters wrote to De Valera for support. In reply he recalled the area and the Frongoch days, even though he himself had never been there.[53]

Articles on the camp and interviews with former inmates appeared in *papurau bro*, the local Welsh-language newspapers, in the early 1970s. To some young Welsh patriots Frongoch may have been as much of a symbol as it was to young Irish nationalists generations previously.[54] But if it was a symbol of republicanism and a celebration of nationalist identity to many Irish and to some Welsh, for others it was tainted with sadness. For supporters of both Collins and De Valera Frongoch held memories of broken friendships and lost comrades, when the unity created in the camp was damaged in the Dáil debate on the Treaty and shattered in the shelling of the Four Courts. Networks created by Collins in the fastness of Merioneth broke down in Dublin.[55]

Yet the differences of opinion that led to the Civil War, and which were enhanced by it, were already in place at Frongoch. Even in 1916 the prisoners there were not in complete agreement and were sneered at by camp officers for not knowing what they actually wanted to achieve.[56] The lines of division were already drawn. It was becoming clear who would wield power and influence in any new Irish society. The Bicycle

Revolution had its brakes applied by its own riders. In particular, the power of the IRB was exerted to create a society within a society, and this at a time when the move towards democracy and self-government was attaining mass appeal. This in itself would harden attitudes during the bitter controversy over whether to accept the limited autonomy of the Free State or to continue the struggle for full independence. An army was created at Frongoch that brought into existence an officer class of commandants and generals who would otherwise have been unlikely to wield either individual or collective authority. Sometimes this power was abused.[57]

It is also worth remembering how youthful were the internees at Frongoch. They were young and impressionable, caught up in a heady period and prone to worship heroes and value friendships with idealism and naivety. Such devotion when abused can result in bitterness and sour disillusionment. Many Frongoch veterans could never forgive De Valera on the one hand or Collins on the other for costing them friendships in the flower of their youth, and such was the longevity of the Irish political class that this bitterness persisted for decades.

In Neil Jordan's 1996 film *Michael Collins*, the Big Fellow's assistant says to another of Collins' circle that the Free State Commander in Chief should not make the fateful tour of West Cork during which he would be assassinated at Beal nBleath. It is dangerous territory, he says, because 'Mick doesn't know the lads down there any more'. Michael Collins had been a young man in Frongoch, and had himself once been relatively unknown, as had many of his influential comrades. But so swiftly had Irish politics moved, and so meteoric had Collins' and his fellows' rise been, that a new generation of rank-and-file activists had appeared. A new army of young, impressionable people had been created. Unlike the Frongoch veterans, who had little option but to listen day and night to Collins in an isolated and lonely camp, this new generation now had a choice of two leaders who were in open and public conflict. Frongoch created an artificial society that had no hope of survival in a wider political arena.

For a few short months in 1916 the greatest concentration of Irish revolutionaries in modern times were incarcerated in north Wales. It was in Merioneth that a brief period of internment laid the ground for the War of Independence, the Civil War, the creation of the Free State and the founding of Fianna Fail and Cumann na nGaedheal and later Fine Gael. British military exigency had resulted in a bleak and desolate Welsh upland becoming a focal point for revolutionary ardour, national symbolism, youthful energy and cultural commitment. The heroic march of modern Irish history ended with the assassination of Collins in the lovely valley of Beal nBleath in West Cork; it may have begun on the dreary slopes near Bala in north Wales.

Notes

1. For a general narrative and description of Frongoch see R. Brennan-Whitmore, *With the Irish in Frongoch*, Dublin, Talbot Press, 1917; Sean O Mahony, *Frongoch: University of Revolution*, Dublin, FDR Teoranta, 1987; M.J. O'Connor, *Stone Walls: An Irish Volunteer's Experiences in Prison and Internment in England and Wales after the 1916 Rising*, Dublin, Dublin Press, 1966; Desmond Clifford, 'With the Irish in Frongoch', *Planet*, 66 (December 1987–January 1988), pp. 37–42; J. Brennan, 'Frongoch', in *Dublin's Fighting Story*, Tralee, Kerryman Press, pp. 112–24.

2. Historians of the medieval and early modern periods have had no such problems, as has been demonstrated in the works of Rees Davies, James Lydon, Ciaran Brady, Brendan Bradshaw and others. Among Wales' modern historians, Paul O'Leary and John Davies have been almost alone in their work on the modern connections. See John Davies, 'Wales and Ireland: Parallels and Differences', *Planet*, 95 (1992), pp. 7–16; Paul O'Leary, *Immigration and Integration: The Irish in Wales, 1798–1922*, Cardiff, University of Wales Press, 2000; *idem*, 'Accommodation and Resistance: A Comparison of Cultural Identities in Ireland and Wales, *c.*1880–1914', in *Kingdoms United? Great Britain and Ireland since 1500: Integration and Diversity*, ed. S.J. Connolly, Dublin, Four Courts Press, 1999, pp. 123–34.

3. Richard English and Cormac O'Mallie, *Prison Letters of Ernie O'Malley*, Dublin, Gill and Macmillan, 1991, pp. 69–71.

4. K.O. Morgan, *Rebirth of a Nation: Wales 1880–1980*, Oxford, Oxford University Press, 1981, pp. 123–55.

5. One famous exception was the article by D.J. Williams in the University College of Wales Aberystwyth students' magazine, *Y Wawr*, in the summer of 1916. This drew a furious response from O.M. Edwards in *Cymru Coch*, 51 (August 1916).

6. See K. Kenny, *Making Sense of the Molly Maguires*, Oxford, Oxford University Press, 1998, passim, and, from the Welsh side, W.D. Jones, *Wales in America: The Welsh in Scranton 1860–1920*, Cardiff, University of Wales Press, 1993, passim.

7. The best-known example is the south Wales miners' leader, Arthur Horner, but others too went with Larkin to America and north Walians joined De Valera. See A. Horner, *Incorrigible Rebel*, London, MacGibbon and Kee, 1960, pp. 25–32.

8. *Aberdare Leader*, 27 May 1916; *County Cork Eagle*, 27 May 1916.

9. Many of their assailants were wives and relatives of men who were voluntarily fighting in the trenches, though the extent of the lack of sympathy for the rebels has recently been questioned.

10. These allegations were made several years later in the Scottish socialist newspaper *Forward*, 4, 11 September 1920.

11. At the height of the later troubles, liaison between Dublin Castle, the

Black and Tans and the Auxiliaries would be overseen by Sir Hamar Greenwood, who, although born in Canada, was of Welsh parentage. One of his senior civil servants would leave and later take up a post with the South Wales Coal Owners' Association. His experiences at 'the Castle' obviously suited him to this task.

12. For the narrative of the rising, see D. Ryan, *The Rising*, Dublin, Golden Eagle Books, 4th edn, 1966; M. Caulfield, *The Easter Rebellion*, Dublin, Gill and Macmillan, 2nd edn, 1995; Kevin Nowlan (ed.), *The Making of 1916*, Dublin, Stationery Office, 1969; F.X. Martin, *Leaders and Men of the Easter Rising*, Dublin, Gill and Macmillan, 1967, and the same author's two major studies, '1916 – Myth, Fact and Mystery', *Studia Hibernica*, 7 (1967), pp. 7–124, and 'The 1916 Rising – Coup d'Etat or Bloody Protest?', *Studia Hibernica*, 8 (1968), pp. 106–37; *Sinn Fein Rebellion Handbook*, Dublin, *Irish Times*, 1917; the 1926 issues of *An Tolagh* have blow by blow accounts of Easter Week and the 1966–67 issues of the *Capuchin Annual* contain reminiscences of participants.

13. A district inspector, three sergeants and 18 constables came to arrest Darrel Figgis and his wife at their isolated home in Mayo. See D. Figgis, *A Chronicle of Jails*, Dublin, Talbot Press, 1917, p. 14. Veterans of the rising talked and wrote about meeting men from other parts of Ireland for the first time: Joe Good, *Enchanted by Dreams: Memoirs of a Revolutionary*, Kerry, Bandon Books, 1997, p. 32. In his famous statement on Frongoch, Tim Healey referred to the coming together of Ulstermen, Munstermen, Connachtmen and Leinstermen who had never previously encountered one another. See *House of Commons Debates*, vol. LXXXIV, col. 1766, 26 July 1916.

14. PRO, HO 144/1455/313106/1, Maxwell to Attorney-General, 9 May 1916.

15. PRO, HO 144/1455/313106/2, confidential note to cabinet, 15 May 1916. The advisory committee was to be chaired by Mr Justice Sankey.

16. PRO, WO 35/69/1, 3 May 1916; PRO, HO144/1455/313106/2, General Byrne, Deputy Adjutant-General, to War Office, 10 May 1916. Good (*Enchanted by Dreams*, p. 87) comments on the respectability of the men. The local Irish press described them as people 'who would be classed as intellectual . . . tall, clean-cut looking whose association in life was probalbly to be found in the professional classes' (*Tipperary Star*, 13 May 1916). Even the popular English press would paint a romantic picture of the clean-cut image for its readers: see *Sunday Chronicle*, 9 May 1916. Tom Garvin discusses the social background of nationalist activists in *Revolutionary Nationalists in Ireland 1858–1922*, Oxford, Oxford University Press, 1987. There is also extensive analysis for the period after 1916 in Peter Hart, *The IRA and its Enemies*, Oxford, Oxford University Press, 1998.

17. PP XV 1916, *Official Report of Conditions in Prisoner of War Camps . . . Frongoch*. There is a small collection of photographs of German inmates in the Dolgellau office of the Gwynedd Archives Service.

18. Others were detained at Gloucester, Knutsford, Reading, Stafford and also in Glasgow.

19. They came back as heroes, but as early as July 1916 Tim Healey was already placing the 1916 men in the pantheon of the Irish revolutionary tradition when he prefixed a question on Frongoch with a request for statistics on the number of Fenians who had been imprisoned in 1867 and 1881–82 (*Kerryman*, 8 July 1916).

20. The women were interned at Aylesbury gaol. They were Winifred Carney, Helen Moloney, Maura Perolz, Ellen Ryan and Bridget Foley. The Home Office agreed that the 'ladies' should not have to consort with German brothel-keepers from Antwerp and that they should have a wing of their own. PRO, HO 144/1455/313106/7, Sir Edward Troup to General Byrne, 6 June 1916. On the women of 1916 and their imprisonment see Ruth Taillon, *When History was Made: The Women of 1916*, Belfast, Beyond the Pale Publications, 1996, pp. 102–106, Margaret Ward, *Unimaginable Revolutionaries*, London, Pluto Press, pp. 88–118.

21. PRO, HO 144/1455/313106/8, Camp Standing Orders.

22. He was Arthur Shields, brother of Barry Fitzgerald, one of the stars of *The Quiet Man*. See Seamus Scully, 'The Abbey Theatre 1916 Plaque', *Dublin Historical Records*, 42.4 (September 1988).

23. In later years code names would be used extensively by Irish prisoners in their correspondence, but the references were simple and fairly easy for intelligence officers to decipher: who else but De Valera could have been the 'Barcelona Brat'?

24. *Kerryman*, 27 July 1916.

25. PRO, HO 144/1455/313106/8, Camp Standing Orders.

26. O Mahony, *Frongoch*, p. 117.

27. Figgis, *A Chronicle of Jails*, p. 51; Tim Healy, *House of Commons Debates*, vol. LXXXIV, col. 1766, 26 July 1916. Even when internment was over there were bureaucratic problems over the supply and payment for food. The canteen account for the camp generally was held at a local bank in Bala, and there was much discussion between the Home Office and War Office over the mutual disbursement of £49 11s 6d.

28. There had probably never been so many Catholics in Merioneth since the time of the Reformation. PRO, HO 144/1455/313106/168, HO 144/1456/313106/638, letters from Heygate-Lambert (Camp Commandant) to Home Office, 3 July 1916; *House of Commons Debates*, vol. LXXXIV, cols. 1662–65, 27 July 1916.

29. Inmates of gaols in England did much the same: for example, there were similar events at Portland gaol where George Irvine was the only Protestant. See J.J. Brennan, 'The Mendicity Institute Ave.', *Capuchin Annual* (1966), p. 192.

30. Thirty Kerry internees said they would rather stay in Frongoch than have their freedom attributed to the good offices of the MP for West Kerry, Tom O'Donnell. Indeed they only agreed to see him when he visited the camp because he was a Kerryman (*Kerryman*, 15 July 1916).

31. PRO, HO 144/1455/313106/61.

32. *Manchester Guardian*, 10 December 1916. Apart from the *Irish Independent*, papers such as the *Kerryman*, the *Tipperary Star*, the *Cork Free Press* and the *Mayo News* all contained details on camp life. The *Cork Free Press* was a proscribed publication in the camp, but for some reason the *Mayo News* was regarded as acceptable, which is surprising given some of its contents.

33. Such men came close to the status of martyrs, particularly in the eyes of exiles. See, for example, the report in the *Gaelic American* of the funeral of Thomas Stokes, which took place at Enniscorthy in 1917 (*Gaelic American*, 27 October 1917).

34. PRO, HO 144/1455/313106/593–598, Collins to Heygate-Lambert.

35. Writing from the Buckingham Palace Hotel in the Strand, she informed the home secretary that she would be calling to see him at 10.00 am on Wednesday 21 June and that he had better answer her questions in full as she wished to be out of London by noon. PRO, HO 144/1455/313106/28, McSweeney to Home Secretary, Herbert Samuel, 19 June 1916. When she eventually arrived at Frongoch she was allowed only 15 minutes to visit her brother and another 15 minutes with Tomas MacCurtain. Both men were to die in tragic circumstances. See F.J. Costello, *Enduring the Most: The Life and Death of Terrence MacSweeney*, Kerry, Bandon Books, 1995, p. 78.

36. *Cork Free Press*, 11 November 1916.

37. The *Irish Independent* and all the major local newspapers carried lead articles on the conscription crisis.

38. For a recent study of the First World War and Ireland see Thomas Hennessey, *World War One and Partition in Ireland 1914–1922*, Dublin, Gill and Macmillan, 1999, and for conscription especially, pp. 108–24.

39. Some, such as Sean Nunan, never lost their English accents. See Good, *Enchanted by Dreams*, p. 84; PRO, HO 144/1455/313106/229. Strictly speaking Michael Collins should have been in the same position as the others who had avoided conscription in England. See 'IO', *The Administration of Ireland 1920*, London, Philip Allan, 1921, p. 141.

40. *Kerryman*, 8 July 1916.

41. PRO, HO 144/1455/313106/168, Heygate-Lambert to Home Office. The receipt of letters in Irish was the subject of debate in Parliament. Tim Healy was particularly incensed at the home secretary's use of the word 'Erse' to describe Gaelic; see *House of Commons Debates*, cols. 1662–65, 26 July 1916.

42. PRO, HO 144/1455/313106/621; *Tipperary Star*, 13 May 1916.

43. Judge Sankey described the IRB as 'a somewhat dangerous society'. PRO, HO 144/1455/313106/272.

44. For example, the release and return of three teachers to Charleville in north Cork was greeted with processions through the town as the men disembarked 'from the 10.20 train from the internment camp in Wales' (*Cork Free Press*, 22 July 1916). Public transport between Merioneth and Cork was obviously better eighty years ago. The authorities pleaded that if men were to be released it would be better if they arrived on the evening boat rather than the morning one, since this would reduce the possibility of enthusiastic demonstrations. PRO, HO 144/1455/313106/220, telegram to Home Office 19 July 1916. The Mayo police thought that eight Westport men were too dangerous to be released at all. PRO, CO 904/157, 3 October 1916.

45. Other prominent Sinn Fein leaders or IRB activists had been imprisoned elsewhere. One such was Ernest Blythe, who had been the subject of intelligence scrutiny since 1914. When Lawrence Ginnell tabled a question in Parliament asking why Blythe had not been sent to Frongoch, the reply was, 'It was considered inadvisable that some of the chief leaders of the movement should be interned with the remainder at Frongoch'; *House of Commons Debates*, vol. LXII, col. 1597, 6 July 1916. In later years Blythe was to be a staunch supporter of the Welsh chapel in Talbot Street, Dublin.

46. The longevity of many of the participants in the rising added to their gravitas in the Irish political structures of later years. De Valera is the most obvious example, but there were others and even Michael Collins' short life did not prevent his prosperous family from establishing political influence.

47. PRO, HO 144/1496/362269/172, Governor of Reading Gaol to Home Office, 1 February 1919; HO 144/1496/362269/3, 27 September 1918, Peter Segure to his daughter.

48. Joop Augenstein, *From Public Defiance to Guerilla Warfare: The Experience of Ordinary Volunteers in the Irish War of Independence 1916–1921*, Dublin, Irish Academic Press, 1996, pp. 87–123.

49. Emmet Dalton, with a laconic humour that he clearly did not feel at the time, later described Collins' attempts to persuade men to carry out assassinations; Dalton MS in the possession of Mr Paul Flatley. I am grateful to Mr Flatley for this reference. Hart (*The IRA and its Enemies*) has a great deal to say about the attitudes and experiences of young people in the IRA with special reference to the Cork brigades.

50. The house was occupied by Mrs Joseph Plunkett and Maeve Cavanagh, who wrote a poem entitled 'The Voice of Insurgency'. She was clearly a favourite with English civil servants, who after a time thought her poetry to be improving. PRO, CO 904/161/10. On the Rajah of Frongoch, see Brennan, *Dublin's Fighting Story*, p. 112.

51. Huw Llewelyn Williams (*Wrth Angor yn Nulyn*, Caernarfon, Llyfrfa'r Methodistiaid Calfinaidd, 1968) has much to say on the old Welsh chapel community. One of the most respected residents of Dublin was John Lloyd-Jones of Dowyddelan, who was Professor of Welsh at University College Dublin, 1910–55.

52. Lists of Black and Tans and Auxiliaries of Welsh birth are in PRO, HO 184/37–41.

53. Einion Thomas, *Capel Celyn: deng mlynedd o chwalu, 1955–1965*, Bala, Cyhoeddiadau Barddas, 1997, p. 35. Inhabitants of the valley referred to letters of support from De Valera when they were interviewed on television many years later.

54. *Pethe Penllyn, papur bro* (spring–summer 1971).

55. Most memoirs are replete with such sentiments, but there are few regrets at the stand taken. On attitudes towards De Valera, see Maryann Gialanella Valulis, 'The Man they Could Never Forgive – Eamon de Valera and the Civil War', in *De Valera and His Times*, ed. J. O'Caroll and J. Murphy, Cork, Cork University Press, 1983, pp. 92–100. As early as 1917 British civil servants had come to regard 'Dev' as the supreme opportunist: 'De Valera is cool and calculating. He is without means and his friends know that he is looking forward to his prospects in an Irish Parliament. He is looking at his own future and the country's afterwards'; PRO, CO 904/24.

56. PRO, HO 144/1456/313106/571, Heygate-Lambert to Home Office, 16 December 1916.

57. Maryann Gialanella Valulis, *Almost a Rebellion: The Army Mutiny of 1924*, Cork, Tower Books, 1985.

Comparing Immigrant Histories: The Irish and Others in Modern Wales

Neil Evans

The Irish migration of the nineteenth century stands at a strategic point in the history of Wales. It coincided with the onset of industrialisation, and the intellectual process of coming to terms with a new social order was confused by the sudden acceleration of Irish immigration.[1] Awareness of a crisis in public health dawned just as Irish immigration reached its peak. It is little wonder that the two were conflated: at least one newspaper referred to an 'Irish Plague'.[2] Public health inspectors concentrated their attention on the areas of Welsh towns that were identified as Irish, while the sporadic riots and disturbances that greeted the arrival of Irish migrants reached a peak around 1848. Frequent disturbances within Irish communities – usually relics of factional fights and feuds from the old country or the result of over-exuberant celebrations of St Patrick's Day – had the further effect of fixing a reputation for disorderly behaviour on the whole immigrant population. They were also identified with criminal behaviour – an ascription that was less unfair than many of the other charges, but which had its roots (like most crime in the period) in poverty and insecurity rather than in racial characteristics. Hostility resurfaced in the later 1860s when the Irish became identified with Fenianism and revolution and further attacks were made upon them as people who stood outside the pale of respectable Victorian society.

But most of these views were inaccurate or at least exaggerated. While it is true that the Irish migration was highly weighted towards poor and working-class people, it was never entirely the kind of lumpenproletariat that writers such as Engels imagined and feared. There were always skilled workers as well as the destitute and always a small middle-class element in the migration. Nor were the Irish the only residents of the central areas of towns in which the poor and migratory population was increasingly concentrated. The so-called 'Little Irelands' were in fact dense conglomerations of Irish, Welsh and English people, although it is true that the Irish were to be found in disproportionate numbers in these areas.

The overwhelmingly hostile environment in which Irish people found themselves led many to make assertive public displays of their respectability. This quickly forced some recognition from the indigenous society that the Irish community was a divided one and that not all of its members were at the head of the queues for poor relief. Irish immigration brought with it a 'devotional revolution' that paralleled the one in contemporary Ireland, bringing a larger proportion of the population within the orbit of the Catholic Church. Many of the values of this 'revolution' were shared with Welsh nonconformity: temperance, religious observance and ultimately a political agenda largely driven by a feeling of religious exclusion. Integration and respectability are well exemplified by a surviving banner of an Irish Hibernian Society in Newport. On its front, on a green background, is a painting of Thomas Grattan, leader of the Irish parliament of the 1780s when it was pressing for a greater role within an imperial context. On its reverse are sentimental images of Ireland. Overall it exudes a proud and respectable image of Ireland.[3]

By the 1880s politics and trade unionism were building substantial bridges between the Irish in Wales and the native population. James Mullin, a doctor who settled in Cardiff in the 1880s, highlighted such themes by leaving us a record of his life. He struggled to gain an education in Ireland and had an appetite for books and knowledge to rival that of any auto-didact from the south Wales coalfield. His social position gave him a prominent place in Cardiff's Irish politics, though one observer of Cardiff's 'Bohemians' claimed that the Cymru Fydd (Young Wales) supporter, Alderman Edward Thomas ('Cochfarf'), was the real leader of the Irish Party in Cardiff.[4] This integration would never be entirely stable in the political dimension, as the pull towards the Liberal programme of Home Rule always faced a counter-challenge from the Tory stress on denominational education.

Only when the Free State was created in 1922 would the political barriers to the integration of the Irish into Welsh society completely come down. In Cardiff in the 1920s Irish areas were among those most closely associated with the Labour vote.[5] Disturbances against the Irish ceased after the riot at Tredegar in 1882, and indeed the Irish were sufficiently integrated with the indigenous population to figure significantly among those who attacked Jews at Dowlais in 1903 and black and Arab settlers in 1919.[6] In 1925 Jim Driscoll's funeral was the largest ever seen in Wales, a symbol of the way in which a man sprung from a once-reviled community could become a symbol of the identity of industrial south Wales.

The Irish migration was the second largest influx of immigrants into Wales and continued at a decreased rate into the late nineteenth century. It was never one of the greatest flows of Irish people into Britain, and could never compare with the much greater migrations to Clydeside and

Merseyside. The social formations and political temper of those areas were shaped by this immigration and the local response to it much more profoundly than was the case in south Wales. Cultural divisions became entrenched in a variety of institutions from Orange Lodges to football teams. Liverpool acquired a deserved reputation as the British capital of ethnic rioting.[7] In Cardiff, by contrast, from the 1870s the annual Corpus Christi parades passed off with hardly a murmur of dissent and ended in the inner sanctum of Cardiff's social elite in the castle. The conversion of the Third Marquess of Bute to Catholicism in 1868 obviously had much to do with this acceptance, but clearly integration at elite level would have been highly precarious if it had not been paralleled by an acceptance at the grass roots.[8]

It needs to be stressed that Irish migrants were integrated into Welsh society rather than assimilated by it. Assimilation implies that individuals adopt the norms, values and behaviour of the wider society – effectively they disappear into it. Integration implies that the group survives but with an assured place in the host society.[9] Indeed the Irish were distinct enough to serve as an 'Other' to Welsh identity in the second half of the nineteenth century and beyond. Irishness has survived through religion and other social institutions and remains a significant part of the identity of many people of Irish descent, including those born in Wales. If it has been weakened at all it is through the lack of 'top-up' migration since the Second World War.

What does this experience tell us about the wider Welsh society? Discussions of immigration in Wales have become a cacophony, in which those who want to sing the praises of the tolerance and welcoming spirit of the Welsh encounter the deafening bass notes that reveal a darker history of anti-immigrant violence and intolerance.[10] As a result of this argument there is now far less recourse to the stereotype of the welcoming Welsh; the occurrence of a number of racially motivated murders in south Wales in the 1990s (two in 2000 while this chapter was being written), in the context of a rapidly escalating incidence of racial attacks, has also presented a serious challenge to the old view. It is plainly inadequate to apply a simple dichotomy of 'tolerance' versus 'prejudice' to all Welsh people and their relations with all the different immigrant groups that have arrived in Wales in the past two hundred years. Paul O'Leary's solidly grounded, subtle and often brilliant account of the relations between the Welsh and the Irish – reinforced by the essays in this book – provides an opportunity to revisit some aspects of this debate. I shall argue that using the experience of the Irish as a model and then as a basis for comparative studies can move us forward into new realms of understanding.

Primarily what we should take from the Irish experience is a sense of the divisions within communities, and a sense of periodisation. The above account noted some divisions within the Irish population and it drew attention to the class position that immigrants occupied. Not all the Irish were unskilled workers and other immigrant groups might have very different social positions. There were also significant changes within the Irish community, especially when the 'swarming' of the mid-Victorian period is compared with the more settled and respectable Irish community of the late nineteenth and early twentieth centuries.

Nor was Welsh society static in this period. The mass migration of the Irish coincided with a profound change in the nature of industrial society in Wales as a turbulent 'frontier' industrialism gave way to a more stable social order. The contours of this change are often depicted rather too starkly but there is little doubt about the underlying reality of the process. So not only were the Irish of the 1890s a rather different population from that which had arrived fifty years earlier, they lived in a Wales that had achieved a more settled sense of its identity and its place within the British Isles than had been the case in the 1840s. To some extent those who had reshaped Welsh identity had achieved this by casting the Irish (both in Ireland and within Wales) as an 'Other' against which to frame their own more peaceful and loyal image.[11] So we should beware of thinking of Welsh–Irish relations – or any host–immigrant relations – in a static and timeless way.

There is a further issue to which we should be alert: that is, the extent to which there may have been divisions within Wales over the proper response to immigrants. In the case of the Irish there seems to have been a fairly united front against the immigrants in the 1840s, which gradually gave way to tolerance and integration. This means that divisions are likely to have occurred in the transitional period. One example of this is the generational conflict over Irish politics that occurred in the 1880s. Older radicals such as Thomas Gee found it difficult to embrace an alliance with Catholics, while younger ones such as Tom Ellis found much to admire in Irish nationalism. If relations between groups were not timeless, neither were they uniform. The Welsh were not a united people and neither were the Irish. If we take this as a model for ethnic relations we may find complex and divided responses rather than a straightforward once-and-for-all choice between tolerance and prejudice.

What this means is that we need to think in terms of the complex connections and conflicts of a social ecology, and one that evolved over time, rather than thinking in terms of a simple and fixed structure. Welsh society was divided enough to exhibit varying responses to the different immigrant groups that arrived, and these also changed with the passing of the years. Accommodation and conflict could coexist and responses have to be set in the full social context rather than being seen as expressions of an unchanging and homogeneous Welsh character.

In the years before the First World War the Welsh identity that had been refashioned in the mid-Victorian years once again came under challenge from the largest immigrant group ever to arrive in Wales, the English. There was little chance that the English, unlike the Irish, could be seen as a uniformly poor and threatening group. The first English settlers were conquerors and many of their followers held elite positions in the gentry or later as industrialists. Indeed, it has been observed that a small number of English settlers in nineteenth-century north Wales had a much greater impact on Welsh society than the far larger numbers of Welsh people who found their way into England did on English society. The explanation lies in the asymmetry of their social, economic and cultural positions.[12] There were few attacks on English settlers despite (or because of?) the numbers in which they eventually came. By the eve of the First World War around one sixth of the population of Wales had been born in England. Half of these were in the county of Glamorgan. Essentially this was a south Wales phenomenon, for north Wales had a net loss of population to England.

The main exception to this record of peaceful relations was in northeast Wales, where English managers were unpopular and sometimes run out of town, and where there was resentment at favouritism allegedly shown to English workers. But even this seems to have passed away by the late nineteenth century, when newer English incomers tended to settle in distinct communities such as Llay rather than in Welsh ones such as Rhosllanerchrugog.[13] In south Wales there was some antagonism towards English workers during the Tumble strike of 1893, but the thrust of this seems to have been directed against blacklegs who happened to be English, rather than being ethnically motivated.[14] Yet anti-English feeling was not totally absent. Much of it was articulated through nonconformist ministers who had decided – in the aftermath of the assault on Welsh morals and culture in the official reports of the Commissioners on Education of 1847 – that the English were irredeemably godless. Henry Richard voiced such an opinion when speaking in favour of the provision of English-language chapels for English incomers.[15] By the turn of the twentieth century this chapel-bred middle-class elite was coming to see the much greater number of English incomers as a threat to the nonconformist Welsh identity that had been so painfully constructed in the nineteenth century. Such people were easy scapegoats for the industrial unrest that began to build up from the turn of the century and exploded at Tonypandy in 1910. Good Welsh colliers were rarely seen as being responsible: it was the heathen incomer who caused unrest.

In some respects the English were 'invisible immigrants' in Wales as much as they were in the USA. They came from the dominant culture in the islands and had some advantages from this position, even if their inability to speak Welsh did produce some local disadvantages and force the earliest settlers to learn at least a smattering of Welsh. In 1891 they clustered close to one another in particular streets in valley communities. One contemporary observer stressed the lack of any tribal feeling on the ground: 'There is no Ulster in Wales.' English settlers were seen as having adopted the politics, traditions and religion of Wales.[16] Soon there were enough of them for English to become the dominant language in virtually all social domains. In many places it was Welsh speakers rather than the English who became the ethnic minority.

Yet in some senses the English were assimilated rather than integrated. Their origins were quickly forgotten and bitter industrial struggles as well as the common deprivation of the inter-war depression forged a regional working-class consciousness that was stronger than any ethnic identifications. Yet it was an Anglo-Welsh identity that arose from this. Valleys culture undoubtedly identified itself as Welsh but its predominant language was English. In retrospect it almost looks like a bargain: the acceptance of a local identification in exchange for the changing of a language. The emergence of a more coherent and organised labour movement from the late nineteenth century – a significant change from the often violent and temporary mobilisations of earlier years – helped construct an arena in which integration could be negotiated. Perhaps it is significant that the attempts at ethnically based unions in the 1870s and the localised ones of the 1880s gave way to the Miners' Federation of Great Britain – known as 'the English union' – in the 1890s.

The fact that the newcomers' language was the dominant language of the Isles, valuable for commercial and academic advancement, while the controllers of Welsh-language culture tended to remove Welsh from the issues of the modern world, undoubtedly eased the complex process of adjustment. It is hard to think of a parallel situation in which the language of an incoming group became the dominant one of a regional society.[17] Perhaps the closest parallel is the impact of Latinos on the contemporary American city. Many refuse to learn English and their presence leads Asian immigrants to learn Spanish rather than English. Their linguistic stance is buttressed by modern communications technologies, which provide virtual contact with home and sustain cultural links.[18] Clearly such links were also easily maintained by English immigrants in late-nineteenth-century and early-twentieth-century Wales. In south Wales English incomers were linked to a long-established process of Anglicisation that had spread from over the border. Some observers saw much more to fear in the Anglicisation of the Welsh rather than from the English incomer.[19] Or perhaps south Wales ought to be thought of in terms of the American idea of the melting pot. This holds that the process of adjustment is neither assimilation nor integration but involves changes on the part of all the groups involved. What emerges is a new and refashioned identity rather than acculturation or the persistence of older identities.[20] In some ways this parallels the process in the north-east of England in the late nineteenth century when migrants from Scotland, Ireland and England were forged into a working class. It has been claimed that such a culture is inherently civic: it can be joined and is changed by the process of joining. Once this regional working class was seen as being English. Now some in the north-east want to stress its Britishness, to reflect its diverse roots.[21]

The relative lack of reaction to English incomers – despite the profundity of the social and cultural change they brought with them – has something to do with the smaller migrations of other groups, such as Jews, Spaniards and black people, that ran parallel with their arrival. In some ways it was they who absorbed the anger and tensions. Certainly these were the people who were *seen* as immigrants and who caught the rough edge of local reactions.

The combined weight of all this migration was to make the south Wales coalfield the prime attractive area for in-migration in late-nineteenth-century and early-twentieth-century Wales. In the first decade of the century only the USA eclipsed it in its capacity to attract incomers. These were immigrants whom we must associate with the upsurge of steam coal production from the 1850s. The Irish were much more closely associated with the earlier iron-making phases of industrialisation – especially its climax and decline – and were largely kept out of the steam coal areas. Often this was by means of violence.[22] The tiny colonies of Spanish workers which began to appear at the turn of the century split between the two phases. The settlement in Dowlais was clearly related to the ore ships from Bilbao and to the attempts to restructure iron- and steel-making to cope with changing world conditions in the industry. Immigrant labour had a place in this process. But some of the Spaniards also established themselves in the emerging anthracite coalfield at Abercrave. Here there was in some ways a microcosm of the process that was going on in the whole coalfield:

> Abercrave, a quiet little mining village of only a few thousand inhabitants at the top of the Swansea Valley, has now become one of the most cosmopolitan in the district. In addition to the Welsh, English, Scotch and Irish residing in the locality, there has been a strong influx during the past few years of Frenchmen, Spaniards, Portuguese, Germans, Belgians, &c, and employment has been found for them in the local collieries. The Spaniards form the strongest colony, and it is computed that there are over 200 in all.[23]

The steam coal phase of growth in south Wales is associated with the arrival of a whole rainbow of different peoples into south Wales, mainly but not entirely in the ports. From the mid-nineteenth century, in the sailing ship era, there were sailors from many European nations, including Greeks, Norwegians and Germans. Steam vessels often added to this black or Arab stokehold crews. Small numbers of Chinese were added to the mix from around the turn of the century, and there were also Jewish immigrants who came to escape East European pogroms and Italians who produced a café culture in the valleys. Many of these settled in the ports but they also spread more widely into the industrial hinterland. Of these groups the Jews and the Italians were quite scattered and hardly formed distinct colonies.[24] The small Chinese community in Cardiff was scattered in the service sector of laundries across the city rather than confined to a particular district of the city. The same was true of the Italians over the wider area of the coalfield. The maritime trades and the Spanish settlers did form more distinct colonies, but like the earlier Irish settlements they were intermingled with the indigenous poor – and also with one another.

When a widespread industrial crisis, exacerbated by the demands of global conflict, struck in the decade 1910–1920 it was people from these groups who would be its victims. The English may have been blamed for it by much nonconformist opinion but they did not suffer at the hands of ethnically motivated crowds. This crisis is the equivalent of the one around 1848 that Paul O'Leary highlights as the climax of anti-Irish violence in south Wales.

In many ways it was a reflection of the world crisis. Industrial militancy and ideas of industrial democracy affected most of the industrialised or industrialising world. Ethnic violence in south Wales was in many ways closely related to this, while the global crisis of the World War led to widespread racial violence.[25] In 1911 there were anti-Chinese riots in Cardiff, closely followed by anti-Jewish riots in the eastern valleys of the coalfield. In 1919 there were anti-black and anti-Arab riots in Cardiff, Barry and Newport, which cost four lives. This crisis bears comparison with the same period in Liverpool, where there were five major riots between 1909 and 1919.[26] The difference resides largely in the fact that in the Merseyside city Catholic–Protestant tensions could still give rise to violence and that there was a much more serious anti-German riot in 1915. Perhaps the more minor anti-German outbreak in Rhyl should really be seen as an extension of this. Yet anti-Chinese and anti-Jewish violence were absent on Merseyside.

These outbreaks need to be considered in the context of the emerging labour movement. Jews and Italians were mainly in the retail sector rather than in mining which meant that they were not integrated into the local community via a trade union. As shopkeepers they were potentially victims of working-class anger in industrial disputes. The tiny Chinese community was split between seamen and laundry work. In the 1911 strike they were branded as strike-breakers, and even those who tried to join the union were refused entry. In the event it was the laundries that were made the scapegoats for the alleged 'sins' of the Chinese seamen.[27] The Spaniards, by contrast with all these groups, were essentially working class and generally trade unionists.

Was violence the whole story of this period? It has recently been argued that the anti-Jewish riots in south Wales are misnamed: there were attacks on shops, some of which were Jewish-owned and some were not. What has been left out of the picture, it is claimed, is Welsh philo-Semitism.[28] Such an argument does well to remind us that Jews were not the only victims of the attacks in 1911. But it seems to be based on an artificial separation between riots seen as arising out of industrial conflicts and those seen as ethnically based. The disturbances in the valleys can then be allocated to the first category while Welsh philo-Semitism takes a bow. The problem with this approach is that ethnic conflicts frequently – in fact almost always – arose during periods of industrial tension of one kind or other. The anti-Chinese riots of the same year were embedded in the seamen's strike of the time and occurred just as many other Cardiff workers walked out to make the strike a city-wide general strike. There seems little doubt that they were ways of ensuring solidarity along the waterfront.

Equally, the race riots of 1919 were closely related to the disruptions of trade and employment that accompanied the ending of the war. What seems to have been different in the anti-Jewish riots was that Jews were not the only victims, whereas only Chinese or black people were attacked in the other two examples. But non-Jewish shopkeepers seem to have been targeted only if they were rackrenters or people who exacted exorbitant prices for goods. Jews, by contrast, were *all* attacked – presumably because stereotypes were strong enough to suggest that all Jews were tight-fisted and exploitative. Some local people did discriminate, in the sense that they protected some Jews from the crowds, but there seems to have been no selective targeting of Jewish shops by the crowds themselves. The attacks were bad for the reputation and trading position of the communities and attempts were made to distance the local population from them by suggesting that they were the work of people on the margins of society ('hooligans'); there were even some hints that the Irish were prominent among the perpetrators. Such views came from people who believed in Welsh philo-Semitism – the elite of nonconformist ministers and journalists.

But there is little evidence of philo-Semitism on the streets, even if there is some evidence that some people knew a good and honest neighbour when they saw one, whatever their ethnic origin. Clearly the riots revealed tensions in Welsh society that were more complex than simply 'Welsh versus Jewish'. In public discussion Welsh nonconformity often made common cause with local Jewish opinion and denied that there was evidence of anti-Semitism in the local population. Their united front was against 'riff-raff' and journalists who were alleged to have misinterpreted the riots. But some Jewish opinion both within and outside south Wales joined with those who felt that anti-Jewish feeling was present in important ways. Yet perhaps it is significant that, as was pointed out at the time, those Jews who worked in the mining industry were not singled out for attack.

Some idea of the complex attitudes that ran through this area can be derived from an autobiography of a Jew who was very young at the time of the riots. He did well in school, was widely praised by his teachers, and seems to have had a close relationship with his headmaster. He went on to be a student at the university in Cardiff. He encountered one teacher who held pronounced anti-Semitic views but extracted an apology from him by confronting his prejudices. The family was victimised in the riots of 1911 but was sheltered and helped to safety by Welsh neighbours. On another occasion he rescued an older Jewish trader from a group of young miners who were beating him up – but his schoolfellows, who were not Jews, refused to help him do so. What is revealed by this individual testimony is a complex social landscape that could include varied experiences.[29] But that landscape certainly included proletarian racism.

A slightly later example helps underline the point. During the campaign against company unions at Bedwas in the 1930s a miner suggested to Arthur Horner that they might launch attacks on all the Jewish shops in the area since Sir Samuel Insole, who was chairman of the coal company, was a Jew. Horner treated this with the kind of disdain that an internationalist and anti-Fascist might be expected to show. But the suggestion, almost a quarter of a century after the outbreaks at Tredegar and in the eastern valleys, is of significance. Horner took it seriously enough to raise the matter at a coalfield conference and threatened to resign from the presidency of the South Wales Miners' Federation if there were an outbreak.[30] Yet at the same time middle-class opinion in the nearby Rhondda valleys could see the departure of Jews from south Wales as a depressing barometer reading for the local economy and could predict that Germany would suffer economically from its persecution of the Jews.[31] As much as the events of 1911, the situation in the 1930s reveals the complexity of responses in south Wales.

What the events of 1911 show is that economic circumstances could make racial stereotyping the basis of popular action. Any discussion of ethnic conflicts must allow for the interaction between attitudes and economic and social circumstances. It is not enough to invoke Welsh tolerance or to decry Welsh intolerance. In which circumstances were Welsh people likely to be tolerant and in which intolerant? And which Welsh people are we talking about? Two vociferous discussions over the place of immigrants in coalfield society on the eve of the First World War reveal something more of the lie of the land in ethnic relations in south Wales.

Towards the end of 1913 the Free Church Council of Aberdare became concerned about the 'desecration' of the Sabbath in the town. There were many facets to this: Sunday bands in the park, Sunday trams, newspapers and the opening of shops. It was feared that Sunday schools might follow the example of one in Cardiff that had seen its attendance decline from 250 to 25. The Revd Cynog Williams made a complaint that foreigners were prime culprits in the opening of shops:

> it was too bad for Italians to come to our country, defy our customs and open their shops and make fortunes on our backs . . . the shops of the Italians and other foreigners and Infidels and pagans . . . were moral and consumptive cesspools . . . Respect for the Sabbath had made Wales the land of the white gloves, and here we were allowing Italians to come and damn our people . . .[32]

A correspondent added to the list of sins by arguing that such shops took many pennies intended for Sunday school collections at the chapels. J. Manley, conductor of a band that Williams had condemned for playing on Sundays, wrote to the local paper to condemn Williams for a lack of consistency (he had preached that all men are brothers) and for his lack of Christian charity.[33] But it was the socialist Wil John Edwards who launched the most wide-ranging and forceful attack. He referred to Williams' 'annual outburst', which was likened to a dose of influenza, and thought he was deranged:

> It is a crime, you say, to desecrate the sabbath. It is a greater crime, sir, to desecrate humanity . . . your swash-buckle talk about foreigners coming to this county reveals a nature which is supremely small . . . Wales is damned – that is the only truism you uttered . . . Before these Italians, Pagans and Infidels had a ghost of a chance Capital had already done the trick. Capital had damned Wales and her people and her greatest representatives are Welshmen. D. A. Thomas and David Davies are familiar enough to your mind. You forgot their existence because your national temperament got drunk . . . I am still religious and moral enough to extend my hand across the seas and continents and grip the hand of my fellow man . . . 'The world is my country; mankind are my brethren; to do good is my religion.'[34]

This controversy fluttered across the pages of the local paper for over a month.[35] It was an argument that generated as much heat as it did light, for Williams was unrepentant at a public meeting in December, proclaiming a theory of 'difference' that is the exact opposite of what modern cultural theorists mean by the term: 'He heard every week of people who differed from him; every infidel did likewise, and so did every Sabbath-breaker, and gambler and publican.'[36]

Wil John Edwards clearly represented a strand of Marxist internationalist thinking in the labour movement that could, of course, be an effective basis for the protection of minorities.[37] Williams, by contrast, displayed the depths of xenophobia to which a besieged Welsh nonconformity could descend. In a sense it was easy for Edwards to be open and international in this debate since no immediate interest of native-born labour was challenged by it: indeed many workers were voting with their feet and payslips for the services that Italian café-owners provided. Yet it was not the only position held in the labour movement. Two months after Cynog Williams' outburst in Aberdare similar views appeared in a socialist newspaper, *Llais Llafur*. The writer used a stereotypical name, 'Antonio', to refer to Italians (though recognising that some were called Dominico!) and stressed that the law-breaking was profitable.[38] Again the concern over Italian shops fed off fears for the rising generation much as it did in the case of Cynog Williams. Italian shops had become enlarged and showed evident signs of prosperity, so that 'Antonio smiles broadly and grows fat'. A pose of protecting the poor and unfortunate was also struck:

> The poor widow struggling to maintain herself and her family by the tiny shop in the obscure street sells a half penny candle, or maybe a pennyworth of sweets on Sunday and pays the penalty which closes her door for ever on Sunday. With even her poor competition removed Antonio, with his well-lighted and spacious premises in the main street goes from strength to strength. He educates his sons, purchases houses, invests his surplus and in the course of comparatively few years returns to the country of his birth a prosperous gentleman. He leaves in the Rhondda our police courts and reformatories.[39]

There are crucial socialist references in this diatribe, mixed in with the ethnic stereotyping and the fears for the newcomers' undermining of the moral and social order. There is, as well as the protection of the poor, the fear of monopoly (or at least the swallowing of smaller enterprises by larger ones) and an implied use of the profits obtained from this to fund further exploitation in the valleys (through house purchase). Beyond this is the creation of a privileged elite (by education and by investment), resulting in 'non-civic' capitalists who cut and run from their social responsibilities.[40]

We are beginning to see the shape of the social landscape and the way in which the ethnic groups interacted within it in an ecology of ethnic relations. Clearly there was a position of internationalism and tolerance: but in the example given here it operated in a context of rejecting the cultural hegemony of nonconformity and its 'Welsh way of life'. Not all in the labour movement shared this position: they could also seek to defend the values embodied in Welsh nonconformity while continuing to uphold more radical positions on many social and economic issues, even if some of these were expressed in ethnically prejudiced ways. The Revd Cynog Williams seems to have been a more straightforward bigot. The mixed perspective that ran through the labour movement can be seen by examining the debate over Spanish workers at Abercrave that erupted on the eve of the First World War.

In 1900 the Spaniards had arrived, heralded as trade unionists who had immediately enrolled in the union. Yet by 1913 there was a sense in the anthracite district that active trade unionists who were of good character and of long standing in the area had been thrown out of work in favour of 'strangers'. This issue of victimisation was seen as a threat to one of the best organised areas of the coalfield. Within a month the number of Spaniards at Abercrave was being commented upon, though with the rider that most were people of exemplary conduct, and enjoyed good relations with the natives. Some of the children were said to speak both Welsh and English fluently, while numbers of the younger men were becoming cultivated through self-education. Less than a month later meetings of workers at Abercrave, International and Gwaunclawdd collieries were considering the advisability of taking steps to remove Spaniards, French and Germans from the local pits. The necessity for this action was mysterious: 'certain occurrences known to the local workers'.[41] In the event, committees were formed to approach management to ensure that no more foreigners would be employed in the three pits. This prompted an intervention from Guy Aldred, who made the Marxist case for internationalism:

> You are workers. So are your foreign comrades of the pick and shovel . . . Your choice is between revolution and increasing slavery. But you will not ensure your emancipation by fighting your fellow-slaves. It is the system, the principle of profit, the aggression of Mammon which you have to war against. Not your fellow workers.[42]

The strained rhetoric reveals just how far removed Aldred was from the world of the anthracite miner. Wil Jon Edwards held a similar position but was wise enough not to advocate revolution in the columns of the local press. From the position of anthracite miners facing depression and victimisation a few foreigners were clearly a rather easier obstacle to remove than were the coal companies that employed them and the political system in which they participated.

The issue continued to worry the anthracite district into the next year, in the same context of economic depression in the area. Just why the local miners objected to the Spanish presence is again unclear, but the argument quickly became mixed up with a dispute about the overcrowded bungalows that the Spaniards, Italians and French occupied. This was a secondary matter because the first issues were clearly related to the workplace, one of them apparently being an assault by a Spaniard on a local worker.[43]

Trade union negotiations were entered into over the issues and it was claimed that the hostility against the Spaniards was nothing to do with their being foreigners but connected to the way that their conditions of labour affected those of other workers. This can be disproved with two pieces of evidence: the complaints about their living conditions, which were featured to a great extent in the press, and the allegation that they were more docile than local workers. The local labour paper commented that it was the duty of the workers to inform the Spaniards of their rights.[44] Yet it seems that all the Spaniards at Abercrave were members of the South Wales Miners' Federation, something that would have fulfilled many unionists' dreams had it been true of all workers across the coalfield. There were also denials that this was undercutting foreign labour, and it is difficult to see how it could have been in an industry so bound by collective agreements. The problem of overcrowding was also denied and M. Esteban, the highly articulate champion of the Spanish workers, made an appeal for international solidarity that was free of Aldred's rhetorical and ideological flourishes: 'Fellow workmen, I think it is despicable of a person who, not having a just cause against a particular class, tries to fan the flames of racial hatred.'[45]

Within days of this statement being made, Britain was at war with Germany and the issue vanished from view. French workers left the area as they were called to defend France; Spaniards were expected to mobilise but in the event Spain failed to join in the European war. At the end of the war the council of the South Wales Miners' Federation recommended to the local workers that they accept back those workers who had gone home to fight.[46]

In the inter-war period Wales was overwhelmingly a net exporter of people, having been a net importer in the period before the First World War. Hence there were few new immigrants to whom exception could be taken or welcome could be given. The main exception to this is the black community in Cardiff and, to a lesser extent, in the other south Wales ports. The size of such populations was clearly greatly expanded during the conflict and it remained stable afterwards, despite the post-war repatriations – though there may have been some turnover in the people involved.[47] In the course of the war the labour movement in south Wales had resisted the importation of colonial labour to jobs within Britain, though its expansion in seafaring was accepted.[48] This black community would place Wales in the first division of early-twentieth-century black communities in Britain. It was at least as large as those of Liverpool or South Shields, though it was distinguished from that of London by its lack of students and intellectuals. Cardiff's black community was ethnically diverse but had few social divisions. Most were seamen and only a few rose precariously above this to become boarding-house keepers. There was also a political elite that was mainly active in the Communist Party. The black settlement was much more of a ghetto than the mid-nineteenth-century Irish settlements had been – its boundaries were policed by many groups ranging from rioters to the city council. Yet it was not a ghetto of a single nationality and had a core of white women who bound the community together and an internally seg-regated area of people of European origin. In some ways it was closer to the ghettos of Europeans in the USA than to those in which Afro-Americans were confined. Organisations tended to follow religious and ethnic lines but an identity based on location also developed over time. The long-term experience of the Cardiff black community was neither integration nor assimilation but rather continuing segregation.

Nor was Wales a major magnet for immigrants after 1945. Settlements of post-war black people and New Commonwealth immigrants were small and located outside the old ghetto of Butetown. South Glamorgan currently has the greatest concentration of black people in Wales, but even this only reaches the UK average for an ethnic minority population. Yet despite this relative lack of settlement after 1945 issues regarding migrant labour did sometimes arise in post-war Wales. One of the key economic problems in the period 1946–1949 was a shortage of labour with which to effect the reconstruction of Britain. The shortage was acute in coal, on which depended much of the rest of the recovery. Hence governments sought to use some of the displaced persons who were left stranded in Europe by the eddying tides of totalitarian regimes. Many were victims of the Nazis, survivors of forced labour regimes; others were refugees from communism. Some 80,000 were taken into Britain as European Voluntary Workers, of whom almost 11,000 were engaged in mining in April 1949. There were 1,700 each in Glamorgan and Flintshire, though these were not all engaged in mining. There was much opposition from trade unions, especially from the NUM, which had an alternative recruitment strategy of attracting indigenous labour through the improvement of pay and conditions. It stipulated that lodges had to agree to the use of European labour, that recruits must join the NUM and that they should be the first to lose jobs in an economic down-turn. In a country that had recently faced severe economic depression – especially in the old industrial regions – and that had no peacetime expe-rience of full employment, the use of such workers was looked upon with suspicion from the beginning. In the mining industry many lodges would retain this suspicion long after the NUM had shown its political support for the Labour government by agreeing to its manpower requirements.[49]

Nationalisation offered new hope for mining communities that had been stretched to – and beyond – their limits in the Great Depression. It offered both new investment (in the form of 'super-collieries') and also the closure of small and unviable pits. Manpower for the new pits was to be drawn from the old ones wherever possible but clearly there were problems in trying to adjust the old workforce to the new pattern of mining. There was a common belief that sick and injured miners, who were commonly given surface work, were the victims of this process. There was also a hope engendered that at least some of the army of exiles who had left Wales in the inter-war period might return home to fill some of the new jobs. In this context attempts to introduce Polish labour into the pits encountered a good deal of opposition. There were fears that foreigners would get preference and that local men would be neglected. At Mardy it was observed that the 'jubilation felt at the good news that Mardy pits are to re-open will change to resentment if the local unemployed are forgotten'. Local people expressed their opposition by the reluctance to offer accommodation to imported miners and eventually by strike action against them.

Some of the opposition was politically inspired. Some Communists saw Poles as enemies of the Soviet Union and displayed a darker side to the tradition of socialist internationalism that was an important part of the south Wales scene. Poles' image in Britain had suffered ever since the entry of the Soviet Union into the war and many of them were clearly anti-Russian and anti-Soviet. In addition, at the end of the war they were frequently portrayed as scroungers, sponging off the state. In Scotland there was some fear of them as a Catholic group but as yet no evidence of this has been found in Wales. Nor is it likely to exist given the lack of entrenched, institutional anti-Catholicism in Wales.

The opposition to Poles after the war contrasts instructively with the position of refugees from Nazi oppression during the war. They were drawn from Germany, Austria and Czechoslovakia in the main and some were of Jewish ancestry. Some opted for forestry work in north Wales in order to avoid internment as enemy aliens. Yet the machinery of the state often caught up with them and they found themselves interned for a period of months. Their British fellow workers resented this action by this state. Further evidence of integration comes from their active role in creating trade unions in the industry and from their development of an international choir that performed in Llangollen, where they also held international dances. The advantage this group had was a clear anti-Fascist identity, something that Poles had had in 1940–41 but had generally lost once the Soviet Union entered the war.[50]

There was considerable trade union opposition to the use of displaced persons in industrial work in post-war Britain and much analysis singles out south Wales as an area of especially strong opposition. It is not too fanciful to link this with the strength of the Communist Party in south Wales and its influence within the South Wales Area of the NUM. In late February 1949 1,800 miners in the Rhondda downed tools in protest at the use of Polish labour. They demanded their withdrawal until local labour had been absorbed. This was enough to turn a bus-load of Poles back from the pits. The problem was that the local unemployed were often people who were not fit enough to do the heavy development work that was required in opening up new pits and headings. The National Coal Board agreed that foreign labour would only be employed when

British labour was not available, and eventually Poles were accepted into the pits. The whole dispute has to be seen in the context of more general discontents with the management of the nationalised industry and a fairly fraught situation in which there were frequent unofficial strikes over many issues.[51]

Eventually many Poles settled well into Welsh society, with well-publicised examples of Polish farmers learning Welsh and playing a full part in rural societies. As we have seen, this was not a painless process in the industrial valleys. But it does seem to have been effected in the medium term through the agency of work and trade unions. An Aberdare doctor recalled that hostility to the Poles 'lasted only as long as it took the Welsh miners to learn that the Poles could be as fine a set of workmates and as solid a body of trade unionists as any other in the coalfield'.[52] This comment seems to have a wider application as an indication of the role of trade unions as integrators of immigrant communities into Welsh society.

Part of the enduring problem for Poles would be the isolation of some settlers from the community organisations that sustained immigrant life. Poles, like many immigrant groups, found life easier if they settled in proximity to one another. Cardiff was the centre of Polish settlement in south Wales. From 1948 branches of the Union of Polish Craftsmen and Workers were established in the area, and within a few years there were ten branches with 1,500 members. Two years later the union put 800 members and their families on the streets of the city in a demonstration of strength and respectability, such as many immigrant groups had used in the past to demonstrate their presence and their culture. There were fraternal greetings from the district organiser of the Municipal and General Workers' Union, while the vice-chairman stressed the need to learn about Britain and its institutions. But there was also time to look forward to an eventual independent, non-Soviet Poland. It was a social life such as this that Poles in the coalfield lacked; hence they were forced to look to Cardiff as their cultural centre.[53]

In the 1970s a jagged faultline opened between the social democracy of the post-war era and the new political economy focused on the free market. In Wales this was associated with a crisis in the economy, as a region with a state sector as large as those of Eastern Europe spiralled into decline. Heavy industry, one of the underpinnings of Welsh identity, was closed, privatised or at least much slimmed down in the 1990s. Prolonged economic stagnation and decline have made the south Wales valleys the least cosmopolitan area of Wales, in contrast to the position in the early years of the century. They have the highest proportion of their population native-born, reaching a peak of over 92 per cent in the Rhondda.[54] Racial incidents have escalated in the valleys of the coalfield as a small group of Asian shopkeepers and professionals (mainly doctors) has found its way into these deprived communities. The murder of Mohan Singh Kullar at Cadoxton in 1994 drew attention to the problem and initiated the public debate that has led to the re-evaluation of the Welsh record on racism.

On the positive side, in the 1980s ethnic minorities began to find a place in the political structures of Wales as a politics of racial equality (what its detractors call 'the race relations industry') began to be established. It has achieved successes, though all who have taken part in it acknowledge the strength of the obstacles. The creation of such a politics is made more difficult by the many divisions that exist within the small ethnic minority population of Wales. But the relevant structures now exist and with them monitoring and pressure. In that sense there is a political integration of ethnic minorities. This is very limited, however, as is shown by the continuing conflicts over the lack of ethnic minority representation in the National Assembly for Wales and the failure to adopt an ethnic minority candidate for any of the six Labour seats that became vacant at the 2001 general election.

While the old industrial areas of Wales experienced only small-scale immigration, rural Wales was the recipient of a much larger flow of immigration from England. By 1981 the English accounted for 17 per cent of the population of Wales, making Wales the most cosmopolitan of the four home countries; under 80 per cent of the population was Welsh-born. Generally speaking this influx of English people has not created much overt conflict, apart from the series of second-home fires that marked the 1980s. These seem to have been the work of a small group of people rather than the kind of communal actions that have characterised most of the historical incidents of anti-immigrant feeling discussed in this chapter. Opinion poll data did indicate a significant degree of public sympathy for the objectives of firebombers, if not for their methods, but contrary to repeated police statements they were not sheltered by communities. When the occasional 'freelance' firebomber took action they were invariably convicted, and the campaign against second homes has now been dead for a decade and more. Other actions such as campaigns against marinas can have anti-English dimensions to them but are not straightforwardly ethnically motivated: there are genuine issues of the defence of a culture that is under threat, and of unsympathetic development that will bring few jobs in return for much environmental impairment. More recently there have been complaints of anti-English racism in Wales.[55] It is hard, as yet, to see what justice there is in these claims. In the past some disappointed job candidates have found it convenient to take their grievances to the Race Relations Board. Perhaps there has been some inappropriate behaviour and actions on the back of the slowly rising confidence of many Welsh people in the aftermath of devolution and the creation of the National Assembly for Wales.

This essay has traversed a long distance from its starting point of Irish immigrants in the mid-nineteenth century. The template that was constructed at the beginning has not been a very good fit for any of the cases subsequently discussed. This means that future research on migration to Wales will have to address the position of particular ethnic minorities rather than discussing immigrants as a general category. This is a lesson that American historians of immigration learned in the 1960s and 1970s. The size of the Irish migration into Wales has perhaps been more typical of the Welsh experience. It was substantial but not a major one in British terms. The same point could be made about Jews, Italians, post-war displaced persons and New Commonwealth immigrants. The exception to this rule is the massive influx of people who came to Wales as result of the late-nineteenth-century and early-twentieth-century expansion of the coal industry. If we take all the incomers together they do form an unusual concentration of new arrivals. Within this general migration, the case of the black people who found their way to Cardiff's docklands on either side of and during the First World War is a special one. At a time when there were few black people to be seen in Britain, it made Cardiff a very distinctive place.

But the largest group by far in this general migration was composed of people from England. This has been reinforced in the post-war period by another large migration, and indeed becomes one of the central themes of the history of twentieth-century Wales. It has no parallel in the histories of Scotland or Ireland and has consequences that rather defy the obvious categories of assimilation, integration and segregation. There is nothing novel in an analysis of the history of Wales that gives prominent attention to its relationship with England – it is difficult to see how one can be conducted without such an emphasis – but to view the English as an ethnic minority within Wales and to examine their impact on the structures and cultures of Wales offers a central avenue from which to explore the twentieth century. At the centre of the ecology of ethnic relations in Wales is the relationship between the Welsh-born and English incomers. When historians embark on the important journey of analysing this twentieth-century ecology they will be well prepared by the volume and quality of research on the Irish that is now available. Knowing so much about one incoming group will greatly help us to understand what is distinctive about the others.

Notes

1. Unless otherwise stated this account of the Irish in Wales derives from Paul O'Leary, *Immigration and Integration: The Irish in Wales, 1798–1922*, Cardiff, University of Wales Press, 2000. I would also like to thank Paul O'Leary

for many long discussions that have helped shape the way I approach these issues and for incisive comments on a draft.

2. *Cardiff and Merthyr Guardian*, 21 April 1849.

3. The banner is on display in the Newport Museum. The society was formed in 1882 and this gives a rough guide to its date.

4. James Mullin, *The Story of a Toiler's Life*, ed. Patrick Maume, London and Dublin, 1921, reprinted University College Dublin Press, 2000; J. Kyrle Fletcher, *Cardiff: Notes Biographical and Picturesque*, Newport, Western Mail Ltd, 1920, pp. 79, 86–87.

5. Neil Evans, 'Cardiff's Labour Tradition', *Llafur*, 4.2 (1985), pp. 77–90.

6. Neil Evans, 'The South Wales Race Riots of 1919', *Llafur*, 3.1 (1980), pp. 5–29.

7. Frank Neal, *Sectarian Violence: The Liverpool Experience, 1819–1914*, Manchester, Manchester University Press, 1988.

8. I have benefited here from hearing Paul O'Leary's important and as yet unpublished paper on the Corpus Christi processions in Cardiff.

9. The distinction is well explained in Bernard Crick, *Socialism*, Milton Keynes, Open University Press, 1987, p. 105.

10. See Neil Evans, 'Immigrants and Minorities in Wales, 1840–1990: A Comparative Perspective', *Llafur*, 6.1 (1991), pp. 5–26.

11. This transition is central to my account of the period: '"As Rich as California . . .": Opening and Closing the Frontier, Wales 1780–1870', in *The People of Wales: A Millennium History*, ed. Gareth Elwyn Jones and Dai Smith, Llandysul, Gomer Press, 1999, pp. 111–44.

12. I borrow this point from Merfyn Jones's unpublished O'Donnell lecture, 'The English in Wales', the text of which he was kind enough to show me.

13. Neil Evans, 'Regional Dynamics: North Wales, 1750–1914', in *Issues of Regional Identity: Essays in Honour of John Marshall*, ed. E. Royle, Manchester, Manchester University Press, 1998, pp. 215–18.

14. Noel Gibbard, 'The Tumble Strike, 1893', *Carmarthenshire Antiquary*, 20 (1984), pp. 77–86, gives a fairly detailed account; Russell Davies, *Secret Sins: Sex, Violence and Society in Carmarthenshire, 1870–1920*, Cardiff, University of Wales Press, 1996, pp. 139–43, brings out the ethnic dimensions more fully.

15. *Cardiff Times*, 1 June 1867.

16. T. Darlington, 'The English-Speaking Population of Wales', *Wales*, 1.1 (May 1894), p. 16.

17. The debt to Dai Smith's many works should be clear here: *Wales! Wales?*, London, Allen and Unwin, 1984, is the most convenient source. I am also influenced by Tim Williams' BBC Wales film of 1995 in the series 'Moving Home' – though I'm sure we see the process in rather different ways.

18. M. Turner, 'How Latin Lessons Revitalised American Cities' (review of M. Davis, *Magical Urbanism: Latinos Reinvent the US City*, London, Verso, 2000), *Independent*, 4 August 2000.

19. L.F. Taylor, 'Welsh v. English: The Position as Revealed in Industrial

South Wales by the Census of 1911', *Wales*, 5.33 (January 1914), p. 162; J.E.T., 'Migration to and from Wales and Monmouthshire', *Welsh Outlook*, 2 (March 1915), pp. 104–05.

20. Milton M. Gordon, 'Assimilation in America: Theory and Reality', in *The National Temper: Readings in American Culture and Society*, ed. L. Levine and R. Middlekauf, New York, Harcourt Brace Jovanovich, 2nd edn, 1972.

21. D. Byrne, 'Is the North of England English?', *Northern Review*, 8 (Autumn 1999), pp. 18–26.

22. Evans, 'Immigrants and Minorities', pp. 17–18.

23. *Western Mail* (hereafter *WM*), 20 July 1914.

24. Ursula Henriques (ed.), *The Jews of South Wales: Historical Studies*, Cardiff, University of Wales Press, 1992.

25. Neil Evans, 'Across the Universe: Racial Violence and the Crisis in Imperial Britain, 1919–1925', *Immigrants and Minorities*, 13.2–3 (1994), pp. 59–88; *idem*, 'Red Summers: Race Wars and the Great War, 1917–1919', *History Today*, 51 (January 2001), pp. 28–33.

26. Again I am drawing on a splendid unpublished paper by Merfyn Jones: 'The Dangerous City: Liverpool's History of Social Disorder' (1987).

27. Neil Evans, '"A Tidal Wave of Impatience": The Cardiff General Strike of 1911', in *Politics and Society in Wales 1840–1922: Essays in Honour of Ieuan Gwynedd Jones*, ed. G.H. Jenkins and J.B. Smith, Cardiff, University of Wales Press, 1988, pp. 135–59, esp. p. 152.

28. W.D. Rubinstein, 'The Anti-Jewish Riots of 1911 in South Wales: A Re-Examination', *Welsh History Review*, 18.4 (1997), pp. 667–99.

29. S. Joseph, *My Formative Years: A Jewish Boy's Childhood in South Wales in the Early 1900s*, London, Multifarious, 1993.

30. Arthur Horner, *Incorrigible Rebel*, London, McGibbon and Kee, 1960, p. 152.

31. *Rhondda Leader*, 1 September 1934.

32. *Aberdare Leader* (hereafter *AL*), 8 November 1913.

33. *AL*, 15 November 1913.

34. *AL*, 15 November 1913.

35. *AL*, 22 November, 6 December 1913.

36. *AL*, 20 December 1913.

37. Hywel Francis, *Miners against Fascism: Wales and the Spanish Civil War*, London, Lawrence and Wishart, 1984, is the classic exposition of this important strand in Welsh opinion and action.

38. *Llais Llafur* (hereafter *LlLl*), 3 January 1914.

39. *LlLl*, 3 January 1914.

40. See J. Cumbler, *A Social History of Economic Decline: Business, Politics and Work in Trenton*, New York, Rutgers University Press, 1989, p. 3, for the idea of civic capitalism, which I have twisted into the negative.

41. *Labour Pioneer* (Cardiff), 5 (June 1900); *LlLl*, 30 August, 20 September, 11 October 1913.

42. *LlLl*, 1 November 1913.

43. *LlLl*, 11 July 1914; *South Wales Daily News*, 14 July 1914.

44. *LlLl*, 25 July 1914; *Brecon and Radnor Express*, 23 July 1914.

45. *LlLl*, 1 August 1914.

46. *LlLl*, 15 August 1914; University of Wales Swansea, South Wales Coalfield Collection, South Wales Miners' Federation Minutes, 25 March 1918.

47. Evans, 'South Wales Race Riots'; *idem*, 'The South Wales Race Riots of 1919: A Documentary Postscript', *Llafur*, 3.4 (1983); *idem*, 'Regulating the Reserve Army: Arabs, Blacks and the Local State in Cardiff, 1919–1945', in *Race and Labour in Twentieth-Century Britain*, ed. K. Lunn, London, Frank Cass, 1985.

48. Alun Burge, 'Banished from Consideration: The Importation of "Coloured Labour" in 1916', *Llafur*, 8.2 (2001), pp. 89–96.

49. For context see J. Zubrzycki, *Polish Immigrants in Britain: A Study of Adjustment*, The Hague, Nijhof, 1956; J.A. Tannahill, *European Volunteer Workers in Britain*, Manchester, Manchester University Press, 1958, pp. 112–17; D. Kay and R. Miles, *Refugees or Migrant Workers? European Voluntary Workers in Britain, 1946–1951*, London, Routledge, 1992.

50. G. Oertel, 'Trade Union Activity of German Refugees during the Second World War in the Forestry of North Wales: Recollections of Personal Experiences', *Immigrants and Minorities*, 14.3 (November 1995), pp. 257–64.

51. *WM*, 30 July 1947; *South Wales Echo*, 4, 5, 7, 9, 18, 24, 25, 28 February 1949; *Rhondda Leader*, 8, 15, 29 January, 5, 12, 19, 26 February, 5, 12 March, 2 April 1949.

52. K. Sword, N. Davies and J. Ciechanowski, *The Formation of the Polish Community in Great Britain, 1939–1950*, London, School of Slavonic and East European Studies, University of London, 1985, p. 347.

53. Zubrzycki, *Polish Immigrants in Britain*, pp. 115–16, 142.

54. J. Giggs and C. Pattie, 'Wales as a Plural Society', *Contemporary Wales*, 5 (1992), pp. 25–63.

55. *Big Issue Cymru*, 20–28 March 2000; *WM*, 3, 7 August 2000.

Index